THE SOCIAL ENTREPRENEUR'S HANDBOOK

How to Start, Build, and Run a Business That Improves the World

RUPERT SCOFIELD

New York   Chicago   San Francisco   Lisbon   London   Madrid   Mexico City
Milan   New Delhi   San Juan   Seoul   Singapore   Sydney   Toronto

1 2 3 4 5 6 7 8 9 10 11 12 13 14 15 16 17   QFR/QFR   1 9 8 7 6 5 4 3 2 1

ISBN   978-0-07-175029-5
MHID   0-07-175029-0

This publication is designed to provide accurate and authoritative information in regard to the subject matter covered. It is sold with the understanding that neither the author nor the publisher is engaged in rendering legal, accounting, securities trading, or other professional services. If legal advice or other expert assistance is required, the services of a competent professional person should be sought.

> —*From a Declaration of Principles Jointly Adopted by a Committee of the American Bar Association and a Committee of Publishers and Associations*

Vignettes and sidebars ("swag boxes") contained in this work are based on real incidents, but the names of the participants in these events have been changed.

Library of Congress Cataloging-in-Publication Data

Scofield, Rupert.
    The social entrepreneur's handbook : how to start, build, and run a business that improves the world / by Rupert Scofield.
       p.   cm.
    ISBN 978-0-07-175029-5 (alk. paper)
    1. Social entrepreneurship.   2. Social responsibility of business.
    3. Entrepreneurship—Moral and ethical aspects.   4. New business enterprises—Moral and ethical aspects.   I. Title.

    HD60.S395   2011
    658.4'08—dc22   2010047466

CONTENTS

Preface   v
Acknowledgments   vii

**PART 1
RIGHTING THE UNRIGHTABLE WRONG
AND FINDING YOUR MISSION POSSIBLE**   1

1 Identifying Your Constituency and Arranging
   Your Apprenticeship   5
2 The Big Idea and Finding a Mentor   19

**PART 2
IT TAKES AN ASYLUM**   29

3 We Few, We Happy Few: The Founding Fathers   31
4 Wanted: Resourceful Humans: Recruiting the Best
   Minds Money Can't Buy   41
5 Still Wanted: More Resourceful Humans: And
   the Interview Techniques to Find Them   57
6 Managing Them: On the Herding, Roping, and
   Hog-Tying of Cats   71
7 Continuing to Manage, and Staying in Touch   85
8 Leading Them: Finding Your Inner Andre Previn   93

PART 3
MONEY DOES GROW ON TREES,
BUT YOU HAVE TO PLANT THEM FIRST   103

9   The Private Pillar: Brother, Can You Spare a Dime?   105
10   Private Pillar Pitfalls: Sponsorship Programs
     and Dealing with Donors   119
11   The Power of the Other Pillars: Public and Internal   133
12   Communication: From "Who?" to Wheaties   143

PART 4
NOT ROCKET SCIENCE: STRUCTURE, SYSTEMS,
TECHNOLOGY, AND STRATEGY   157

13   Your Organization's Structure and Business
     and Financial Models   159
14   Systems: Give Me Liberty, or Give Me Systems!   173
15   Strategy: Getting Beyond "Everybody Go Long"   185

PART 5
THRIVING AND SURVIVING   197

16   But It Used to Work So Well!: The Time and Place
     for Innovation   199
17   Governance by Dummies: Wise Counsel or
     Micromanagement by the Ignorant?   211
18   Humanitarians at the Gate: Surviving and Thriving in
     the Treacherous World of the Modern Nonprofit   229

     Afterword: The Next Phase of Social Entrepreneurialism:
        Expanding, Diversifying, and Scaling the Model   247
     Index   259

PREFACE

"How did you do it?" *The Social Entrepreneur's Handbook* is my attempt to answer that question, whether posed by a recent college graduate, a professional midcareer in the private sector, or even a retired person seeking to enter the fascinating and rapidly growing world of social entrepreneurship. Derived from my forty-year career as a social entrepreneur in international development, my promise in this book is to offer practical advice on where and how to find your mission, how to finance it, and how to attract, motivate, and manage the "fellow travelers" who make the journey with you. By sharing my experiences, I hope to inspire others to follow in my footsteps, while avoiding the many costly mistakes my colleagues and I made on our long road to eventual success. At the same time, I hope to show you that screwing up is a useful and even necessary part of this learning process, which, I guarantee, never ends.

As we will learn in this book, the modern nonprofit must adopt many of the same strategies, policies, and best practices employed by successful enterprises in the for-profit world, but not at the cost of its soul. To achieve this balance, it must draw also on human resources from the commercial world, successfully assimilating these into the nonprofit culture. As my own experience with the creation and management of FINCA International, a global microfinance network currently serving more than 750,000 clients in twenty-one of the poorest nations on earth, demonstrates, this process, while necessary, is fraught with risk, for both the organization and the people trying to govern and manage it.

ACKNOWLEDGMENTS

I keep a copy of *Don Quixote*, in the original *castellano*, in my bathroom. It weighs about five pounds, and I get through it at the rate of about a page per day. One reason is that one of my favorite authors, Gabriel Garcia Marquez, said that no person could consider himself or herself educated unless he or she had read it. The second reason is that I wanted to remind myself while I wrote this that all missions are "A Possible Dream."

Far more than the fleeting satisfaction derived from completing a work like this, it is the act of creating it that brings true satisfaction. I take this step now, in contradiction to pages and pages of preaching about the importance of results and deadlines, to remind myself of that fact. Often I found myself stumped in the middle of a section, unsure as to what the meaning or lesson was of the experience I was relating. I would find myself believing I had completed the section, only to be haunted by a deep, vague feeling of dissatisfaction and a lurking suspicion that I had shortchanged both myself and the reader. Then hours, sometimes days, later the deeper significance of the experience would come to me. Indeed, the title of the final chapter came to me when I was beginning a walk up in Maine on a beautiful August morning. I had been looking for something that adequately summed up my experience of the past thirty-five years, spent in more than fifty nations on this small world. When I came to the top of the drive, in my mind's eye I saw them gathered there: humanitarians at the gate.

This is what I love about the process of writing: how it allows you to restore order to your thoughts and, in a real sense, to your life.

I wish to express my thanks to Alex Counts of Grameen Foundation, who facilitated my introduction to the best agent in the business, Jessica

Papin of Dystel Agency, who patiently guided my "Big Idea" for this book through its various iterations, from business book, to memoir, and finally to business book memoir. I would also like to thank the crack editorial team of Leila Porteous and Zach Gajewski at McGraw-Hill, who showed the utmost respect for my work and always asked my permission before removing the more over-the-top diatribes and tirades and who improved the final version in ways I had not believed possible.

I want to thank the indigenous people of Guatemala, the most generous people on earth, whose nobility in the face of grinding poverty set me on the path to the most fulfilling and useful life one could imagine. Of course, I cannot forget my brothers and sisters in the Latin American trade union movement, to whom I owe my political education. Above all, let me add a loud shout out to my fellow board members, FINCA donors, and supporters everywhere, and my sixty-five hundred FINCA colleagues around the globe, who collectively improve the lives of our millions of beneficiaries. Our journey has just begun.

Finally, I want to thank my beautiful family—Lorraine, my wife; and my children, Julie, Michelle, and John—who forgave my prolonged absences all these years, only because they believed in and supported my mission, and constantly inspired me by telling me how proud of Dad they were.

PART 1

||||||||||||||||||||||||||||||||||||||||||||||||||||||||||||||||||||||||||||

RIGHTING THE UNRIGHTABLE WRONG AND FINDING YOUR MISSION POSSIBLE

At some point on the drive back to Kampala from Jinja, Uganda, I realized Sam had stopped talking and was focused intently on the approaching rear of the sugarcane lorry about fifty yards ahead of us. His left foot pumped the brake pedal, which was worn down to a drop of shiny metal about the size of a quarter. His valiant efforts had so far failed to decrease our speed.

"Sam, is there something you want to tell me?"

"I'm afraid the brakes have gone."

"Sam, you can't pass him! There's a truck coming in the other direction!"

"What can I do, then?"

"The cornfield! Into the cornfield!"

In the seconds before Sam jerked the wheel, my mind hailed back to three previous times I was certain I was going to die in a foreign land, thousands of miles from home.

The first was in 1983, when I sat in a darkened house in a suburb of San Salvador with two union organizers. Outside, two carloads of paid assassins tried to figure out if we were armed and dangerous or, like so many other death squad victims, defenseless and ripe for the slaughter.

As it turned out, we were armed. Pancho, my Salvadoran colleague, had a .22 revolver. Larry, who had just joined my team a week previous, had a good-size rock from the garden. I had a broom.

The second was in 1985, when the pilot of our Burma Airways flight came on the intercom to say, "Well, ladies and gentlemen, some nights it just doesn't pay to fly. I can't get the goddamn landing gear down. We're going to try to do it manually, and hopefully we'll have this crate on the ground in a few minutes. But in the meantime, I have to ask you to prepare for a crash landing by fastening your seat belts and placing your heads against the back of the seat in front of you."

The third time was in 1987, in Somalia, when an altercation we had with a UN driver resulted in me and my colleague, a livestock expert from Texas, running for our lives from a sympathetic (to the driver) mob through the streets of Mogadishu.

Well, Sam's timely diversion into the cornfield of an astonished Ugandan farmer spared me from becoming one more victim in the lethal game of chicken played out daily on the Kampala-Jinja highway.

In the case of the Salvadoran hit squad, extinguishing all the lights in the house apparently dissuaded them from carrying out their mission. Not so our call to Embassy Security, which didn't arrive until two hours later.

Timely action on the part of the Burma Airways flight crew obviated the need for a crash landing on the Dhaka airport runway. As we passengers watched, two flight attendants studied what was presumably an owner's manual. Then, one of the attendants descended into the compartment that housed the landing gear while his colleague shuttled back and forth from the cockpit, carrying sometimes tools and other times instructions from the pilot. After a brief eternity, a grease-and-oil-blackened head emerged, grinning: "Landing gear down, and I think locked."

My survival in Somalia I attribute to the last hour of lacrosse practice at Brown, when our coach made us run up and down "Harvard Hill," a near 45-degree incline meant to put us in superior condition when we met the Cambridge milquetoasts for our last game of the season.

What prompts a man who would have otherwise pursued a comfortable middle-class life in America, perhaps selling insurance for AIG or bonds for Lehman Brothers, to repeatedly and knowingly place himself in jeopardy?

It begins with a noble cause. Which morphs into a passion. Which becomes a mission, worth risking your life for.

Of course, not all missions will require you to put your life on the line. But they will entail sacrifice, over and over again. The good news is, you will be rewarded on a daily basis in ways you would not be as just another "factor of production" in a for-profit company. Probably not with great financial gain (although you may be surprised to know this can come as well), but definitely with the satisfaction of knowing that yours is a life worth living, and, most important, that you are helping many others to achieve the same.

1

IDENTIFYING YOUR CONSTITUENCY AND ARRANGING YOUR APPRENTICESHIP

The world abounds with noble causes, and there is one that is just right for you. If you're reading this book, you have taken the first step in that discovery process.

As a second step, identify your constituency, a group of people who are getting a raw deal. Most people have an innate sense of justice and are offended, even outraged, when they see people less fortunate than they being exploited or taken advantage of. But to really help them, you have to get to know them, walk in their shoes. You would be surprised at the number of organizations that espouse this or that noble cause in which the personnel seem only dimly acquainted with the facts on the ground. Many large, publicly funded development agencies are criticized, and rightly so, because they are populated by "experts" who have never known poverty themselves, nor immersed themselves in the world in which four billion people survive on less than four dollars per day. These agencies may be well meaning and full of brilliant people, but unless they close this "empathy gap" their work will forever be hobbled by a fundamental lack of understanding of what their constituents need and desire.

Groups like the Peace Corps (international) or AmeriCorps (U.S. based) are ideal for this purpose of experiencing, firsthand, the lives of your identified constituency. You live on the level of the people you are trying to help. You lose your fear of poor people. You learn to speak their language and communicate with them in terms they can understand. You identify with their problems.

Think that the Peace Corps or AmeriCorps is exclusively for newly minted college graduates? Think again. Five percent, or 350 of the 7,700 Peace Corps volunteers, are over the age of fifty. AmeriCorps has ten times as many volunteers and no upper age limit.

Just because you are accepted into the Peace Corps or AmeriCorps does not mean your mission will be gift wrapped and handed to you upon arrival. Some assignments are more appropriate for finding your mission than others. Try to get involved with a privately funded nongovernmental organization (NGO) rather than a government agency. The NGO will make much better use of you and your talents, while providing the possibility of offering you a "real" job when your voluntary assignment ends, if you've proven yourself useful. A government agency, on the other hand, may not know what to do with you.

Government jobs, especially in developing countries, are often the creations of political patronage. They pay poorly and often don't address real needs. Moreover, they tend to be at a loss as to what to do with another body, however willing and able. A great many Peace Corps volunteers end up teaching English, which is a real job, but not necessarily great for finding your mission. Still, your formal job description doesn't need to prevent you from finding something else useful to do in the community during your abundant spare time. You need to take matters into your own hands and not think the Peace Corps or even an international NGO will have a junior executive training program waiting for you. Read the swag box "From Zero to Hero" to see how I found my mission as a young Peace Corps volunteer in the highlands of Guatemala.

From Zero to Hero

In my case, I had what sounded like a real job as a Peace Corps volunteer: credit officer for an agricultural cooperative in the highlands of Guatemala. The problem was, having been born and raised in Levittown, New York, I didn't bring a deep knowledge of agriculture to the table. Two months of technical training in growing corn and beans in Costa Rica rendered me more of a threat to the Mayan Indian farmers' crops; I was not the Second Coming of Dr. Norman E. Borlaug. In retrospect, my Guatemalan counterpart, Edgar, could be forgiven for his reluctance to introduce me to the co-op members. He and I had weekly meetings at the co-op office in Chimaltenango, and at each meeting he would tell me to wait for him the following day so we could ride together out to the countryside to see the clients. But when the appointed time would arrive, no Edgar. This went on for two months, and I couldn't figure out why.

Then one morning I came out the door of my house to see him stealthily driving his jeep down the main street of my pueblo, headed out to the countryside. I kept watch on the street all afternoon. When I saw him returning, I planted myself in the middle of the *calle* and flagged him down. He sheepishly rolled down the window.

"Look, Edgar, if you don't want to work with me, that's fine. But I'm not going to sit on my ass for the next two years and do nothing. Introduce me to the co-op members, and I will figure out what to do for them."

"Come on, gringo. Let's have a drink."

That day, over much rotgut sugarcane alcohol, I broke the ice with Edgar, but it wasn't until another two months had passed that I found a way to make myself useful to the farmers. When I was learning Spanish in Mexico, our trainer made a big deal about something called *confianza*. It translated literally as "confidence," but really it means "trust." Until you earned the trust of the people you were trying to help, the trainer warned us, they would not admit you to their culture and whatever noble project you were trying to accomplish, however well intentioned, would come to grief. Unfortunately, our instructor was not too specific as to how one went about earning the *confianza* of the people. He gave us to understand it was a somewhat mysterious process, but we would know when we succeeded.

And when we failed.

I will never forget the day I achieved my "*confianza* moment." The co-op had promised to deliver credit in the form of fertilizer instead of cash, but the head of the program had screwed up and ordered it too late. The rains started, and the farmers were desperate to plant. Every day they came to my house asking, "*Don Ruperto, dónde está el fertilizante?*"

The fertilizer finally arrived in the country, but then we had another problem. The dirt roads out to the *aldeas* (hamlets) where the Indians lived had been turned to mud by the heavy rains. The branch manager in Chimaltenango told me he could get the truckers to bring the fertilizer as far as my house in San Martín Jilotepeque, but no one was willing to go out to the *aldeas*. Week after week, the fertilizer piled higher and higher in my house, and the Indians sent their delegations, asking me when I was going to make good on my commitment to deliver it to their communities.

Finally, I took matters into my own hands. I went into Chimaltenango and found a trucker who, for ten *centavos* extra per bag, was willing to drive the final leg from my house to the *aldeas*. I paid him out of my own pocket from my meager $150 a month salary.

I still recall the looks of jubilation on the faces of the farmers when, covered with mud from head to toe after digging the truck out of one slippery morass after another, we finally rolled into their communities with our truckload of fertilizer.

For the first time in my life, I felt useful.

▮▮▮

Aside from volunteering through the Peace Corps or AmeriCorps, you can also offer your services directly to an NGO. All foundations welcome volunteers as "force multipliers," a free resource, and this can be a great way to gain your "poverty experience." However, be forewarned: surprising as it may seem, not all nonprofit managers know how to use volunteers, and many actually avoid them, having learned that even free resources have a cost. Time is a precious commodity in nonprofits, and orienting and training volunteers so they become a value-added resource rather than a burden requires an investment not all managers are willing to make. Volunteers can help by arriving at the doorstep of the foundation "field ready," meaning they have fully researched the organization's mission, structure, and methodology and can provide a clear proposal for how they can contribute to its success.

Oh, and if your first words are "And I will fully cover all my costs, including travel and living expenses," this will dramatically increase your chances of being accepted as a volunteer. The initial experience you gain as a volunteer will prove to be invaluable in the future and, in the end, outweigh the expenses you incur starting out.

What kind of money are we talking about? If you are willing to live on a level with the people, à la Peace Corps, then your monthly outlay, once you reach your destination, should not exceed a few hundred dollars. When I was a Peace Corps volunteer, back in 1971, I was paid the princely sum of $150 a month, and I was able to save $100 of that each month, with my rent being $10 a month and my food a dollar a day. Amazingly, since per capita income in the poor part of the world has changed little since then, your expenses should not be much more than that. The airfare, of course, is the wild card. It can be substantial, even if you man an oar in economy, but you can find bargains if you look hard enough.

So let's say, all in, you would need about $2,000 to live and between $1,000 and $3,000 for the roundtrip airfare. Where would you find such funding?

If you have been working for several years or more, you would hopefully have this amount socked away. If not, you could budget for this expense monthly, and when you hit the critical mass, make your move. If you are a student, many schools have funding for internships, both domestic and overseas. If your school doesn't offer such internships, or if you are just beginning your career, try pleading your case to your local church or service club. Consider finding a way to finance your poverty experience a first test of your marketing and promotion abilities.

Failing those options, turn to the two people who are likely to believe in you most: Mom and Dad. That's right, those same wonderful philanthropists who supported you by financing everything from your First Communion to your wardrobe; from braces to piano lessons; and even took out a second mortgage to pay for your college education. Tell them they aren't done yet: you need this poverty experience to understand how the rest of the world gets by on just a dollar or two a day. Tell them your attitude toward money will never be the same.

Once in the door of an NGO, figure out how to make yourself indispensable. The best way to do this is to get deep into the provision of services to the organization's beneficiaries. Build a constituency that will raise hell with the organization if they hear you're leaving. Make allies and supporters of your salaried counterparts who will testify on your behalf as to your value to the organization. The Big Boss is probably too busy to have taken the time to even realize you've been working there. Six months after you've hit the ground, inform the boss that it's been fun and rewarding, but you have to get back to the real world and earn a paycheck. Note with satisfaction the alarm on his face as he says, "Where the hell are you going? You can't leave! Sit down, let's talk."

There is no substitute for this poverty experience. If you don't have it, you can still work in a mission-driven organization, but you will always lack that real passion and understanding of the world the poor inhabit. Your solutions will be more theoretical, less grounded in reality, and, as a result, less effective. If you get hired by a nonprofit without having had this seminal experience, condition your acceptance of the job on getting into the field to meet the constituents within the first ninety days of your employment. Offer to pay for it yourself if necessary. Your boss will be so impressed she may tell you to put in a voucher afterward to get reimbursed.

Big Pond, Little Pond, or Your Own Pond: On-the-Job Training and Becoming a Social Entrepreneur

Once you have your poverty experience under your belt, there are two paths you can take on the road to becoming a social entrepreneur. You can move immediately toward the creation of your own mission-driven organization, or you might want to do what most people who eventually go into business for themselves do: learn the basics of the trade you want to ply on someone else's dime. This would mean working for a period of months or even years at a nonprofit before you strike out on your own. The amount of time spent there depends on how long it takes before you feel comfortable going it alone. Alternatively, you could find an organization where you believe you can rise to the top in a relatively short time frame and put your own stamp on it. In either case, you are spared the work and trouble of immediately having to create an organization from scratch.

Let's take a look at the overall landscape and what your options are to obtain this kind of on-the-job training.

There are more than a million charities in the United States alone, and millions more overseas. Most participate in a local capacity and create a small impact. Some, however, have developed an innovative approach to solving a particular problem, have managed to scale it up, and are improving the lives of millions of people. In considering the size and overall impact of an organization, you need to ask yourself:

- Where do I want to work to gain my initial experience?
- Where will I best fit in?
- Do I want to be a big fish in a small pond or part of a large school of fish in a big pond?
- Where can I learn the most in the shortest time frame about what I need to know?
- Do I already have my own Big Idea that I know will change the world and just need a platform to launch it?

Each option has its advantages and disadvantages.

The Little Pond

The biggest plus of the "little pond" organization is that small, local foundations make a huge difference in the lives of the individuals they serve. Examples include working at a shelter for the homeless or serving food at a soup kitchen. On the international level, a small organization could be one that cares for war orphans in a conflict country. Your experience could be writ small but rich and satisfying nonetheless.

If you're good and display great aptitude and energy while producing valuable results, you could rise quickly and easily to the top of a small organization. You might see potential for growth the current leadership doesn't, and figure out how to turn the little pond organization into a big pond one. See the swag box "Crossover Craig: Going, Going, Going . . . Green!" for an example of someone who had worked all his life in the commercial sector and then, at the tender age of fifty-five, crossed over to a small pond nonprofit, helped take it to scale, and found both job satisfaction and, ironically, greater financial reward than in his previous career.

The biggest disadvantage of a small organization is that, unless it is lucky enough to have an endowment or the founder gets a spot on Oprah, it is likely to be undercapitalized and living hand to mouth. If you join such a group, make sure you are willing to live with the prospect of the president coming into your office on payday with a long face, asking if you don't mind taking an I.O.U. this pay period.

Keep in mind that there may also be a good reason the organization is small: the founder might like it that way. Beware of joining an organization that is someone's personal ego trip or meal ticket. It may have the potential to grow but won't under the current leadership, either because the leaders don't have the skills to take it to scale or they won't let someone more qualified run it. Several FINCA programs that disaffiliated in the first decade of our development did so because the founding managers of the programs lacked the managerial skills or vision to grow the operation. To quote a former director of a FINCA program in Central America, the managers preferred to be "the head of a mouse rather than the tail of a lion."

||||||||||||||||||||||||||||||||||||||||||||||||||||||||||||||||||||||||

Crossover Craig: Going, Going, Going . . . Green!

Craig is a perfect example of someone who crossed over from the private to the nonprofit sector, jumped into a small pond late in his career, and, catching it on the upswing, is today the number two man in a big pond that is still growing larger.

Craig began his career in banking before moving on to work in real estate, insurance, systems integration, and architecture, always in the role of finance and operations manager. While all these opportunities appeared promising initially, none provided the job satisfaction or financial rewards he was seeking. Age fifty and disenchanted, Craig returned to graduate school, earning a master of science degree in organizational development. It recharged his batteries. Through networking with one of his professors, Craig responded to a job posting from an environmental firm. U.S. Green Building Council (USGBC) is a nonprofit whose lofty mission is to "transform the way buildings and communities are designed, built, and operated, enabling an environmentally and socially responsible, healthy, and prosperous environment that improves the quality of life."

At the time, USGBC was a small nonprofit with $15 million in annual revenues and fifty employees. Like many nonprofits, it was the brainchild of visionaries who over the previous twelve years had brought the organization from zero to the point where it had a precarious grip on financial sustainability. It had something else, however: a Big Idea. And it was not just a Big Idea, it was an idea whose time had come: a system for rating the design, construction, and operation of green buildings. Since buildings in the United States are responsible for 39 percent of CO_2 emissions and 40 percent of all energy consumption, anything that could contribute greater building efficiency was destined to become a very "hot" idea— pun intended. The visionaries, one of whom became CEO in 2003, had positioned USGBC perfectly as the preeminent certification program for green building ratings. However, the CEO needed a partner to manage the exceptional growth that the company was experiencing. Otherwise, it might miss or mismanage the incredible opportunity presented by the growing international interest in a promising program to address global warming.

Enter Crossover Craig. With his experience in both large and entre-preneurial organizations, plus his freshly minted degree in state-of-the-art organizational development, Craig took command of the situation. Over the next five years, in his role as chief operating officer, Craig reorganized the staff and systems at USGBC. The operation transformed from a "process-free zone" into a well-run, competitive organization, while keeping the energy and enthusiasm of the young, idealistic staff intact. Revenues grew fivefold to $100 million. Staff grew from 50 to 220. Requests for USGBC's proprietary Leadership in Energy and Environmental Design (LEED) Green Building Rating System grew not just in the United States but also internationally, with one million square feet of space certified each day.

"It's funny," says Craig, "while I didn't take this job for the money, I'm doing very well by doing good. People, planet, prosperity—the triple bottom line is not a fantasy. It's a remarkably powerful driver of constructive change, so irresistible that an increasing number of global companies are embracing it.

"I love my job."

The Big Pond

The big pond generally has all the upsides and downsides of large organizations. The advantages include financial stability, job security, good benefits, a better-defined job description, plus a clear career path. The chief disadvantages include bureaucracy, less entrepreneurial opportunities, and less ability to shape the strategy and future direction of the organization. You may acquire the skills you seek faster in the big pond, but beware of getting too comfortable and overstaying. You might discover that in the process your entrepreneurial ambitions have been extinguished.

Make sure if you choose a big pond you have done your due diligence and are joining a growing concern, not an organization in a death spiral. Organizations have life cycles just like products and people, and you need to find out where your prospective employer sits on the continuum. The most important feature of the big pond is the leadership, and leaders also have life cycles. Is the CEO one of the founders of the organization with a strong personal commitment to the mission but with enough energy and enthusiasm to keep adapting to changes in the competitive environment? Or is she an aging matriarch on a glide path toward her retirement, surrounded by "yes men and women," padding her nest and preparing to pull the rip cord on her golden parachute? Or is the leader a recently promoted eager beaver with a notion of how to grow the organization, but maybe not enough experience to pull it off? These are hard things to learn during an interview, but you should ask if you can talk to some of the employees to see how they feel about the leadership before you sign on.

In the international domain, most of the big pond organizations fit into one of two categories: relief or economic development. Some organizations, like Save the Children, CARE, Catholic Relief Services, World Vision, and Mercy Corps, do both. It's important to consider what kind of work you want to do. The big relief organizations are designed to respond rapidly to short-term emergencies and disasters of both the natural and manmade kind: hurricanes, tsunamis, famines, civil wars, and genocide, to name a few. They also fulfill a humanitarian role in the less visible, slow-moving tragedies like malnutrition and the AIDS epidemic. These are worthy causes, but the emphasis is on short-term responses, not prevention or making the victims of these tragedies self-sufficient and capable of meeting their own needs in the long run.

The financial model of these organizations reflects this short-term bias. They depend on income from large "feeding programs" financed by the United Nations, USAID, and other governmental or multilateral relief agencies. They also have large, private fund-raising operations that can generate a reliable income stream, based on small donations via direct mail, but are also able to generate huge spikes in contributions, depending on the profile of the disaster. Hurricane Katrina in New Orleans produced a fund-raising bonanza for the American Red Cross initially, followed by a public relations disaster when it was unable to deploy the resources rapidly and effectively. The tsunami in South Asia, which devastated the coastlines of Thailand and Sri Lanka, produced the largest outpouring of public philanthropy in history, far more than the one hundred thousand affected families required and leaving the benefiting foundations with an embarrassment of riches they have yet to find ways to spend effectively.

Development-oriented foundations, on the other hand, focus on long-term, sustainable solutions to the problems of poverty and conflict. People who are frustrated by the seemingly bottomless needs of the poor—and endless solicitations from the relief organizations—are drawn to this sector, as are most social entrepreneurs. The impact of these organizations is usually less immediate and less visible than the smiling child in a refugee camp spooning rice into his mouth. Their funding flows tend to be less reliable and can be "fad driven" in the sense that the donor agencies tend to pounce on the latest intervention showing promise, lavishing resources upon it only to pull the plug when some nay-saying research organization produces a study debunking the practitioners' claims.

The best development-oriented organizations find ways to involve the poor in their own economic and social development, creating sustainable institutions that continue their good works after the subsidies end. The microfinance industry is one of the best illustrations of this phenomenon, where, after three decades of intense investment by the donor community, more than ten thousand microfinance institutions continue to provide small loans and other financial services to more than 150 million of the formerly unbanked poor. Industry analysts argue about the extent to which individual organizations have achieved true financial sustainability, but most have weaned themselves off donations at this point and earn the bulk of their income from interest and fees charged on their loan portfolios.

Your Own Pond

The third, and most challenging, path—also, if you have the tempera-
ment, the most rewarding—is to come up with your own Big Idea and
implement it yourself. In retrospect, recalling all the hard work of all the
people who helped build FINCA into what it is today, I can only shake
my head at what naïve fools my partner John Hatch and I were to embark
on this journey in the first place. When John first told me of his idea to
start a foundation to raise money to fund his village banking concept, I
asked him how long this might take. "A few months" was his answer. Six
years passed before we landed a $9 million USAID grant, and were, for
the first time, able to pay ourselves salaries and hire a few other full-time
employees. Before that, we raised money in small amounts, just enough
to keep our handful of pilot projects going. After each small contribution
John would call to give me the good news: "We're almost there, partner!"

I realize now John's sense of time was more geologic than calendar.

It is important to note that John and I both took this leap midcareer,
after we had worked for several years in big pond organizations. We also
worked as private consultants to both big pond, mission-driven organizations and large bilateral and multilateral international aid agencies. In this
latter capacity, we had the opportunity to see scores of development initiatives, some that worked but many that didn't. By the time we launched
FINCA, John was convinced he had the chops to start, build, and run his
own business that would change the world.

The advantages of the entrepreneurial path are as compelling as the disadvantages are daunting. The greatest boon by far is the joy of being your
own boss. (Probably everyone who has ever had a boss, even a good one,
could agree on that one.) The second is the thrill of building your own
organization and the pride you feel as you see, first, the foundation being
laid, then the walls going up, and, hopefully, the roof finishing it off. You
have control over all the key decisions. One of the greatest frustrations of
working for someone else—waiting to be recognized and rewarded appropriately for your hard work—goes away when you sign your own paychecks.
Oh, and regardless of how bad the job market may be, you can't be fired!
(Well, you could be if you have a Board of Directors, but hopefully they
would put you in another role in the organization versus unceremoniously
sacking you. More on this when we discuss governance in Chapter 17.)

The chief disadvantage of the entrepreneurial path is the high probability of failure. The failure rate for purely commercial start-ups is more than 90 percent. To my knowledge, no one tracks the failure rate for philanthropic start-ups, but considering you have even less ability to control your income than in a commercial venture, it must be so high only a fool or a visionary would try to beat the odds.

If this doesn't dissuade you, be prepared to deal with the next greatest disadvantage: continuous rejection. If entrepreneurs are a rare breed, then people who can recognize a great concept when they see one are even rarer. Be prepared to have total idiots smile condescendingly as you present your brilliant idea and dismiss you with a cavalier "It'll never work." Unless you are absolutely convinced of the worth of your idea *and* stubborn as hell, this path is not for you.

Finally, being an entrepreneur is a lot of work. Even if it's great to be your own boss, you'll soon discover, if you are going to succeed, you have to be a greater tyrant to yourself than the worst "boss from hell" could be.

Regardless of what size pond you enter, and apart from drive and work ethic, the key factor that determines whether a social entrepreneur will eventually succeed or not is the Big Idea.

2

THE BIG IDEA AND FINDING A MENTOR

The Big Idea is the development of a unique product, a "killer app," that actually works and no one else has yet thought of or implemented. If powerful enough, the Big Idea can be the driver of growth and success for many years, but it is not by itself a guarantee of success—the social entrepreneur may screw it up through poor execution, or the competition may eventually steal it and do it better. Big Ideas, however, are surprisingly resilient and tolerant of early failures, and it often takes the competition a long time to wake up and start copying you.

Speaking of the competition, another way to become a social entrepreneur, if you don't have your own Big Idea, is to borrow one from some struggling small pond or social entrepreneur, and do it better and bigger.

Coming Up with Your Big Idea

Where do Big Ideas come from? The process is mysterious and could be the result of years of trial and error or a momentary flash of inspiration. In the case of miracle rice and wheat, the research took years. In the case of microcredit, the solution arose spontaneously, and more or less simultaneously, on two different continents: Latin America and Asia. I made my first microloans in Guatemala in 1972.[1] Muhammad Yunus, several years later, pioneered microlending in Bangladesh. More than a decade later, John Hatch, founder of FINCA, claims to have come up with his group-lending village banking methodology en route to Bolivia while swilling bourbon thirty-five thousand feet over the Andes.

So, how do you recognize a Big Idea when you see one? First, it has to work on a small scale. Harken back to those Mayan Indian farmers to whom I provided fifty dollars' worth of fertilizer on credit. On their slave wages, they would never have amassed that amount of money in a lifetime of working on the oligarch's plantation. Simple as the intervention was, microcredit produced an immediate and huge impact on the beneficiaries' welfare. To continue, it then became a matter of figuring out how to replicate that success and scale it up.

The second big clue your Big Idea might work is that, once you have succeeded with your demonstration project, customers beat a path to your door. For years, naysayers questioned whether microcredit was really a Big Idea or just hype. The millions of poor people who benefited never had such questions. They were too busy queuing up to get their loans.

Some Big Ideas remain trapped in a small program because neither the founder nor anyone else recognizes them as such, and, therefore, no one dedicates sufficient resources to them. When I was a Peace Corps volunteer working in my microcredit program, an American general practitioner, Dr. Berhorst, set up a clinic to attend to the Mayan Indian population in the town of Chimaltenango. His Big Idea was that since few in the indigenous population could afford health care or they were not welcome at the *ladino*-run clinics, he would train a number of Indian paramedics in the basics. Under his guidance, the new paramedics could treat the most common maladies affecting rural Guatemalans: malnutrition and diarrhea. It worked brilliantly, saved the lives of thousands of children, and was an idea that could have been replicated widely. Instead, people assumed Dr. Berhorst was an aberration on the landscape, a crazy gringo doctor who for some reason had abandoned a lucrative career in the States to attend to these worthless Indians.

With time, Dr. Berhorst's Big Idea was vindicated. Paramedics, like China's "barefoot doctors," have become the solution to the disastrous

---

1. The actual concept came from David Fledderjohn, chief of party of our USAID-funded Agricultural Credit Cooperative project.

shortage of doctors in developing countries such as in Kenya, where there are only fourteen doctors for every one thousand people, and far fewer in rural areas.[2]

The final proof of a Big Idea is when other people begin to copy it. Many social entrepreneurs, like Muhammad Yunus and John Hatch, actually encouraged and enabled imitators. Despite their years of work and self-sacrifice, neither Muhammad nor John is bothered by the fact that thousands of organizations have borrowed or downright purloined their "intellectual property" without asking permission. Both believe it belongs in the public domain (John would say it belongs to "the movement," meaning the microfinance industry). John facilitated the process of adoption by traveling around the world holding workshops to teach other large international NGOs the village banking methodology. He reasoned that FINCA had neither the financial nor human resources to roll out the model on a large scale. This strategy worked reasonably well in that a number of large international relief organizations, including Save the Children, CARE, World Relief, Catholic Relief Services, and a myriad of local NGOs, became enamored of the methodology. At this writing, village banking has been adopted or adapted by more than eight hundred organizations, or almost 10 percent of the microfinance institutions worldwide. To this day, John considers it one of his proudest legacies.

Crossover Craig from Chapter 1 had a similar experience. He was invited to Beijing by the Chinese government, who professed an interest in USGBC's green building certification program. Once there, a congenial Chinese official began to describe "their" green building program. "It was identical, down to the most minute detail, to USGBC's program," said Craig. If imitation is the highest form of flattery, then USGBC had been paid the ultimate compliment: its Big Idea was copied by the Chinese.

Can You Be Trained as a Social Entrepreneur?

Many institutions of higher learning apparently think so. In the United States and Canada alone, more than two hundred universities have estab-

---

2. Ironically, the demand for trained paramedics in the United States and Europe has created a "brain drain" among professionals in developing nations and renewed shortages in those countries. Time for another Big Idea?

lished centers, courses, competitions, scholarships, or speakers' series focusing on the field of social entrepreneurship.[3]

At first, I was somewhat skeptical as to whether these programs could really make a difference in swelling the ranks of "real" social entrepreneurs, whom I considered more born than made. Like the famous joke about the waiter trying to complete his chicken soup delivery to a patron who has died of a heart attack, my attitude was "It might not help, but it can't hurt." My perception began to change several years ago, when I got out into the academic community more and started meeting the students and professors involved. The best of these programs combine course work with the opportunity to gain hands-on experience, and they can be a great way for young, aspiring social entrepreneurs to gain their poverty experience. Many have done so at FINCA. In 2008 I did a tour of business schools at Stanford, Berkeley, UCLA, and USC with the actress Natalie Portman to describe the work of FINCA and the importance of microfinance in developing countries. These and other universities have supplied hundreds of interns to FINCA to conduct research and even populate the lower levels of management both at headquarters and in the field.

One of the best programs, where I gave a talk once, is the Social Enterprise Program at Columbia Business School. It has a near ideal mix of course work with opportunities for summer internships; loan assistance programs to support students working with mission-driven organizations in the United States and abroad; consulting opportunities, where students can provide advice to nonprofits; mentoring opportunities with nonprofits; and, my special favorite, Microcolumbia, which provides opportunities for students to travel to see microfinance organizations and even invest in them.[4]

Many FINCA people have MBAs or master's degrees from Georgetown, the School for Advanced International Studies at Johns Hopkins, Wharton, London Economics, or Thunderbird School of International Business in Glendale, Arizona. Nobody laid out the extra bucks for a doctorate. I polled the MBAs in FINCA as to whether that sheepskin actually was relevant to their day-to-day work, and their response was a unanimous *sí*, but with a caveat. All said that while the MBA was useful in providing

---

3. David Bornstein, *How to Change the World: Social Entrepreneurs and the Power of New Ideas* (Oxford, England: Oxford University Press, 2007), xiii.
4. Ray Fishman, The Social Enterprise Program at Columbia Business School, http://www4.gsb.columbia.edu/socialenterprise.

a frame of reference for understanding any kind of business or company, they attributed their success to the work experience they acquired before or at FINCA.

Timing is also a factor. If you have a golden opportunity to work in the field, you may want to put that master's degree on hold for a couple of years. Don't believe those who say, "If you don't do it now, you'll never go back" (think Crossover Craig). You may even be able to persuade your nonprofit to finance that MBA. FINCA has done so for many of its high-performing employees.

The Importance of Finding a Mentor

Another critical step on the road to becoming a social entrepreneur is identifying and recruiting a mentor (or mentors). Mentors are people who have been in the field for a while, know the players and the politics, and will help you navigate your way toward your career objectives. They are more than just people who will give you advice now and then. They are people who are interested enough in your career that they are willing to invest valuable time in you. If you are in a big pond, with well-defined career paths (such as program officer, program manager, program director), your mentor can help you find the time and means to develop your skills and competencies to get promoted to the next level. If you are in a little pond or start-up, where the career development ladders are less well defined or even nonexistent, a mentor can help you anticipate and jump to the next open position for which you are plausibly qualified. Mentors can also advise you as to the right time to make your big move and strike out on your own.

Does the mentor have to be your boss? That would be ideal, but unfortunately not all bosses believe they have the time for mentoring, nor feel it is an important part of their job. If you have such a boss, you must find someone else within the organization to play the role of mentor. This is trickier. You will have to recruit your mentor in such a way that your non-mentor boss doesn't feel as if you are whining or being disloyal.

Is your ultimate goal to go to work for your mentor? Absolutely. Otherwise, you'll have to wait to realize your full potential until your current boss needs you in a different role, and that could take a long time. You need to be proactive.

Assuming the mentor you want to work for also wants you, you will have to arrange a transfer to the new team. If you're good (and of course you are) your current boss isn't going to want to let go of you, because you're making *him or her* look good. But since transfers happen all the time in organizations, most places have protocols for this type of situation. In FINCA it entails the boss you want to work for requesting your current boss to release you, thereby permitting you to make the transfer. Sometimes this can result in your being blocked from a promotion, but successful big bosses realize that preventing someone from moving up the ladder is a way for an organization to lose its best talent.

How do you recognize potential mentors? First, they notice you. You've said or done something to stand out; maybe it is something your current boss takes for granted but your potential mentor realizes is special. You can almost read the bubble coming out the mentor's head: "Wow, this person is really great. Sure wish she worked for me."

You're on first base now, taking a long lead toward second, but your eye is still on the pitcher. After all, you don't want to burn your bridges with your current boss, in case your mentoring plan fails. Now what? How do you make known your interest in working for your mentor without appearing to be a disloyal opportunist? First, by lavishing praise on your mentor and refraining from criticizing your current boss. Couch the move in terms of what you think is best for the organization. Explain why moving you into this new position, even if it's a lateral move, is both a better use of your abilities and a win for the company. Your mentor will get the idea.

Do you have to be a sycophant? Just a little. The first rule of politics is to learn what the other parties want and figure out how to give it to them. The second rule is that 99 percent of people succumb to flattery. In the case of your mentors, what they want is your brain, but it never hurts to let them know what a genius you think they are (especially if they really are a genius).

Let's say you pull it off, you've done it, and now you're working for your mentor. You can just kick back now and take advantage of having a boss who cares so much about promoting you that she'll step aside, if necessary, to get you to the next level, right?

Never forget that the mentor-acolyte relationship is a two-way street. You can't look at mentors merely as people to help your career; you need to ask what you can do to further theirs. Make sure you reward their faith in you on a daily basis.

If you've picked the right mentor, when the moment comes for you to make the next move—even if it means leaving the department or, the ultimate betrayal, leaving the organization—you can count on her to do the right thing. So you better do the right thing as well, including having identified and prepared your successor, so you don't leave your boss in the lurch. If you haven't, sorry, you can't move yet. If you do, you're a shameless opportunist. Good luck finding your next mentor.

Good mentors are like good leaders (as we shall see in the following chapters): unselfish and always ready to put the interest of the organization ahead of their own. If you are lucky enough to work for one, don't screw it up. As the song goes: "Once you have found her, never let her go. Once you have found her, never . . ."

John Hatch was my first mentor, and you'll read in the next chapter the interesting way we came to work together, seven years before we launched FINCA. John taught me how to overcome my insecurities as a consultant, just out of grad school, when I didn't think I had anything of value to impart to my clients. He also taught me how to extract information from people high-born and low, with a combination of backslapping camaraderie and 100-proof Kentucky Bourbon.

After John, I met the second major influence on my life, Mike Hammer, while working for the AFL-CIO as a Cold Warrior supporting democratic trade unions in Latin America between 1978 and 1984. The swag box "A Battlefield Promotion" recounts Mike's story as a passionate union leader who died tragically in El Salvador, pursuing his vision of a better, more just world.

||||||||||||||||||||||||||||||||||||||||||||||||||||||||||||||||||||||||||

A Battlefield Promotion

While working for the American Institute for Free Labor Development (AIFLD), Mike Hammer, a union leader who ran the Agrarian Union program, noticed my grant-writing skills and asked me to write a funding proposal for his Guatemalan program. It was successful, and I was pulled into Mike's team to continue writing proposals for a number of programs.

I was one of the few technical people in an organization filled with wily union bosses, but Mike helped me navigate through it. I needed a political education in order to survive and thrive in those waters; otherwise, I would have always been seen as an outsider. Mike was there to give it to me. But what really made me want to work for him was the same thing that put off many of his colleagues: his over-the-top passion for justice and dignity for the *campesinos*. He was out to make a real change in their lives. I wanted to be a part of that crusade, that mission.

Tragically, Mike's passion for his work ultimately cost him his life. In the wake of a sweeping land reform program Mike and I helped to orchestrate, there came a vicious backlash from the landlords. Mike was sitting in a private dining room at the San Salvador Sheraton Hotel, along with the head of the Salvadoran *campesino* union and a young Seattle lawyer, when two men in ski masks entered, armed with Ingram machine guns. A burst from one assassin's weapon riddled the *campesino* leader's face. The young lawyer was hit twice in the chest, dying instantly. Mike was found lying facedown by a locked exit door with two bullets in the nape of his neck.

To this day, my work is powered by his memory.

■■■

I keep Mike's picture on my desk to remind myself of the ultimate cost one can pay when choosing a life dedicated to pursuing justice for the disenfranchised people of this world. But I also use the photo to remind myself of the joy I felt working for this wonderful man and the incredible excitement I experienced being at his side as we made history together in El Salvador, enabling more than a million people to gain access to the land that was their ticket to a better future, with dignity for themselves and their children. Occasionally, when traveling to El Salvador, I will meet a taxi driver or waiter in a hotel who was the beneficiary of a small parcel of land under the land reform program and who tells me what a difference it has made in his or her life. If I had never done anything else with my life, I would feel satisfied with that memory.

I purposely bracketed these first two chapters with some cautionary anecdotes about the risks involved in undertaking this kind of work, especially internationally, because I want the reader to go into this very serious business with his or her eyes wide open. Throughout this book, and particularly in Chapter 18, "Humanitarians at the Gate: Surviving and Thriving in the Treacherous World of the Modern Nonprofit," I offer some advice on how to mitigate the various personal, financial, professional—and, yes, physical—risks aspiring social entrepreneurs may encounter in pursuit of their mission. These risks must be weighed against the enormous upsides of a life devoted to helping others. Every aspiring social entrepreneur must also be honest with himself or herself as to how important financial gain and a comfortable material lifestyle is in the short term. My personal philosophy is that all we really have during our stay on this earth is time, and expending it chasing things like money, beyond what is required to meet one's basic needs, is like pursuing those fin-backed whales Derick De Veer's crew occasionally hunted in vain, thinking they were the real quarry.[5]

Picture coming to work every day, excited about the impact you're having on people's lives. Imagine the satisfaction you'll feel knowing you're doing something to further social justice or solve the big problems of the world, not just reading about them or watching the latest disaster unfold on CNN and feeling helpless. Think about being involved in a workplace where everyone is pulling for the same, noble mission.

Sound good?

Then as T.S. Eliot said in his poem "The Love Song of J. Alfred Prufrock," "Oh, do not ask, 'What is it?' Let us go and make our visit."

---

5. One of Melville's best lines in *Moby Dick*: "Oh, many are fin backs, my friend, and many are the Dericks!" Herman Melville, *Moby Dick* (Indianapolis, IN: The Bobbs-Merrill Company, 1964), 465.

PART 2

||||||||||||||||||||||||||||||||||||||||||||||||||||||||||||||||||

IT TAKES AN ASYLUM

You've had your poverty experience, found your mission, identified your Big Idea, completed your apprenticeship, and built your skill sets and competencies, thanks to a mentor or two. Maybe you have even risen to the top of your small or large pond and are ready to take command, put your stamp on it, and "make it your own." Alternatively, you see a long road ahead, littered with obstacles (your competitors and colleagues) with no guarantee that you will ever be anointed with the CEO job or have the opportunity to turn your Big Idea into a reality. It's time to make your move. It's your "own pond" moment.

Gathering up your courage, you decide to strike out on your own. But are you really going to do this all on your own? Even Jesus Christ, who may have had the Biggest Idea of all time, realized he needed a disciple or two to help get the word out. The analogy is not as far-fetched as it might seem. You are, in a sense, creating a new religion around your Big Idea, and to implement it and take it to scale, you will need to attract a large flock of fellow believers.

Where do you find these people? Or do they find you? What are the values, qualifications, and competencies you should look for in a person that will help meet the needs of your growing organization at each stage in its development?

Once you have recruited your A team, do you manage them in the same way as in any other organization? How do you establish your credibility as a leader? Once you have, how can you get this motley crew to take your direction, allowing you to remain, as Sinatra put it, "king of the hill; top of the heap"?

Part 2 answers these questions. In it, we will meet the kinds of people your mission-driven organization needs to attract in order to succeed. We will also meet the kinds of people you need to avoid.

First, to understand what we are getting into, let's be present at the moment of conception, that blinding flash of inspiration that sets in motion the chain of events leading to the creation of a new mission-driven organization, in this case FINCA. We'll meet the man responsible, the person without whom none of this would have existed: the Essential Visionary. In any such organization, this is the person who sets the "tone at the top," makes the organization unique, and leaves the company indelibly relieved with his or her footprints, long after coming up with the Big Idea.

Then we'll meet the rest of the team at FINCA whom the Visionary and I acquired along the way, who helped the organization survive its birth trauma and has continued to guide it along its tortuous—and, at times, torturous—journey.

3

||||||||||||||||||||||||||||||||||||||||||||||||||||||||||||||||||||||||

WE FEW, WE HAPPY FEW

The Founding Fathers

The year is 1984, and John Hatch sits in the economy section of a Boeing 727, hurtling above the Peruvian Andes at six hundred miles per hour, bound for La Paz, Bolivia. At nine o'clock the following morning, he must present a million-dollar proposal to the Agency for International Development (AID) related to their Food for Work program, something to help the impoverished Bolivian farmers who scratch out a living growing maize and quinoa or tending llamas in the rural highlands.

Thus far, the normally reliable stimulus of two double bourbons has failed to dissolve his writer's block. Then, like a lightning bolt striking the fuselage, inspiration hits. Hatch grabs a legal pad and hand calculator and starts writing feverishly.

A former Peace Corps volunteer, Hatch had his poverty experience apprenticing himself to a group of thirty Peruvian peasant farmers for sixteen months, as part of his Fulbright doctoral research. Later, he hooked up with a Peruvian from the indigenous highland pueblo of Ayacucho named Aquiles Lanao, who taught Hatch (and me) most of what he knows about communicating with people from other cultures. Lanao served as

Hatch's faithful *escudero* as they traveled throughout Latin America in the 1970s and '80s, designing projects to benefit peasant farmers.

I first met Hatch in 1977, when, as the recent recipient of a master's degree in agricultural economics at the University of Wisconsin, I spied a help wanted ad on the bulletin board at the student union. Hatch was looking for "former Peace Corps volunteers who speak fluent Spanish and have good writing skills" available for consulting assignments with his newly created firm, Rural Development Services. I fit the profile. And I was available.

Without expectations, I sent out my absurdly thin résumé and a writing sample, along with my end-of-tour report from the Peace Corps. Cavalier in tone, poking fun at the more bureaucratic aspects of the Peace Corps, it bristled with red flags for any potential employer with the most rudimentary early warning system.

A week later I got a letter from Hatch. Inside was a check for $1,500, a plane ticket to the Dominican Republic, and a yellow Post-it with a brief message: "You're hired. See you in Santo Domingo."

Back on the plane, Hatch's pen flies over his legal pad, his other hand tapping out numbers on his calculator, sketching out the concept for what he calls a "Community Rotating Loan Fund." It resembles the credit scheme I managed in Guatemala a decade earlier, as well as the one Muhammad Yunus was pioneering on the other side of the world in Bangladesh, but it is more daring. He plans to send five teams out to as many regions of the Bolivian highlands distributing stacks of rapidly depreciating Bolivian pesos into the waiting hands of some seventeen thousand small farmers living in 431 rural communities. He will tell them they can spend the money on anything they want, as long as they pay it back four months later. The fifty dollars' worth of pesos is more money than they have seen in their entire lives. Hatch knows they will put it to good use.

He's right. After proposing his plan to the Agency for International Development and receiving the funding, he and his teams follow through with the program, dispersing the money throughout the Bolivian highlands. When he returns twelve months later to the communities that received the loans, 97 percent of them pay him back. That's the good news.

The not-so-good news is that despite having indexed the loans to potatoes, and sometimes even sheep, the galloping devaluation has smelted the dollar value of the Bolivian pesos he collects from one million dollars down to less than $600,000. But considering that all the commercial banks in the country have closed their doors, unable to figure out how to operate in such an environment, Hatch's program still looks pretty good by comparison.

The new AID director, however, is not so impressed. After two years in operation and having become the most popular rural program in USAID/ Bolivia's portfolio, the Community Rotating Loan Fund program is shut down by AID, prompted by a critical evaluation report from an outside consultant.

The Bolivian experiment has met an untimely end, but an idea—and a mission-driven organization, the Foundation for International Community Assistance (FINCA)—is born. Encouraged by the near-perfect repayment rate, despite the complete absence of traditional banking controls and procedures, Hatch realizes he has tapped into something powerful. He charters a New York–based, 501(c)(3), tax-exempt foundation to serve as the funding vehicle for his concept, which he rechristens "village banking." Over the next decade, Hatch pursues his vision with a passion bordering on obsession.

This is what it means to be a visionary and what it takes to turn that vision into a reality. No mission-driven organization worth a damn would exist without such a person. Focus, passion, and a stubborn insistence on viewing all setbacks as temporary are the positive qualities that create an Essential Visionary. The question becomes: are there negative ones as well?

You know there are. The main issue is that the Visionary cannot be controlled. Note: the Visionary is not difficult to control; he or she is *impossible* to control. That is because these same attributes that are required to launch a new idea—independence, hatred of convention, the need to constantly be creating something fresh and original—seldom play well with their opposites, the kind of traits typically required to build an organization.

Oh, dear. So how will John ever get his foundation up and running? Enter the Carpenter.

The Carpenter

John's older brother, Bob, is John's polar opposite. Carrying the same entrepreneurial DNA, Bob took a different path, buffeting with hearty sinew the shark-infested waters of Corporate America, where money rules and the issues debated ad nauseam in the nonprofit world—those of social impact and mission—are of little or no concern.

While he knows little about working in developing countries, Bob has a vision and understanding of what it takes to build an organization. He also has a small fortune, built up through years of climbing corporate ladders. He started as a major player in the food industry, surviving a "rank and yank" process that winnowed one hundred promising Ivy League MBAs down to less than a dozen. Years later, forced out of the company in a power struggle, Bob was hired on as CEO of a Fortune 500 bakery, where he turned a $50 million loss into a $50 million profit in three years. A grateful board then forced him out in a leveraged buyout (LBO) when he resisted selling the company to a group of outside investors whose intention was to break up the company, fire half the employees, and sell the pieces.

Astutely, John asks his older brother to join him and me on the board of the fledgling foundation and serve as its first chairman.

Bob serves perfunctorily as chair the first year. He observes his younger brother's attempts at institution building with detached amusement. Reluctantly, at John's insistence, he makes time to visit the project in El Salvador. He meets Dona Amelia, a fifty-five-year-old single mother of eight who used to sleep on a straw mat in the market in San Salvador. After several FINCA loans, she now has her own restaurant and guest house. All her children are in school. Her oldest daughter is at Tulane University in the States. What FINCA is doing, Bob realizes, is saving the next generation, the children, from being condemned to live in poverty as their parents and grandparents did.

Bob is hooked. At the next board meeting, energized by what he has seen in the field and excited by FINCA's potential, Bob announces that "it's time to get real." Recognizing his younger brother's Achilles' heel as a manager, Bob fronts the money for them to hire an executive director. It is this poor soul's job to bring focus to the wild gyrations of Bob's younger brother as he criss-crosses the Southern Hemisphere, training people in his village banking methodology and writing them checks to finance the project.

Mr. Bean

Bob convinces Richard, an Arthur Andersen accountant who performed FINCA's first-ever external audit, to take the job of executive director. Richard has worked for Arthur Andersen for the past ten years. He knows how to say no, and he questions everything. Even when he agrees with you, he doesn't, really. He and John eye each other warily.

Richard proceeds to put FINCA's house in order. He balances the books. He hires more staff. FINCA lands a few small grants from AID, John's former client in the consulting firm, so there are actually some beans to be counted.

FINCA then lands a $9 million grant to launch a microfinance program in the El Salvador. Suddenly, resources are no longer a problem. Uncle Bob's largesse is no longer needed. John is dispatched to El Salvador to implement the project and manage the unexpected embarrassment of riches. Well, of course, John is the natural choice to head the project. But to be placed in charge of a $9 million budget? The man who can't say no to a good idea, and to whom everything seems like a good idea?

We try the usual strategy of surrounding the Visionary with accountants and administrators in an effort to "keep him under control." The project agreement with AID stipulates that FINCA won't disburse a dime in loans until our auditor, Arthur Andersen, signs off on the accounting and internal control systems. But John can't wait and creates a number of pilot village banks, which to his mind don't count as actual loans, although he finances them with AID funds.

Meanwhile, in Washington, Richard has hired a former AID official to keep tighter control over the funding. She starts disallowing some of John's expenses, including the funds invested in the "pilot village banks," which means FINCA has to cover them with its own funds. She warns Richard he needs to manage John more closely and hold him to the letter of our cooperative agreement or we risk AID yanking our funding. Richard tries to talk to John, persuade him to be patient and refrain from creating any more "pilot village banks" until we have the green light from AID. John agrees, but then keeps doing it anyway. Richard is getting desperate. He's never had to deal with a situation before where he is nominally in charge but is being ignored by the person he's supposed to be supervising. He doesn't know where to turn for help.

Enter the Monkey in the Middle.

Monkey in the Middle

Recognizing he needs an ally to help him manage John, Richard asks me if I will dedicate one week a month to FINCA. At John's request, while he has been devoting all his time and energy to getting FINCA up and running, I have been managing our consulting firm, Rural Development

Services. As John's partner in the firm, I learned to recognize the signs when John was wandering off course and to have a heart-to-heart talk with him to get him back in line. Reluctantly, I agree to play this same role now, helping Richard to keep control but without reining John in so much he feels he's actually part of an organization.

It works. John stops defying Richard, AID green-lights the "first" loans, and the project starts to take off.

Who is this Monkey, and why is he key to the success of the organization at this stage? If I wasn't so enamored of the primate metaphor, we could have alternatively called him "the bridge," or the "synapse" between the Visionary and his more practical colleagues, Bob and Richard. The Monkey's secret is this: he knows what John knows, and he knows what Bob and Richard know. He has shared John's poverty experience, but he also understands the credit business.[1] Though he may not be as creative as John, neither is he as fearless when it comes to taking risks.

The Monkey has some management experience, having risen through the ranks of a trade union organization from a lowly program officer to a country director in El Salvador in the space of five years. Granted, his "professors" were former union bosses who prized political skills above management science, but they taught him how to jawbone people and defend himself against potential assassins, skills they don't teach you at Harvard Business School. The Monkey's real value to the nascent organization is his ability to translate for John with Richard, and vice versa. Without him, they would be endlessly talking past each other.

As you may have guessed, the Monkey, as interlocutor between his three colleagues, is positioning himself to run the organization one day, even though he might not have thought of himself in those terms at the time. What qualities do you, as an aspiring Monkey-in-Chief, need to be effective in this role?

First, while you may have already decided where you are going to land on an issue, you need to give a fair hearing to all legitimate points of view and allow each of the contending parties to make his or her case. If people feel their ideas are rejected out of hand, they will shut down on you and you will build a cadre of "yes men."

---

1. Note that this does not mean he knows the banking business, which will have interesting consequences for both FINCA and the author down the line.

Second, you need to establish yourself as a "net listener" in the organization. This means you hold back on your own opinions until everyone else has had his or her say. This will immediately set you apart from 95 percent of the rest of the human race, who are "net talkers."

Third, you need to try to get your colleagues to *listen to each other.* What makes this so difficult is that very few people are capable of putting themselves in someone else's shoes and seeing things from their perspective. They simply can't admit that the person they have a conflict with may have a legitimate point of view.

In FINCA people speak so many languages, literally, and come from such diverse cultural and professional backgrounds, that getting them to understand each other as a starting point is a massive challenge. Which brings us to the final and perhaps most important trait you will need: patience.

Let's return to the drama playing out in our young foundation. For three years, the FINCA program in El Salvador prospered, becoming the largest microfinance program in Central America. In 1993, however, the project is infiltrated by criminal elements, who, having perceived in John's trusting nature a golden opportunity for industrial-size fraud, siphon off more than a million dollars through the manufacture of thousands of "ghost loans."

John is crushed. He makes one more effort at managing a program, this time in poor neighborhoods in Washington, D.C., but this too ends in failure. In this case, it isn't John's trust in our employees that is his undoing. The borrowers of FINCA USA cleverly march up the credit ladder John designs for them, borrowing and repaying their first two or three small loans, but when they take out a larger loan of a thousand dollars or more, they simply disappear with it.

Neither John nor FINCA can avoid facing the harsh reality that one of the qualities that makes John such a revered and lovable leader—his boundless trust in just about everyone—also sets him up for the villains and knaves of the world to take advantage of him and FINCA's resources.

Meanwhile, Richard has returned to the private sector, leaving the Monkey in the Middle in charge, just in time for a troika of calamities to strike FINCA. The organization rights itself, and, riding on the success of some of its other programs, lands a series of large AID grants and starts to grow, rapidly.

But with the Monkey at the helm, where does this leave the Visionary?

Whither the Visionary?

The Visionary views the organization taking shape with a bittersweet mixture of pleasure and something else he can't immediately put his finger on. Aha, that's it: *boredom*. As he sits in strategic planning meetings, discussing things like the need for more systems and policies, his eyes glaze over. Something like the reticular membrane anacondas deploy before submerging back into the Amazon after consuming some hapless farmer's goat, slides down over his eyes. His mind wanders back to that happy moment when inspiration struck like a lightning bolt hitting his airplane over the Andes. Since then, he has tried to re-create that moment on a daily, hourly basis. It is growing harder and harder. He still has lots of ideas, but the rest of the people in the organization don't receive them with the same alacrity as they used to. They mumble words like "distraction" and "focus" and move on. True, the organization is growing by leaps and bounds, all powered by his original concept. But village banking is so yesterday, he thinks; time for something fresh and new.

But the organization doesn't have the resources, human or financial, to fund something new. The implementation of the original concept consumes all the resources we have. We could use ten times that amount and it still wouldn't be enough.

No problem, thinks the Visionary, when his latest brilliant idea gets the budget axe. I will raise my own money for it. I did it before; I will do it again.

And it works fine, until the director of development, calling on one of her biggest contributors, hears him say: "Oh, didn't John tell you? I'm not going to contribute to your Focused Program this year because I already gave John a hundred thousand dollars to launch his new Distraction Program."

Why not put the Visionary out to pasture at this point? He's no longer essential to the smooth operation of the organization; in fact, he's an anathema to it. Don't you dare! You still need him. Someone needs to be constantly reminding everyone in the organization why they are there, and that's the role of the Essential Visionary, the one who started it all. The one whose soul and spirit still permeate the place, keeping it real.

Create a space in the organization where the Visionary can still add value without disrupting the daily operations. Don't keep putting him into positions that play to his weaknesses. Forget about trying to control the Visionary, because you can't.

In John's case, we put him in charge of social research, where he was responsible for creating the tools FINCA uses to determine the poverty level of our clients. Then we surrounded him with hard-core social scientists who knew how to design surveys and carry out field search in a way that guaranteed the integrity of the results.

John remains unpredictable, and he still likes to build grand theories based on a handful of data points, but it's a small price to pay for his enormous contribution to the industry.

Still Together (and Crazy) After All These Years

As of this writing, twenty-five years since the founding of FINCA, the Visionary, the Carpenter, Mr. Bean, and the Monkey in the Middle are still together, and that same foundation, originally operating out of a two-bedroom apartment on Broadway and West 66th Street in Manhattan, now has 7,000 employees and offices in twenty-one countries in North America, Latin America, Africa, Eurasia, and the Middle East. Indisputably, these "strange bedfellows" built something new and useful under the sun. Obviously, it wasn't the only way to do it. Some have even had the temerity to ask "Why isn't FINCA bigger and *more* successful?" (They are called mistakes, dearie, and we will read about a lot of them later in these pages.)

Much as I would like to, I cannot take credit for having assembled this cast of characters by design. If any of us had the winning formula in his head it was probably Uncle Bob, the Carpenter.

Diversity was the key. The ability to work with someone whose worldview was starkly different from our own in every respect save one: we were all down with the mission. Because of that, we could live with the diametric points of view on just about everything else. But more important, we complemented each other, all of us having different strengths and weaknesses and bringing different skill sets to the table.

We will pick up the further adventures of the Visionary, the Carpenter, Mr. Bean, and the Monkey in later chapters. But first, let's see how the mission-driven organization attracts other resourceful humans to its cause.

4

WANTED:
RESOURCEFUL HUMANS

Recruiting the Best Minds
Money Can't Buy

Many fascinating species of fauna inhabit mission-driven organizations. Most are looking for something that has been missing in their lives. Some never considered doing anything else and, for them, a nonprofit is "normal." Others are refugees from the private sector, who may consider the way a nonprofit operates "dysfunctional." Others have simply answered a help wanted ad. When they arrive, their reaction is likely to be, "Oh my God, what is this place?"

Today more than ever before, human capital is what counts, not financial capital. In the nonprofit sector, you probably don't have the ability to offer either the short-term big bucks or the whispered promise of future riches that equity provides. In microfinance some have been able to do that through "transforming" their organizations from nonprofits to for-profits, and in the process distributing shares to their directors and employers. We have eschewed this path at FINCA, believing that it creates an impossible conflict of interest between the mission and the goal of personal enrichment. But you do have a card of equal power, if you know how to play it. How does the mission-driven organization attract and retain great people? Not with the promise of big money, that's for sure. Not with the promise of a career in sackcloth and ashes, after which you retire, well, in sackcloth and ashes.

It's the mission.

In this chapter and the following one, we describe ways of using the mission to attract and keep the employees engaged and how to let them experience for themselves what the organization is accomplishing. We describe how to position your organization to access the largest possible pool of candidates—and, conversely, how not to make the mistake of defining yourself in such a way that you drive whole groups of potential talent away. We also identify the types of people you need to build the organization, take it to the next level, and keep it moving forward. Tips on how to identify "builders" versus "maintainers" are presented, and we'll consider how to sort out the potential high performers from the duds, hopefully before the latter have worked for you for several years and cost you lots of money. A tremendous amount of time will be given to the concept of how to find the right chief financial officer (CFO), as more than any other position, this is the one that can bring you and your vision to grief if you don't get it right.

More Men Die for Ribbons than for Gold: Hiring and Retaining Talent

We have already talked about the importance of the Big Idea and how the first test of whether or not your organization has a really powerful concept is how many people are drawn to it. The second test is how many are willing to work for submarket wages or even nothing, accepting instead a "psychic" paycheck, to advance your mission. In my experience, people who work for nonprofits follow a normal distribution: those demanding full market compensation and those willing to volunteer for zero monetary compensation fall at the extremes, while those willing to take equal parts cash and psychic income form that big camel hump in the middle.

Where do you find good people, or do they find you? While the nonprofit world is vast, the specializations within it are many, and the number of successful organizations within those specializations is limited. When it comes to attracting talent, word of mouth is still a major factor. The lesson here is to treat your current employees well, whether you view them as long-term prospects or not, because they will be out there talking to your potential future hires about the positives and negatives of their experience at your organization. Satisfied employees will also be your ace recruiters. Both of my deputies were brought in by other FINCA employees. But don't leave it to chance: offer a recruiting bonus to your existing employees if someone they refer gets hired and makes it to the six-month mark.

These days, your website is the second most important way to attract new talent, and it's the best investment you can make, both in fund-raising and in recruiting. Every candidate I have interviewed in the past several years replied to my opening "What interests you about this opportunity?" question with: "Well, I visited your website and . . ." A tireless, twenty-four-hour workhorse who lurks in cyberspace like a giant sea anemone, your dot-org casts its tentacles across the globe, pulling in good people and money. Make sure it tells your story as well as any of your best field people can. Furthermore, post videos of your beneficiaries explaining, in their own words, how your organization has directly helped them.

In the course of your talent hunt, beware of the fake crossover. This is a person who presents an impressive résumé and, during the interview, tells you that, after a long, distinguished (and by the way, very lucrative) career in the for-profit world she wants to give something back. She stays in the recruiting and interviewing process to the very end, sometimes even to the point of accepting your offer. Then she doesn't show up.

"Oh, I'm so sorry, Rupert, but my current boss gave me a big raise I just couldn't refuse." Or: "I got another offer that was just too good to turn down."

Congratulations. You just got shopped.

Others, it turns out, are just window shopping, like people who look at houses they never intend to live in. Some will even work for you for a while, to avoid a gap on their résumé, until something better comes along. This could be one day (it has happened) or even several years. While this probably happens to every business now and again, for the resource-strapped organization, this can be especially egregious.

Even for those who seem like they will be dedicated to the organization's mission, psychic income doesn't work in all cases, or if it does, it can't always overcome the pull of good old-fashioned greenbacks. To lessen the chances of people bailing, be transparent with your prospective employees at the hiring stage as to what they're signing up for. You don't just need "self-starters": you need "self-finishers" who can do everything in between. Explain to candidates that the only resources they will have are those they obtain through their own efforts. When and if resources do begin to trickle in, they will never be sufficient to get the job done in the normal meaning of the word *done*. Be clear that this period of austerity can last a long time in a nonprofit, possibly forever. In the meantime, they will get little or no support from headquarters, because everyone there is underpaid or volunteering as well. If they can work under these conditions, they are either truly committed to the mission or insane.

Once you have them on board, continue to use the mission to retain your best people. But if you use psychic currency to make payroll, don't make the mistake of assuming everyone in the organization is paid equally. People on the front lines have the benefit of working shoulder-to-shoulder with the company's beneficiaries and seeing the impact of their work. A FINCA employee once summed up the impact of our work as "the smiles on the faces of the women." Having a FINCA client grip your hand, look you in the eyes, and say "God bless you!" can be worth a lot more than the biweekly credit to your bank account.

The folks who toil in the boiler room at headquarters, however, are not so fortunate. It can be difficult to feel the reward when you aren't seeing it firsthand. To help share the wealth, try to move people between headquarters and the front lines as much as you can, even if it's only as a tourist. In an international organization, this can be expensive, and you'll think you can't afford it, but just watch the productivity of that person soar. Watch the morale in the back office rise as she relates her experience to the rest of the team.

If you can't bring the people to the field, bring the field to the staff. Profile a successful client or beneficiary at the monthly staff meeting. Use pictures, video, and personal testimonials. People from the field probably come through headquarters all the time for different reasons. When they do, grab them and corral them into a brown bag lunch to relate stories from the front. Make your work come alive for those who also serve, or wait, on the home front.

Bottom line: Your mission is, literally, worth money. Over the long run, it will save you millions, because people who want to participate in accomplishing your mission, and feel that they will be effective and appreciated, will come to work for you at a deep discount. Other people will give you their valuable time and expertise for free. Use it. But take good care of that halo you have built around the organization's head: if you tarnish it, all that good can disappear overnight.

The mission is the glue that will help you retain your best employees. It serves as the Teflon to ward off appeals from their former employers who, if your new hires are good, will keep in touch with them, asking every six months if they aren't tired of the nonprofit thing and want to come back and earn some real money.

What if these new hires succumb to their former bosses' siren songs? I don't know a single manager who doesn't view the departure of a key employee as the rankest of betrayals. Bite your tongue. Give the traitor a big send-off. Celebrate his contribution. After he discovers the grass wasn't actually greener back in his old job, maybe he'll come back. Many have to FINCA over the years.

Build a Large Tent, Not a Partisan One

One advantage FINCA has in attracting people and donations is the appeal of its business model to both liberals and conservatives. Liberals like it because it addresses a problem they care about: world poverty and social injustice. Conservatives love it because it encourages self-help versus subsidies for the poor. In the job market, FINCA does not ask you to check your party affiliation at the door, but we make it plain that we don't care for whom you vote as long as you do your job and do it well.

This situation works because at FINCA we respect each other's political leanings, even as we engage in passionate and futile efforts to convert each other. In today's political environment, inflamed by vitriolic talk-show hosts, promoting this atmosphere of civility is increasingly difficult. People are paid big bucks to drive wedges between us and exaggerate our differences at the expense of our common values.

Think about your cause, to whom it appeals now, and then, with a little tweaking of the message, to whom it *could* appeal. Granted, some causes will be more difficult to repackage than others, but most people are in the middle of the continuum and can be recruited to your cause with the right message.

Frank Lloyd Wright or Conan the Destroyer?: How to Tell a Builder from a Maintainer, and a Fixer from a Human Wrecking Ball

When an organization is young, or in the creation stage, it needs builders, not maintainers, to take it to the next level. When it gets into trouble, as it surely will, fixers will be necessary to put Humpty back together again. What a new organization never needs is a destroyer, unless it has an institutional death wish.

To avoid costly mistakes, it is imperative that you and your organization are able to distinguish between a destroyer and a fixer. Often, in its desperation to find a savior, the organization will make the wrong hire, picking a destroyer in the guise of builder. You must be able to tell the difference, even when the destroyer has no track record of destruction.

Builders and Maintainers

There are two types of builders required by the mission-driven organization: The mission builder and the organization builder. The traits of mission and organization builders are the same, although they express themselves differently. The first trait of builders is a vision of what they want to accomplish. In the case of mission builders, the vision is of something that doesn't exist yet, anywhere—it's something entirely new under the sun. In the case of organization builders, the vision is something that has been built before—it's what the house will look like when it's done.

The second trait of builders is an impatience with the status quo and a desire to leave something with their name on it, something they can point to and say, "I did that." For mission builders, this is a long-term, steady state that can last for decades. Organization builders, however, have a shorter attention span and horizon; they need to finish the house in a few years and then turn their hands to building another one.

A third and related trait is a monstrous, almost inhuman work ethic, without which the builder will never last. Here there is little space between mission builders and organization builders, but the contrast to the maintainer is striking.

Maintainers are those employees who get to work on time and leave on time. Builders, on the other hand, have already put in four hours of work before arriving at the office because they couldn't sleep the night before thinking about how to solve an organizational problem no one else could. Maintainers go out to lunch with their colleagues every day, while builders eat alone at their desks. Maintainers achieve a nirvana-like peace of mind from repeating the same process, like closing the books each month, over and over. Builders get restless if two days are ever the same. You need both builders and maintainers if your organization is to thrive. While the former may be your high-profile, high-maintenance employees, your less visible maintainers are also making a big contribution, just by keeping the wheels turning. And if you ignore them, you may learn, to your regret, just how big.

John, the Essential Visionary, is the best example of a mission builder. He had a clear vision of what he wanted to accomplish, and he wasn't going to stop until he got there.

Does the organization need more than one mission builder? If it's a local effort with limited outreach, it probably cannot withstand more than one as the founder most likely would not appreciate a second center of energy in the organization. If it wants to scale up and have a significant impact—especially a global outreach—then it will need a host of little mission builders (LMBs). Since the Essential Visionary can't be everywhere, and, especially in the early days it is critical to replicate the founder's passion, LMBs may prove to be invaluable. Who is the best person to identify and recruit these LMBs? The Essential Visionary, of course. Understand, however, that what you will get in these LMBs is a clone of the Essential Visionary, with all his good traits and liabilities as well. The "They Were the Best of Times" swag box describes how Hatch and I went about recruiting a quartet of LMBs throughout Central America, getting at once exactly what we had hoped for and more than we had bargained for.

Keep in mind that when the time comes to build the house, unless you want to live the rest of your life in a tent, you will need to find an organization builder to move the project, or projects, forward to the next stage.

They Were the Best of Times

With an initial investment of ten thousand dollars per country, FINCA launches pilot programs in four countries of Central America. To manage them, John and I recruit local entrepreneurs, offering five hundred dollars per month. They all take the deal. The chance to work for a messiah like John Hatch is worth it.

Our LMBs are an interesting mix, occupying different loci on the spectrum between mission and organization builders. One of the two John chooses, Irma from Costa Rica, shares his unbridled passion for the mission and has an over-the-top energy and work ethic.

Though Irma is a great field person, she is a zero at institution building. The promoters in the field love her, but none of the managers in the head office working with her last for very long. She also jealously guards her prerogatives as executive director of the program and ignores my suggestions that she needs to build a stronger management team and learn to delegate responsibilities and tasks. Sometimes a troublesome thought creeps into my head: is Irma building an organization for FINCA or for Irma?

Pablo, another of John's picks, is in charge of FINCA El Salvador and in many respects a carbon copy of his mentor. A brilliant promoter, he quickly lands a number of grants and builds a big staff. Unfortunately, similar to Irma, Pablo is less effective as a manager. He doesn't stay focused on microfinance and branches out into housing and anything else the donors will pay for.

Carla, in charge of FINCA Guatemala, is one of my hires. She is organized and cautious; more of a manager. She grows the program slowly and with quality, and she doesn't talk about grandiose things like saving the world and ending poverty. Unlike our other country directors, she is no good at fund-raising and relies on FINCA International to bring in the money. While she relates beautifully and without prejudice to the indigenous women clients, she can become aloof and testy when dealing with headquarters staff. Like Irma, she doesn't appreciate people telling her how to run "her" program. But it seems like a small price to pay; she's getting the results we need.

Monica, my choice for FINCA Honduras, is a patrician from the Latin American aristocracy who needs to overcome her fear of poor people before she can be effective in organizing the village banks. Once she does, she grows the program quickly and with great quality. She is the only one of our four who "has it all": she can do the field work, manage the personnel, and raise funds. Her connections within the ruling elite are helpful in this regard. Unfortunately, two years after we hire her,

her husband is relocated to the States. She hands the reins over to her hand-picked successor, leaving FINCA Honduras in excellent shape.

Sadly, none of those founding four LMBs is still with FINCA today. Irma and Carla, as we might have foreseen, took "their" programs private, turning them into de facto family foundations and in Carla's case, as we will see later in the book, creating big problems for FINCA in the process. Pablo got FINCA so deep in debt he eventually tried to rescue it with his own personal resources and went bankrupt in the process. Monica is enjoying retirement somewhere in the southern United States. We owe them all a great debt. They got FINCA off to a great start in Central America: they earned us the reputation we needed to spread our wings and launch other programs in Latin America and, eventually, the rest of the world.

||||||||||||||||||||||||||||||||||||||||||||||||||||||||||||||||||||||||||||||||

The best example of an organization builder we have met thus far is FINCA's chairman. You remember Uncle Bob, the Carpenter. Bob didn't know what a mission-driven nonprofit looked like, but, as all houses have a floor, walls, and a roof, all organizations have recognizable structures as well. And yes, if you have a decentralized organization with many operating units, you will need many little organization builders (LOBs) as well.

Fixers

Fixers are builders with a twist: they like to clean up other people's messes. They love coming into an organization laid waste by a mismanagement cyclone, surveying the wreckage, and ferreting out those responsible. While the CDOs (chief destruction officers) may have already been sacked or moved on, fixers know their accomplices are still out there, lurking among the toppled columns, peeking out at them.

Most managers dread firing people. The first time I had to do it, I spent the afternoon in my office, door shut, weeping. I can't say it has grown easier with the years, although I have constructed an elegant rationale around it. If it is performance related, I cast myself as the defender of FINCA's high standards. If it is born of financial necessity (as during the global financial crisis), I console myself with the knowledge that I had no choice and the innocent victims will eventually find work elsewhere.

Fixers, however, have no such qualms. I don't know what narrative plays in their heads, if any. They have the ability to view the process through a Darwinian lens: they are natural selection at work.

After fixers have done what you hired them to do, don't make the mistake of leaving them in charge of the unit they fixed. Remember, they're not maintainers. They will get bored quickly. If you want your fixers to stay around, give them something new to fix.

Hiring Builders and Fixers

How can you be sure the person you are interviewing is the builder or fixer you are seeking and not a maintainer or, God forbid, a destroyer? Builders and fixers have definite skill sets and competencies, but they aren't always easily detectable. Plus, when you are starting out and have little or no money, you don't have the luxury of buying an experienced builder or fixer with a long track record of success. So you take a chance on some young, untested talent.

Luck and instinct play a role in your ability to pick winners. But you can tilt the table in your favor by knowing what questions to ask during the interview.

In interviewing potential builders, first ask what they consider their greatest accomplishment in their career or life thus far. If they have to think longer than a few seconds before answering, it could be they have too many from which to choose. More likely, you should excuse yourself, go out to your secretary, and ask her to interrupt you in five minutes with an urgent phone call.

If they do come up with their greatest accomplishment, see if it's an example of something they built over time or if it's a new sales or profit record. Then, if his name is Carl, for example, go job by job down his résumé, asking him to describe the situation of the company or organization BC (Before Carl) versus AC (After Carl). What was the situation he came into, and what was it like after he left? Look for people who came into situations where there was little or nothing going on, who, by the time they left, had created something that survived their departure.

Fixers can be identified in much the same way. However, they should also be masters of change management, which has a well-defined prescription for getting the employees behind the effort. The fixer must be able to first create a sense of urgency among the staff. The team members need to know that the fixer is there because unless the organization radically changes course, it will not survive, and they will all be out of a job. Second, depending on their reaction to this message, you will need to classify your personnel into three categories: (1) those who accept the need to do something different, and potentially support the fixer's new effort, (2) "fence sitters" who may be scared, curious, or even skeptical, but could be won over by the fixer, and (3) those with a stake in the status quo who will definitely undermine your efforts, if given the chance (they could be looting the organization or taking advantage of weak internal controls). The fixer needs to win over groups 1 and 2 and have no qualms about terminating the employees in group 3. If your fixer knows and follows this methodology, she still may fail, but at least she has a fighting chance.

Sometimes you will be lucky enough to hire mission builders who have a good dose of organization builder in them. They can take you far. But what do you do when your loyal mission builder has constructed the best house he can, yet the roof still leaks and he won't bring in a fixer to replace it?

Cut your losses. Replace the mission builder with an organization builder. Yes, the mission will suffer under this change and you will have to compensate for that somehow, but if you don't make the change, your organization—and the mission—will remain forever captive to the limitations of your first mission builder.

It hurts to say good-bye. You feel like an ungrateful son of a bitch for kicking your mission builders to the curb after all their sweat and years of loyal service. Maybe you can find another role for them. Some mission builders will accept this solution, and others will not, choosing instead to, hopefully, move on to their next Big Idea. Before they do, make sure to honor their contribution.

Destroyers

Finally, let's look at the fourth category of new recruit, the kind no one seeks to hire but everyone does at some point: the destroyer.

There are two main species of destroyers: inactive and proactive. Inactive destroyers (IDs) bring down the organization through neglect, failing to make even the minimal efforts required to maintain what they have inherited from their predecessors. Proactive destroyers (PDs) are actually often well intentioned, and might even be a perverse form of builder, the difference being PDs build with faulty materials and hire incompetent subcontractors.

Destroyers are good talkers. That's how they keep getting employed; they have brilliant excuses for why they failed in their last job, or they may even be able to paint their failures as successes. Once they are on board, even though the evidence is clear they aren't performing, you have a hard time giving up on them. They develop a convincing narrative that goes something like this:

Month One: "Oh, Rupert, you didn't tell me how bad this program really was! This is going to take longer than I thought. How long? Well, give me another month. I'll give you an assessment."

Month Two: "Yes, the decline has continued. It's going to take some time to turn this baby around, as I warned you. I know, I know, I promised you a timeline, with specific targets. I've been so busy just keeping the wheels on! The big problem, you see, is my staff. They aren't cutting it. Why haven't I fired any of them? Good question. I will have to do that eventually, but I have to be careful about it in order not to make things even worse."

Month Three: "Yes, the decline has continued, but the *rate* of decline is slowing. No, perhaps .01 percent is not a significant improvement, but at least it has not accelerated! No, I have not fired anyone yet, but I have made up a list. No, I don't have it here; I keep it at home since it's so sensitive."

Month Four: "Yes, another month of decline. And, yes, the rate of decline appears to have accelerated somewhat, although I believe it is too early to call it a trend. External factors played a role, I believe. We had some heavy rains this month that destroyed the maize harvest in a third of the country. No, none of our people grow maize, not that I am aware of, but the crop loss affected the overall economy."

A tell-tale sign of many destroyers is that they don't fire anyone, or if they do, it's only the most egregious nonperformers. Why would this be? Because, unbeknownst to you, he has made an alliance with them. Unlike you, the staff works with him on a daily basis and has figured out that this guy is no miracle worker. In fact, they can't believe you were stupid or cruel enough to impose this incompetent fool on them. But what's the point of blowing the whistle on him? You probably wouldn't believe them anyway. Besides, he's not all bad. He doesn't push them, he tolerates their subpar performance, and he even seems to be turning a blind eye to those employees in the most remote office (that he never visits, of course) who everyone suspects may be stealing. All things considered, it's not a bad arrangement. At least until the company goes under, after which they will all have to find other work.

Be the Dumbest Person in the Room

Some managers are afraid to hire people smarter and more ambitious than they are, thinking these new hires will knife them in the back and steal their job. Elsewhere in these pages, we will provide advice on ways to remain on top and in control, even when the person you are managing thinks—no, *knows*—he's smarter, more qualified, and more capable to perform your job than you are. For now, let's discuss why you need these people.

You may wonder why you would even take the chance of hiring someone more qualified in their area, let alone *your* area, and risk having your boss recognize your comparative lack of worth. As it turns out, however, hiring such employees is the only way for managers to keep their positions. If you don't hire the right person, or people, your boss surely will fire you.

If you hire mediocre, manageable people who always take direction and never talk back, eventually they will screw up and take you down with them. Count on it. The most dangerous thing about obsequious, under-qualified bootlicks who are only in their positions because they tell you what you want to hear, is that *they* will not recognize the warning signs when the wheels of a program, or an entire organization, are coming off. If they are in a strategic position in the organization, when they fail, you fail. They may have the best of intentions, but if they aren't up to the tasks they have been assigned, they will do hidden damage just like termites. And one day, you will walk into the office and the floor will collapse beneath you.

The swag box "But He'll Saw the Floor Out from Under Me" relates the story of Gloria, the director of FINCA Honduras, who had to be replaced because she could not bring herself to trust anyone smarter than she and build a competent management team.

But He'll Saw the Floor Out from Under Me

Gloria, the woman who runs FINCA's program in Honduras, has the makings of a star. She is down with the mission, tough but fair with her employees, and a terrific promoter of the program with the donors. During the past six years, she took FINCA Honduras from a small operation with a few hundred clients to become the best microfinance company in the country. Gloria has unlimited potential. She has the headroom to go all the way.

But Gloria has one tragic flaw. Being a woman (no, that isn't a flaw) in a *macho* society, she knows she has to be twice as good as any man in order to keep her job. She also suspects that, *ceteris paribus*, Hondurans *prefer* to have a man in the top job and will find any excuse to replace her with one. This, of itself, is not a problem. A certain amount of paranoia, as Andy Grove, CEO of Intel, describes in his book *Only the Paranoid Survive*, is not only healthy but desirable. Gloria's problem, however, is that she lets her paranoia take the wheel to the point that she refuses to hire anyone smarter or more capable than she, even in areas like finance, her Achilles' heel.

For years, FINCA Honduras has succeeded largely on the strength of Gloria's personal skills at promotion and outreach. She is a field person who loves to meet with the clients, get out to the branches, and kick the tires. She loathes accounting and the boring back-office stuff. Over the years, FINCA Honduras has built up a number of "transitory accounts," on both the debit and credit sides, whose balances have grown to be significant: several hundred thousand dollars. A transitory account is a wonderful thing, invented by accountants who couldn't do their job. Got a one-legged transaction comprised of a debit but no credit? A disbursement from the administrative account with no record of what it was for? Got a loan that someone collected, then lost the deposit slip so we don't know which client it was from? Dump it into the transitional account.

Had we not trusted Gloria completely, and her ability to sniff out evildoers, we would have suspected fraud. As it is, though, even with Gloria at the helm, we are taking a big risk.

Gloria's CFO is a congenial, marginally competent guy who in the early years, when FINCA Honduras had a few hundred clients and a portfolio of less than a million dollars, was doing an adequate job. As the organization grows, the CFO and his team (he also hired people dumber than he) begin to fall behind. The financial statements that used to be available fifteen days after the end of the month are now not available until after forty-five days. Plus, like Marley's ghost, they drag a long chain of unreconciled transitional accounts.

No amount of mentoring or additional training is going to bring the CFO up to speed fast enough to deal with this problem. Fire him, the board urges Gloria. She agrees but drags her feet, claiming she can't find any good candidates. The situation grows more and more dire. We risk flunking the external audit and having our funding cut off, so we send a board member to find candidates. Some are very qualified, but Gloria doesn't like any of them. Finally, we have no choice. We fire Gloria.

▐▌

Organizations have grown so large and the environments they operate in so complex that you cannot possibly become an expert in every area. Be the dumbest person on your management team and the least specialized. Yes, it will be hard to master some areas to the point that you can manage your specialists effectively, but we'll give you some tips on how to do so in Part 4, "Not Rocket Science: Structure, Systems, Technology, and Strategy." When all is said and done, you will find that being the "dumbest" in the room will not make you an ineffective leader. In fact, it may be what saves your organization and your job.

5

‖‖

STILL WANTED: MORE RESOURCEFUL HUMANS

And the Interview Techniques to Find Them

A final word on the importance of the recruiting process, before we move forward: Darwin Eads, a member of FINCA's Advisory Board and an industrial psychologist, complains that while organizations will often spend many hours working on the specifications and procurement of a vehicle or piece of equipment, they will hire a key employee on the strength of a brief interview or their "gut instinct." Yet during his tenure this key employee may generate millions of dollars in profits for the organization or, conversely, lose millions. Keep this in mind while reading the following sections leading up to the interviewing portion of the chapter.

The Bar Raiser: There Will Be Blood

Sometimes you have no idea of what can be accomplished in a position until someone new comes in and shows you. A bar raiser, that is, a builder with a turbocharger, sets a new standard and forces everyone, including you, to rise to it—or else.

It is not easy to recognize a bar raiser right away, although there are signs in the interview process. At some point, usually very early, you realize it is *you* who is being interviewed. The candidate is trying to discern whether or not you are the kind of boss who will "give him wings," as the Salvadorans say, and enable him to fly high. He is also trying to figure out who is in your organization right now and if they will be obstacles to what he wants to accomplish. At some point, if you have succeeded in satisfying his concerns and piquing his interest, you will sense a restlessness setting in on his side of the table. Now he really wants this job. And he's itching to start tearing into the guts of your organization and fixing it.

Bar raisers will also likely attach conditions to their coming on board. They may immediately require a waiver of some sacred policy, like the signing of a noncompete agreement, or they may want a downside parachute if it turns out you can't get along. They will ask for the maximum number of vacation days (and then won't take any the first two years), even though the policy says new hires only get two weeks.

If you agree to this and you have an authentic bar raiser, you won't regret it. The swag box "Out of the Park" relates the story of Werner, who tripled the size of FINCA's Eurasia region in three years and forced everyone else in the organization to raise their game in order to keep up with him.

While some bar raisers give themselves away during the interview, it is *after* they come on board that you really know that you have landed one. They throw themselves into their work and make things happen immediately. There is no waiting for months, as with the destroyer, to see if they are getting results. Bar raisers instantly classify their direct reports into keepers, maybes, and the ones they feel won't be worth the effort to reach their high standards. Conflicts with the rest of the team and their peers emerge early, and although you haven't asked, they will offer their opinion as to who needs to be replaced on your team. You will also have a nagging suspicion that maybe they think *you* are not up to standards and need replacing.

This is when you have to remind yourself: be the dumbest person in the room. Chill the paranoia. The bar raiser is going to take the organization to a whole new level, and he's going to elevate you and everyone else who cooperates with him.

I don't have to tell you the fate of those who oppose him.

Out of the Park

One glance at Werner's résumé tells me this is the person I have been looking for. The search has not been easy; we are looking for a new regional director to take over our most challenging region, Eurasia. Normally a six-month gap in someone's résumé would be a red flag, but in Werner's case, his explanation that he left his last job voluntarily checks out. His previous boss has nothing but good things to say about him, although he cautions that he is very stubborn. "You argue with him, he disagrees, you make your case, he still disagrees, you insist he sees it your way, and in the end . . . you give in." Another reference expresses doubts that Werner will be a good fit for FINCA. She thinks he's too high powered for us.

This is my concern as well. To get an initial reading, I ask Werner to meet with my country director in Kosovo. "I actually liked him," is the feedback. I take a deep breath and go ahead with the hire. FINCA's tag line is "Small Loans, Big Changes." I sense some big changes coming.

Werner's predecessor had grown the region modestly, but with excellent quality. When Werner looks at FINCA Eurasia, however, he sees something altogether different: vastly unrealized potential. His diagnosis is simple: given the unmet demand for credit in the seven countries where we work, FINCA Eurasia is a fraction of what it should be. To grow, FINCA Eurasia must lever up and attract debt capital on top of the millions in USAID grant money that originally capitalized the region. To accomplish this, Werner needs a credible business plan, one that shows potential investors (many of whom know and respect him from his previous job at our competitor) that FINCA Eurasia will become large and important enough to justify the costs of making the investment. As far as the execution of the business plan—Werner surveys his team, shaking his head—he has a lot of recruiting, retooling, and training to do.

Werner moves from the planning to the execution stage with blinding, near inhuman speed. He hires two former colleagues who, like him, want to move from their current employer, a network of commercial microfinance banks, to FINCA in order to work with poorer clients (the mission!). He makes other good hires and identifies a number of promising people internally whom he promotes. He makes a number of changes to the credit methodology and streamlines the loan approval process, making our product more attractive to our clients.

Then Werner turns his attention to his existing team of seven country directors, whom he has inherited from his predecessor. There are no clear keepers, he tells me; at best they are all maybes. At the first Eurasia regional meeting, the country directors meet their new boss. The atmosphere is tense. This is not going to be an easy adjustment. I brace myself for major turnover, either driven by Werner through resignations or flat-out terminations.

It doesn't happen.

I'm pleased to see that Werner bends over backward to retool his team of country directors rather than take the easier step of just replacing them. From the CDs' side, while Werner is more demanding than his predecessor, everyone recognizes there is a lot they can learn from him. Ultimately, we have only one CD who is transferred to another region, and no one is fired.

Over the course of the next three years, Werner more than triples the portfolio and the number of clients in Eurasia. He is not infallible of course, and we end up suffering a sizable fraud in Armenia. But Werner owns up to his failings, learns from them, fixes the weaknesses in the internal controls, and moves on.

He raises the bar.

▌▌

The Faustian Pact: When the One You Need Isn't Down with the Mission

To maintain your company's culture, all new hires should be screened for their interest in the mission. You can't assume because they are applying to your organization that they are down with its values. Nor should you persuade yourself that, if someone is a great candidate in every other sense, you can indoctrinate her later. If candidates lack commitment to your core values, they won't fit into your top team and you won't be able to count on their support when decisions must be made that involve the mission. In the worst case, they may undermine you in subtle ways, behaving in a way consistent with their reading of what the mission of your organization should be, not what it truly is.

Sometimes, however, the organization needs someone's expertise so badly you are willing to take a chance. In this case, commit candidates to an immersion plan, wherein you take them to the field to witness your work firsthand while you observe their reaction. If you can manage to do this *before* they come on board, all the better. One CEO of a Latin American NGO, working with orphans in inner cities, will not hire anyone, even a back-office person, unless the candidate has first spent a full day with members of the organization in the poorest barrio in the city, a place where people live in cardboard shacks clinging to the edge of a rat-infested ravine that stinks of garbage. In such a situation, people do come around. At FINCA, I have witnessed former bankers with ice in their veins being transformed into ardent supporters of the mission.

There are other times, however, when you suspect your candidate will never come to the light, when you've clearly spotted the cloven hooves inside his tasseled loafers and the bulge of the tail tucked into his trousers. You've been looking for months, and the "mission fit" person with the skills you need is just not out there. Meanwhile, the organization is slipping into chaos. In that case, you might hire him anyway.

If possible, try not to have more than one of these "mission misfits" on your team at the same time. There is such a thing as making your life too interesting. The swag box "Double Trouble for Rupert" relates the brief but incandescent narrative arcs of Tomas and Jerry, each of whom came to FINCA from the corporate world and for a time struggled to adapt to the ways of the mission-driven organization, ultimately unable to transcend their corporate DNA.

||||||||||||||||||||||||||||||||||||||||||||||||||||||||||||||||||||||

Double Trouble for Rupert

In 1998, after four years at the helm, I find myself in the unenviable position of occupying the top three jobs at FINCA: CEO, COO, and CFO.

One upside of performing these jobs myself is that I have a clearer vision of what I want in these positions. In the case of the COO, many microfinance institutions are transforming into regulated commercial banks to gain access to the capital markets. I want FINCA to follow this same path. It's time to hire a banker as my COO.

Tomas is a refugee from the collapse of the banking sector in his home country in South America, when many people lost their life savings and bankers fled into exile rather than face criminal prosecution. He may be just what FINCA needs, but he is a shock to our system. Entering a regional meeting while he is describing his expectations for this team is like walking into a funeral parlor. "Every FINCA affiliate should have a loan portfolio of at least $10 million," he tells his terrified audience. At the time, our biggest program has total loans of a little more than $3 million. While I believe the changes Tomas is making are the right ones for the organization, I don't like what he's doing to the culture of FINCA. One of best regional directors resigns, unable to stomach Tomas's authoritarian management style.

In the meantime, I have identified a CFO candidate. Jerry is the hard-charging chief accountant of a big government contractor. He has experience going into screwed-up companies and putting their books in order in record time. His references testify to his insane work ethic. He tells me this is his dream job. I want to believe him, but I find it to hard to fathom how someone with his background could adjust to FINCA.

Over the next two years, FINCA makes major progress. All the affiliates grow dramatically. On the financial side, Jerry hires a small army of accountants who put the house in order. For the first time, I have confidence in the financial statements.

But something else is going on. Both Tomas and Jerry have brought their "command and control" management styles with them from the private sector, which grates on their employees. We have more resignations.

When Tomas and Jerry aren't tormenting their employees, they are training their guns on each other. Though each has clear areas of responsibility, they keep getting in each other's way. My other managers warn me the conflict between Jerry and Tomas is splitting the organization into two camps.

I have a talk with Uncle Bob. "Fire them both," he advises me.

The idea is unthinkable. The organization is at a whole new level, thanks to Tomas and Jerry. But their pissing match is destroying FINCA. By tolerating it, I am making a mockery of the organization's values.

I take half of Uncle Bob's advice and fire Tomas. With Tomas gone, Jerry settles down a bit. But with a change in the White House, our government grants begin drying up. We go through a wrenching downsizing at headquarters, and Jerry, sensing coming hard times at FINCA, returns to his previous employer.

The question now is, would I do it again? I made my deal with the devil and moved the ball down the field. The organization paid a price but then righted itself.

The answer is yes, I would make the same decision.

▌▌

I learned another valuable lesson from my Tom and Jerry experience: never allow too many filters to get between you and the rest of the employees and, above all, the beneficiaries. With Tomas managing the operations and Jerry in charge of finances, my job was reduced to serving as referee between them. By removing Tomas I reestablished my relationships with my field team, just in time to learn many of them had been putting out their résumés.

When Beans Bite Back: Getting the Finance Director You Need, Not the One You Deserve

You've heard the expression: accounting is not rocket science. True, perhaps, but there have been times when I wished I were planning a manned mission to the moon rather than unraveling a hairball of one-legged bookkeeping entries. And I don't think I'm the only nonprofit CEO who dreads those final weeks of an audit as my finance department works behind closed doors with the auditors cajoling those last, obstinate beans to jump into their proper boxes.

You'll recognize good chief financial officers (CFOs) during the interview process because, like the bar raiser, they ask more questions than you do. They have been around enough to suspect your dirty little secret: you're hiring them to clean up a mess. Now they want to know how big it is and how long it will take to do so. They realize that regardless of how honest and transparent you are trying to be, even *you* don't know the true dimensions of the disaster.

There are also several odd features of nonprofit accounting, such as the treatment of grants, which is optimistic in the extreme. It assumes that every pledge translates into an actual donation and therefore requires you to register it as income *before you actually receive the money*. This is the nonprofit's version of "The check is in the mail." Similarly, there is the treatment of restricted grants, which *can't* be registered as income until you actually spend the money (according to the terms of the grant/contribution) *even though you have already received the money*.

There are financial types who don't find this odd and, even more unusual, get excited when the sadistic pooh-bahs of the Accounting Standards Board change the "generally accepted accounting principles" every couple of years.[1] If you find such a person, chain her to a heavy safe in your basement. Better yet, send me her résumé.

The swag box "When Beans Bite Back" recounts the good, bad, and disastrous picks the author made in filling this key position, which, nevertheless, followed a jagged trajectory ever upward.

‖‖

When Beans Bite Back

During its formative years, FINCA doesn't need a bean counter because it has few beans. When the beans finally do begin to roll in, Mr. Bean himself is on hand to record them and put them in their proper places.

It's when Mr. Bean returns to the private sector and hands the reins over to the Monkey that things get complicated.

FINCA's first director of finance, Frijol Uno, is a good old boy from the Department of Defense. Why did we think that the DOD, which has so much money its rounding errors begin at a trillion dollars, would be an appropriate place to find our finance director? Good question. At his first board meeting F-1 presents a balance sheet that doesn't balance. He makes a big splash when we throw him overboard.

Frijol Uno's successor, Frijol Dos, not only can balance a balance sheet but also wants to fix everything else wrong with FINCA. F-2 is a ball of energy, and he is indisputably getting things done. The only downside is that he clashes frequently with other members of the team, whom

---

1. At this writing, we are struggling to convert to something called International Financial Reporting Standards. To put it mildly, not everyone in the financial accounting world believes this is an improvement over the last set of principles and standards.

he feels don't rise to his high standards. He successfully orchestrates a complicated conversion to a new accounting system and volunteers for all the toughest assignments, like going down to rescue our troubled program in Guatemala, which is behind schedule on delivering a customized accounting software program. His heroics, however, end in tragedy.

On a rainy night flight over the Central American highlands, the pilot becomes disoriented and crashes into a volcano at six hundred miles per hour. F-2 and two colleagues die in the crash. In a tragic replay of events from a decade earlier, I find myself attending a funeral, consoling family members of fallen, cherished colleagues.

FINCA, in the meantime, experiences a hormonal growth spurt. Grants pour in. The torrent of beans overwhelms FINCA's skeletal accounting crew. The Monkey's goal now is to find another F-2, equally high powered but with a more collegial style.

Frijol Tres is definitely more easy-going than his predecessor. He is so low-key, in fact, sometimes the Monkey has to poke him to see if he's still alive. Bank wrecks pile up, as in a financial demolition derby. The monthly close, forty-five days late when F-3 arrived, slips to three months late. Less than a year after we hire him, F-3 goes on vacation to the Caribbean and never returns.

Next!

Frijol Cuatro hails from the commercial banking world, which supposedly holds its bean counters to a higher standard. During the interview, Mr. Bean expresses doubts as to whether F-4 will "get his hands dirty." Mr. Bean's reservations are prescient. F-4 goes into his office the first day, closes the door, and rarely emerges. Somehow, the work gets done, but after a year, things begin to slide. Basic errors crop up in the financial statements. Observing F-4's declining performance, the Monkey enters into familiar territory: a dangerous state of desperation. Someone stop him! He's going to make another bad hire, we just know it! He conducts furtive interviews with his latest prospect, a congenial accountant whose main appeal is that he is not F-4. The Monkey reasons that, albeit by random walk, each time he has changed CFOs, the new one has taken the organization to a higher level. He has forgotten that his initial benchmark, Frijol Uno, was not exactly the gold standard. He is about to learn a hard lesson: not every change is for the better.

As you were reading about Frijoles Uno through Cuatro I could hear you thinking: "I recognize these types." You recognized Frijol Dos as a fixer, and Frijoles Tres and Cuatro as maintainers. The maintainer's thinking goes something like this: "Hmm, this is a bigger mess than I thought it was. I *could* take on that huge tumbleweed of six years of screwed-up transactions, but that would be a lot of work. I would have to put in several months of twelve-hour days to unravel it, and in the meantime I would be falling behind on the day-to-day. Plus, when would I have time to day trade and play Halo during working hours? Best leave sleeping dogs lie. Stick around for a while until something better comes along, and then bail before the roof caves in."

F-5 was followed by Jerry, whom we've already met. Jerry pertains to a special category: hero fixers, or in this case hero CFOs. Hero CFOs are fixers who have outsized egos that, like black holes, have a gravitational pull that sucks all praise into them and still needs more. The hero fixer's thinking goes like this: "This place is a disaster. The systems are nonexistent; the staff is worthless. I'm going to have to build everything from scratch, hire all new people. As it is, I will have to work miracles to keep us from going over the abyss. And my boss? Hiring me is the first right thing he's done." Jerry had a point there, and he did do a lot of great work, taking us to a whole other level in terms of the quality of our financial reporting and control.

Hero fixers don't mind thinking out loud, especially at board meetings. So be prepared to see some of your board members stealing looks at you as the hero paints the situation in the starkest, most alarming terms. You can almost see the thought bubble coming out of your board members' heads: "Why didn't the Monkey tell us this? Wow! Thank God we have the hero on board!"

A hero CFO may also want your job. The problem with CFOs who aspire to be CEOs is that their solution to every problem is the same: cut costs and close operating units. In the mission-driven organization, this is a serious issue. Jerry wanted to close our struggling programs in Haiti and Malawi because they were losing a lot of money. But those are the places where FINCA is most needed.

Why did I have such difficulty recruiting and retaining good CFOs in the early days? Let me start with a mea culpa: as a program guy, I didn't pay enough attention to what was going on (or not going on) in my finance department. I bought the myth that accounting was simpler than rocket science or brain surgery. Big mistake. While that may be true, if neglected, accounting issues can become the source of debilitating problems that devour your time and your organization's resources when you finally get around to fixing them.

A more systemic problem is that in a rapidly growing organization, like FINCA, finance directors have a shorter half-life than other managers. This is because they have been hired to manage an organization at one size and level of complexity, only to discover six months later that they have to manage an organization twice that size. Well, you ask, why hire someone for the present size and not someone for the level you will reach in the future? Easier said than done. Compensation is one issue. Another is that when your operation is small and uncomplicated, it's hard to attract and retain "next level CFO" types because they won't feel sufficiently challenged.

Steps to Making the Right Hire

How do you spare yourself all the travails we went through and protect yourself from making the wrong hire?

First, assess the stage of development your organization is in. If you are going through a growth spurt, don't hire a maintainer (much less a destroyer); hire a builder. If you are broken, hire a fixer, but a hero CFO only if you have to and are prepared to watch your back. The hero CFO and the fixer can serve your needs for a time and take the organization to a whole new level, but the day will come when the hero is tired of being *your* hero and wants to be her own person. The fixer will eventually just get bored and check out. Oh, and neither of them will leave you with a successor, no matter how much you nag them to train an understudy. Why? A hero by definition is irreplaceable, and a fixer is too busy fixing to worry about who will maintain the thing after he's gone.

Second: Don't try this alone! Assemble a panel of experienced financial people (you should have at least one on your board and/or audit committee) to help you make the selection. Ultimately, you will have to make the decision, but at least you will feel more confident after someone else has looked over your candidates.

Third, check those references. This is especially important if you are suffering from "search fatigue" and are feeling desperate, as I was when I hired F-5.

Finally, sit yourself down and promise you will monitor your new CFO like no other. Even if you believe things are going well, have monthly face-to-face meetings with your CFO in which you go over the latest financials and ask dumb questions. If there are questions your CFO can't answer, make sure he comes back with the answer before the end of the week. Take a surreptitious meeting with one or two of his subalterns and ask how the new guy is doing.

Following these simple guidelines could prove invaluable in hiring the right CFO, and I'm happy to report that I was eventually able to snap my losing streak, hire some world-class talent, and turn Finance into arguably FINCA's strongest department.

When Dumb Luck Plays a Role

If it's any consolation, the odds of your finding the perfect, defect-free employee is close to zero. I can think of only a few in FINCA who have asymptotically approached perfection, and, sadly, I did not hire any of them. Someone else in my organization did. Even more tragic, some of them were too good, and if we didn't have adequate opportunities for them at the time, they moved on.

On the brighter side, you do occasionally land walk-ons who seem to have been tailor-made for your organization, possessing every skill set and experience you are seeking at the time. In this case, your only challenge is to recognize them as a perfect fit and do what you have to do to get them to accept your offer.

Also in the dumb luck category are the less conventional paths to employment, such as that taken by Guy, a young Australian. Having been told "no thanks" by the regional director for Africa in response to his offer to volunteer for FINCA's program in the Democratic Republic of the Congo, Guy showed up at the door to FINCA's office in Kinshasa anyway. By the time the regional director actually met him, Guy had been working for FINCA Congo for six months and had rendered himself indispensable.

Guy's is an extreme case, but more than a few people have found a home at FINCA just by showing up at our doorstep. If you have too many of these, where people have to take extraordinary measures to go to work for you, it tells you two things. First, you've done something right and built a great organization. Second, and more important, you are making it *too* hard for good people to work for you and leaving a lot of talent on the table.

Interviewing Candidates

Before leaving the topic of recruiting, let's check out a few tips on that time-honored ritual that produces so many disastrous hires: the interview. Here we refer not only to the interview of potential employees but of references as well. We covered some of this in the section on distinguishing a builder from a maintainer or destroyer in the previous chapter, but here I will describe in more detail what I call my "flip side" approach to interviews.

For example, after I ask the candidates to describe for me their greatest accomplishment, I ask the opposite: What was their greatest failure? If they hem and haw and say, "I can't really think of one"; describe a failure that they attribute to forces beyond their control; or give you the classic failure that is actually a success ("I once made the firm so much money everyone got jealous of me"), watch out. If they can't admit they have made mistakes in their career, then, ipso facto, they can't learn from them, and they will probably continue to make them.

Other "flip side" questions go like this:

Who was your best boss, and why? Who was your worst boss, and why?

How candidates answer the first question will help you understand what they value in a boss (possibly you) and how to motivate them. How they answer the second question will tell you what they find difficult to deal with, and what de-motivates them. Their response could also raise a red flag: perhaps the worst boss has some qualities you share. Or maybe they didn't get along with any of their bosses. If they have to think a long time before they can recall their best boss, this could mean they simply don't like to be managed.

Ask who their best employee was, whether they hired the person, and whether they turned the person into a great employee or if the person came to them already formed by someone else. Then, ask who their worst employee was, how hard they tried to turn that person around, and how long it was before they finally cut their losses. This will tell you two things: is this someone who is going to try to develop his people (good), or is this someone who can't bring himself to fire people and will therefore tolerate subpar performance for a long time, costing the organization money (bad)?

One of my favorite killer questions that really cuts to the chase is "Tell me about a time you made a mistake that cost your company a lot of money." And the flip side: "Tell me about a time you did something or had an idea that made your company a lot of money."

I really like the flip side approach because you get to the positives and negatives quickly and succinctly. Employing the flip side method also helps you identify a major problem in many people: denial. If someone has a denial problem, do you automatically pass on her? The problem is, many people with denial problems are also high performers. Despite being brilliant and competent, they are also deeply insecure. Their belief system rests on the idea that they are infallible, and to admit to the merest flaw, like the microscopic crack in the dyke, will cause the whole thing to be swept away.

It also depends on what you need at the time. The problem with deniers is that if things go south, they won't tell you. You will have to be vigilant and triangulate with other sources of information (you need to reach several levels down into the organization; more on that in the next section) in order to avoid nasty surprises. But maybe it is a risk you are willing to take. For a time, deniers may actually *be* infallible and deliver amazing results.

View the interview process not as a means of identifying the perfect person for the job but rather as a way of identifying the weaknesses and flaws you know exist, so that you can later manage to them.

That said, recognize this important law of physics: the more defects you accept in a candidate during the vetting process, the more energy you will expend trying to manage that person.

Which tees us up perfectly for the next chapter: "Managing Them."

6

||||||||||||||||||||||||||||||||||||||||||||||||||||||||||||||||||||||||||||

MANAGING THEM

On the Herding, Roping, and Hog-Tying of Cats

Once you have recruited and hired good people your job is over, right? Sorry. To paraphrase the Carpenters: "You've only just begun . . ."

You need to first start with the basics and understand how to manage the elusive normal employee. There are many good books on managing performance of normal employees, but I don't summarize them in this one. Instead I deal mainly with what I have learned about managing *abnormal*, but high-yield, employees. In my experience, the higher you go in the hierarchy of an organization, the fewer "normal" employees you will find. I will, however, go over some of the basics that I have learned from my good friend and member of FINCA's Advisory Board, Darwin Eads. As mentioned in the preceding chapter, Darwin is an industrial psychologist with many years of experience advising companies in the area of managing performance.

Darwin tells us that we get what we:

- Expect
- Inspect
- Discuss and talk about
- Evaluate
- Reward

This is simple enough, in theory. In practice, however, the formulation of clear, measurable goals is something of an art in itself.

Managers often confuse activities or processes with goals. For example, if you are managing a fund-raiser, you might set a goal to "send out a million pieces of direct mail." However, this is in fact an activity. What you actually care about is how much money this activity will raise, so your goal should instead read: "Raise a million dollars, net of costs, from the direct mail campaign." Try to visualize the desired *outcome* of all the activities that contribute to the achievement of the goal—this is the crock of gold at the end of the rainbow and what you really want your employees to accomplish.

Unfortunately, not all goals are as easy to articulate as those that can be readily quantified. Anything to do with professional development of your human resources can be particularly challenging. But you still need to try to quantify all goals, however difficult. For example, you might set a goal for one of your managers to "train one hundred credit officers," but what you really want as your outcome is one hundred *good* credit officers. What do you mean by "good"? You want credit officers who can manage a certain size loan portfolio and recover a certain percentage of the loans disbursed. You also want a specific percentage of those credit officers to still be around in two years so that the resources you have spent on training will not be wasted. So your goal for your manager could be: "Train one hundred credit officers who have an average portfolio of $50,000 and a portfolio at risk of less than 3 percent, with an employee retention rate of 80 percent." Would a result like this make you happy? If yes, that's your goal.

Darwin's main point about inspection and feedback is that employees watch carefully what their bosses pay attention to. If bosses put something on their employees' work plan but then never check their progress on it or bring it up at their evaluation, then the employees get a clear message: Boss doesn't care about this, so I don't have to either.

Evaluations

Darwin recommends doing at least two sit-down, face-to-face evaluations per year (FINCA follows this system). The goal of the evaluation is to:

- Review how people are doing
- Recognize all the accomplishments they are making
- Clarify, redirect, or renew expectations for things not being accomplished
- Discuss what the person will do to meet expectations

This one-on-one time with the boss aims to motivate employees, making them feel like they matter. It is a formal and structured opportunity for the boss and employee to have uninterrupted time for a two-way discussion, and for the boss to demonstrate interest in the employee's progress, accomplishments, career, and job satisfaction.

Many managers hate doing evaluations because it means they may have to confront their employees with their failures. But this is your best and, if you have a lot of direct reports, as I do, only real opportunity to put on record where your employees are coming up short, while impressing upon them the need to "raise their game." The primary objective is to get your employees to focus on missed targets and their other deficiencies, then reach agreement on what they are going to do differently during the next grading period to accomplish all of the set goals.

To leaven this sometimes painful, awkward message, I begin the session by praising them for their accomplishments and the things they've done right. This doesn't always work, especially with high-performance employees. But even normal employees hate criticism, and their first reaction may be defensiveness or, its more pathological companion, denial. This is the moment when you will discover how well you have articulated their goals. If there is any vagueness or room for interpretation, you may have already lost the battle. Examples of vague goals that any wily employee can squirm out of include "Make the office run smoothly" or "Improve the quality of the Financial Reporting System." If you haven't defined "smoothly running" or "improved quality," this could be a long evaluation session.

In between evaluations, it is important to do other things that give employees feedback on their performance so the grade on the evaluation doesn't come as a shock. You should also be providing guidance on how to improve their performance. Darwin recommends a staged approach, with escalating consequences if there is no improvement. This strategy begins with coaching, which, as the term implies, means providing friendly, on-the-job training and direction to the employee. If this fails, you escalate to counseling, which homes in on a specific problem or weakness and provides suggestions for how to correct it. The counseling phase is different from coaching in that it is formal and documented, and consequences for not correcting the problem are laid out. This process lets employees know of the choices facing them: either correct the problem(s), produce successful results, and keep your job or face the consequences discussed. (The consequences can be interpreted as a threat that will be carried out. This is OK because you want employees to know what will happen if they choose not to correct the problem.) Most employees will make the desired changes at this point because they truly do want to be successful.

If counseling does not work, discipline must be implemented, that is, enforcing the consequences. If suspension or other disciplinary actions do not produce the desired results, terminate the employee and hire someone who will do the job needed.

People will concentrate their efforts based on what their boss pays attention to. If, as a manager, you do not have written expectations of what you want done, then the task is at risk of not being completed. If there are written expectations but you neglect to review, discuss, report, and comment on a specific expectation, then employees will think it does not matter. Even if you bring it up at the annual formal evaluation time, it is too late, since what you wanted to happen did not. All you can do at this point is beat up the person for not completing the task, or beat yourself up for not doing anything about it for a whole year. Evaluations are the end result of what a person has done, or not done, for the evaluation period. In the end, just give people what they earned, good, bad, or mediocre.

Hire Good People and Just Get Out of Their Way . . . and Other Myths

Perfect employees do exist. However, most employees, as we have noted in the previous section, will come with flaws that you will have to live with or correct. Is it realistic to think you can manage the imperfections out of otherwise good employees, making them even more valuable?

Let's assume you didn't make any mistakes in the hiring process and chose only great people. What would be wrong with just "getting out of their way"?

This approach could be a good one if everyone worked 100 percent independently and never had to rely on someone else's deliverables to achieve his or her own objectives. I, however, know of no organization or company that fits that description. In any normal organization, the employees will have to work together as a team at some level. This doesn't mean they need to like each other and enjoy working together (although this would be ideal), but they do need to *behave* as if they at least respect each other. At the same time, they shouldn't be so courteous to each other that bad ideas or subpar performance is tolerated.

In any organization, there are several reasons why employees can't all just get along. Probably the most common one is that they get in each other's way. Something they do, or the way they do it, may constitute an obstacle to another person's ability to do his or her job. This usually has a solution, and it usually involves one or both of them changing their behavior.

Another common problem is one that arises when two or more people are competing for a promotion. Ideally, they would compete fairly, but some employees play dirty, resorting to so-called office politics—by which we mean sucking up to the boss, running down a competitor, or even undermining a colleague's work. If you allow a dog-eat-dog culture to take root in a nonprofit organization, whether explicitly or implicitly condoning it, you are asking for trouble. You will kill the mission.

The other problem with "just leave them alone" is that many of the best employees don't *want* to be hired and forgotten. They may be unsure as to whether or not they are doing what you want, or maybe they simply crave recognition. You might think it is obvious that, because you are ignoring them and giving them little or no feedback, you are happy with their performance. But even if you tell them they are doing a great job and that you are leaving them alone so you can focus on your problem employees, part of them could suspect the real reason is that you don't place much value on their work or, even worse, you don't appreciate them.

Your best employees are good precisely because they know how to "get it done." They also know how to get what they want *for themselves.* If you aren't providing the praise they seek or the attention they crave, they will figure out how to get it. Like your five-year-old son, they will act out. And, just like the kids on the playground, the easiest way to draw attention is to pick a fight with a rival. One way to get two feuding employees to work out their issues is to add a new project to each of their work plans, one that cannot be accomplished unless they collaborate.

At the risk of seeming to contradict myself, there is a time to "just leave them alone," and that is during the first few months of a new hire's tenure. Some managers believe in controlling their new hires tightly from day one, to ensure a minimum of missteps. I prefer to give people some rope and see how they can do, unsupervised. If they thrive in that space, it may be months before the need arises to rein them in, if ever. Some people just have a good sense of where the boundaries are without their boss having to spell it out to them. Even if they do appreciate your staying out of their way, though, it doesn't mean they don't want to hear the occasional "well done," just to be reassured they are on the right track.

One Madman Begets Twenty: Managing the High-Performing Psychotic

Mission-oriented organizations attract passionate, driven people and a lot of perfectionists. But many are truly crazy, and they can destabilize the entire organization with their antics. As Benuto Chellini warns us: "One mad man begets twenty."

It's OK to bring high-performing psychotics (HPPs) on board, as long as you do so wittingly and are prepared to put yourself and the rest of the organization through the wear and tear that comes with them. Is there a way you can manage them in order to minimize this?

Let's talk first about what doesn't work, beginning with compensation. You can try to buy them off, but because they perceive themselves as so valuable to the organization—something money can't buy—they will take whatever you offer but it will never be enough. Don't expect any gratitude, even when you bestow an over-the-top raise upon them.

Another thing you can try is to cast yourself as a coach, playing the buddy as opposed to the boss, but this strategy will bump up against the same problem the NFL coach has with his overpaid, prima donna wide receiver: high-performing psychotics don't think you have anything they can use. You can also try the "we are a team" approach, but this will only work if you accept being a member of the HPP's team and not vice versa.

Meanwhile, the other members of your management team will be grumbling big time. They will resent the HPP, especially how he always seems to get his way. The old-timers will grouse about how this newcomer is the one getting the big raises while their years of loyal service go unrecognized. They will not sympathize with your plight and won't understand why you put up with this guy.

Another trait of HPPs is that, while they don't accept being managed, they demand absolute loyalty and obedience from those who report to them. They pay lip service to things like inclusion and transparency, but if you work for them you must accept them as the undisputed leader.

How do HPPs get away with this?

They are good. Very good. They are bar raisers with a turbocharger.

Forget about trying to manage HPPs. Focus on utilizing their upsides while minimizing their downsides. This means, above all, recognizing that the time will come when the negatives will outweigh the positives. Why is that? Because you and the HPP are playing a game of "chicken," seeing who will ultimately use whom to the greatest advantage. HPPs are with you only for as long as you meet their needs. At some point, you see the negatives growing at such a velocity you can foresee the moment when your HPP pulls down the columns of the temple and wipes out all the good he has done. You don't want to wait that long to cut the cord.

The swag box "From Hero to Zero" describes how Donaldo, FINCA's star country director in Latin America, performed brilliantly but erratically for years only to explode in a supernova crisis that nearly destroyed our best-performing program.

▐▐▐

From Hero to Zero

Donaldo comes to us from an international commercial bank, where he worked for many years before a banking crisis caused his employer to withdraw from the country. He has experience in absolutely every area of commercial banking: credit, risk management, IT, treasury, sales, and capital markets. I sense a manic energy during the interview for the country director position. As he speaks, his eyes spin about the room, briefly visiting the ceiling then striking glancing blows off the eyes of his inquisitors as he describes his vision (destination) for the program. I think to myself: "This guy is a little crazy, but he has more energy than a hectare of transformers. If we can harness it, he could do big things."

During Donaldo's first two years he doubles the outreach and triples the loan portfolio for his country. His credit officers average five hundred clients each, the highest productivity in the network. Only one in every hundred loans is in arrears. Donaldo generates more than a million dollars in net revenues. Even in the one area where I had anticipated some work on my part, his commitment to the mission, it's all good news. "Until I came to FINCA, I never realized there were people so poor in my country," he tells me.

The only smoke on the horizon is Donaldo's relationship with the regional director. "What can this guy teach me if I already know ten times more about banking than he does?" Donaldo says with a chuckle. "Do me a favor; just tell him to leave me alone."

Donaldo's words remind me of another country director, also a former banker, who ran our program in El Salvador. She presided over the biggest fraud in the history of microfinance. "What can FINCA teach me if I already know everything?" she used to say.

Donaldo is correct that he is several notches above my regional director. Still, one has to maintain the chain of command, right? I hear a rustling in the corner, behind the curtain. A pitchfork clatters to the floor. Him again.

I tell my RD to ease off and give Donaldo the space to show what he can do. In fact, perhaps because of the overwhelming aroma of sulfur permeating my office of late, my mind is already moving in a more diabolical direction. My current RD is not making much headway with the programs in Central America. What if Donaldo could give me six more programs that looked like the one he's running? Donaldo accepts my offer to take over the RD position, but he wants to retain his country director job, too. Coming from anyone else, I would have laughed in his face. But perhaps Donaldo truly is the superman he claims to be.

It's a mistake. In the first year of his tenure as regional director, Donaldo makes one or two trips to the other countries, but spends 85 percent of his time in his home country. He also dismantles the regional team, which he claims adds no value. The other country directors love Donaldo's "hands-free" style. But they are not Donaldos. Things begin to deteriorate. When I do Donaldo's evaluation, I ding him hard, hoping he will take my criticism to heart and rebuild the regional office. My assessment is all wrong, he insists. A week later, he resigns as regional director.

The next three years of Donaldo's tenure as country director bring declining performance and increasing conflict. Board meetings grow increasingly contentious, sometimes erupting in shouting matches in which Donaldo accuses the board of trying to micromanage him. When we propose that we hear from the rest of the management team during the board meetings, Donaldo pushes back. "Doesn't the board trust me anymore?" he asks. Meanwhile, a populist president has been elected in the country and declared war on all the banks. The financial sector is doomed, Donaldo warns us. He presents the board with a radical proposal: sell Banco FINCA to outside investors. The lead investor is well known in the country, having engineered a number of deals in which he has profited and the other investors lost their shirts.

We are being set up. I realize my deal with the devil is about to backfire. I have given Donaldo his head far too long.

Eventually, we have to fire Donaldo, but he has another big surprise for us. The day after we let him go, his entire management team plus two-thirds of the rest of the staff walks off the job to join him in a parallel finance company he has established on the sly. For the next several months, we fight trench warfare against Donaldo and his band of traitors, staffing Banco FINCA with volunteers from our other programs in Latin America. We win: ironically, Donaldo and his team had done such a good job building Banco FINCA's brand, the clients stay with us.

If you are going to hire strong personalities, make sure you have the skills and stomach for it. A degree in psychology (I have a B.A.) helps, and it's not a game for everyone. With your high-performance psychotic, it's always touch and go as to who will take advantage of whom.

Heirs Apparent: Managing and Retaining Those Who Aspire to the Throne

An occupational hazard of a hiring strategy based on the "be the dumbest person in the room" principle is that you will inevitably hire people who aspire to occupy the top position: yours. They might be patient enough to wait for you to retire, but that could be a long time away, either in real terms or from their perspective. If you have a strong team, as I always have, you may have several aspirants to the corner office at the same time, each with different "career clocks" ticking away. These people are not going to be patient. They need to feel that every day, month, and year they spend with you is doing something to advance their ultimate career objective: to run an organization. If the day arrives when they don't feel that way anymore, two things happen. First, their productivity begins to tank. Second, they start spending at least a few hours of each workweek looking for their next opportunity. Neither of these developments is good for you or your organization.

Unless your organization utilizes the European "management board" model, where the three top executives share the authority and responsibility for decision making, or some hybrid power-sharing structure, there can be only one CEO at a time. Though I have never suffered the frustration of having to wait for a promotion or, worse, being passed over for one, I can imagine it is an extremely difficult experience for any ambitious person.

The obvious danger to you, as the manager of the heir apparent (HA), is that you will lose her to the competition. If this happens, extra work will be created for you. First, you have to figure out who in the organization might fill the vacancy, and how to get him or her up to speed quickly. Worse, maybe there is no internal successor, and you have to go through an external recruiting process, which, even if you are an ace interviewer, is a process fraught with risk. An even greater downside to the loss of an HA is that you now have fewer candidates to succeed you. Your best heirs will probably depart in the worst possible order: BIFO (best in, first out). You want to do everything you can to retain your lineup of HAs for as long as possible.

The swag box "Ready When You Are, Boss" describes the trajectory of Terry, one of my first hires, a talented builder who made vast contributions to the organization, but for whom I ultimately ran out of new challenges and failed to retain.

||||||||||||||||||||||||||||||||||||||||||||||||||||||||||||||||||||||

Ready When You Are, Boss

Terry comes to FINCA from another international nonprofit, where he was trapped at the lower levels of a huge bureaucracy and found it difficult to be entrepreneurial. FINCA is the small pond he's been looking for, the perfect place for someone of his talents and energy.

He works a room like no other, instantly sizing up the occupants, ranking them in order of importance, going in and closing the deal. He has a born politician's gift for making you feel you are the center of the universe while he's talking to you.

Terry also has a fantastic eye for talent. He populates his small policy and research shop, which has the broad mandate of raising public funds and promoting microfinance-friendly legislation, with exceptional employees. He plays a key role in uniting the microfinance community to speak with one voice in Washington. His skill as a compromiser and deal maker wins him accolades throughout the industry. When the Soviet Union disintegrates, Terry's shop brings in millions in AID grants to establish FINCA programs in Central Asia, Russia, and the Caucuses.

In the course of his tireless networking, Terry gets introduced by a member of Congress to Queen Rania of Jordan. He gains an entrée to the entertainment industry through Hollywood agents Stephen Rivers and Michelle Kydd Lee, through whom he ultimately meets a young, up-and-coming actress named Natalie Portman. Terry persuades both Queen Rania and Ms. Portman that the microfinance movement could greatly benefit from their advocacy. Queen Rania joins the FINCA board, and Portman becomes our first "Ambassador of Hope."

As the organization grows in size and complexity, Terry goes through something of an identity crisis. The management team has grown and contains some other potential heirs apparent. Terry's eagerness to be involved in everything and plug holes is not as welcome as it was when the organization was small and thinly staffed. With the unexpected change in the White House in 2000, many of Terry's valuable "assets" are swept out of office. Government grants, which Terry used to land on a regular basis, dry up. Meanwhile, elsewhere in the microfinance sector, one of his longtime friends and colleagues gets promoted to the position of CEO of her organization. I can feel Terry getting antsy. He needs a new challenge. The tragedy of September 11 provides it. FINCA enters Afghanistan, and I ask Terry to lead the effort.

Terry is reenergized by his new challenge. His fund-raising skills land us major grants from the World Bank and USAID, both of whom are pouring money into the country. But the challenge of finding good talent willing to work in Afghanistan is daunting. We go through a number of country directors, even losing one to a credible Taliban kidnapping threat. The program suffers a major fraud. Steve McQueen, a colleague who helped bring FINCA to Afghanistan, is gunned down in a bungled kidnapping attempt. Terry wonders if his dream of bringing microfinance to this tormented part of the world is achievable. When someone from the Gates Foundation headhunts him, he's receptive. I agree it looks like a great opportunity. After more than ten years, Terry leaves FINCA.

Another heir apparent whom I held as long as I could was my first deputy, Monique. Described by Chairman Bob as "the smartest woman on earth," Monique had grown to the point where she became, in every sense, my alter ego, understanding telepathically how I would handle a given situation and being able to take action and make decisions on her own. This was greatly liberating for me, allowing me to focus on the big picture and strategy.

How could I let such a prized colleague go? My daughter had an answer when, having heard me extol Monique's virtues one time too many, she asked me, "What makes you think Monique's objective is to be your deputy for the next ten years?" There were also more immediate causes that sparked her departure.

First was the entrance of an extremely high-powered CFO who not only took over the reins from Monique (she was acting CFO at the time) in the finance function but also began encroaching on some of the other roles Monique had played for me. Instead of looking like it would grow in the future, Monique's responsibility appeared to be shrinking. I tried to mitigate this by giving her one of the most challenging jobs in FINCA: country director for Afghanistan. As a retention strategy, this backfired. Not only was Afghanistan a ruthless master in terms of the time and effort it demanded, but asking Monique to manage it remotely (her family obligations didn't permit travel) proved to be totally unrealistic. My hope had been this would give her the "street cred" of having managed a program, and while she did ultimately thank me for the experience (I don't think she was being sarcastic), I think it was another factor pushing her toward the exit. When Women for Women Foundation came headhunting, as they had several times before, this time Monique answered the call.

What can you do, then, to try to retain your heirs apparent until the moment of succession arrives?

- Honor their ambition. Recognize ambition as natural and even desirable in the high performer, and don't feel annoyed when your HAs pester you at every review as to what your plans for them are. Better yet, be proactive and tell them what you think would be the next good career move for them.
- If the HAs are low in the hierarchy but with obvious potential to someday succeed you, make sure you have mapped out their career paths to the next two or three promotions.
- If the HAs are already in the top team, analyze the feasibility of a lateral move, an exchange of roles functions with other members of the top team, which would help better prepare them for the top job.
- If a lateral move isn't feasible, think about what functions you perform that could be delegated to them, both to keep them engaged and to better prepare them to become the CEO.
- If no change of position is feasible, think about what new challenge you could give the HAs in their current position that would require them to stretch their abilities in a new and productive direction, giving them valuable experience.
- Finally, think about retiring. That's right, move over and give someone else a shot. As my friend Al once said to me: "Rupert, you need the experience, and I need the rest."

7

||||||||||||||||||||||||||||||||||||||||||||||||||||||||||||||||||||||||||||||||||||

CONTINUING TO MANAGE, AND STAYING IN TOUCH

As we have seen, there are many variations of the high performer, each with their embedded idiosyncratic personality traits that, like ticking bombs, may explode down the road, spraying the unsuspecting manager with shrapnel or even putting the whole organization at risk. We put up with these downsides, however, because of the extraordinary value these people provide during their extended runs of sanity.

Too Smart by Half: Beware of the Super Smart, Highly Educated Who Don't Know How to Work

One thing the high performers share is brilliance. But while every high performer is brilliant, the converse is not true. Some very intelligent people prove to be a total waste of your organization's time and money. How can you spot them? One "false positive" is their academic degree. People get into Harvard for many different reasons: their great-grandfather endowed the law school, they can kick a 60-yard field goal, or they are the only person in the Aleutian Islands to have filled out an application. Nor does the fact they graduated magna cum laude necessarily mean you've landed a prize hire. One thing I noticed during my tenure as a professorial lecturer at Georgetown University is that the modern student at the top school has mastered, not necessarily the subject matter, but the *methodology* for obtaining high marks.

I don't contend that our top schools are turning out legions of people who don't know how to work, only that the skills that come into play when seeking admittance to Harvard or Stanford are not the same ones that prepare you for life on the outside. A bright, articulate mind can often conceal a mystifying inability to solve problems or produce results.

The first person I came across who pertained to this category, let's call them Too Smart by Halves (TSBHs), was Bailey, who worked for me at AIFLD. I did not actually hire Bailey but rather had him thrust upon me by my bosses, owing to the fact that he was the son of a former highly placed official in the government who was calling in a favor. This should have aroused my suspicions immediately. Bailey was extremely intelligent, articulate, and personable. After a while, however, I noticed a strange thing. Whatever task I assigned to him remained unaccomplished or left short of the goal line. Bailey was not good at owning a problem. He liked "teamwork" because it was a way to fob off responsibility to someone else. He always had a brilliant excuse for his failure to complete the assignment, usually that some other person or department failed to do its part.

Results-based employees always find a way to get things done, regardless of the box you put them in or how you define their job. They take as part of their job getting what they need from their colleagues to put a task over the goal line. It need not be said, but Bailey was not a results-based employee.

He had another quality common to the brilliant nonperformer: he was skilled at hiding out in an organization until someone ultimately came along and realized, "Hey, this guy isn't doing anything." He lasted quite a while at AIFLD, and to my knowledge he never accomplished anything. One skill the TSBHs have is identifying organizations where it is easy to hide out, so if they have chosen yours you should be concerned.

If you suspect you may have hired a TSBH, you don't have to give up on him immediately, but you need to force him to address his disability head-on. Structure an early test of the TSBH's ability to deliver a specific product or solution that has a clear, unambiguous, measurable result. Pay close attention to how you articulate the goal so there can be no doubt as to whether it was achieved or not. Put a deadline on it and don't renegotiate. Provide all the coaching and moral support your conscience dictates. If you have to let the person go, don't feel any remorse. TSBHs will find happy homes somewhere they don't have to make decisions or complete projects with defined deliverables and deadlines.

Come on, Everybody, Do the Del-e-ga-shun: Coaching the Recovering Perfectionist to Hand Off Without Dropping the Ball

Perfectionists and workaholics abound in mission-driven organizations. The two attributes frequently coexist in the same person, one enabling the other. What attracts the perfectionist workaholic to the mission-driven organization is the fact that they never have enough resources to accomplish the tasks set before them. They face that daily mountain of work with much whining and feigned dread, but if you took it away they would pace the carpet restlessly until you refilled their in-box.

Initially, you might consider yourself fortunate to have people working for you who fit this profile. If these traits are accompanied by a large dose of self-confidence, they can add up to a highly productive individual. Often, however, the perfectionist is powered by huge feelings of insecurity. To reject her work is to condemn her as a person. To avoid rejection she postpones judgment day as long as possible, polishing the brief over and over until you have to literally tear it from her hands. The perfectionist is not big on delegation, either. She knows no one can do the job as well as she can. When she does delegate, don't be surprised when she "undelegates" it at the end, checking and rechecking for imperfections and producing the final product herself.

Perfectionists can be difficult to work for. They can drive off some great human resources who may feel insufficiently challenged or never allowed to prove themselves. They tend to be turf conscious and unable to see what is in the best interest of the organization. They are so identified with their work that taking away part of it is the same as amputating one of their limbs.

All perfectionists have a hard time accepting criticism. It clashes with their need to be infallible. They will go on the defensive at the merest suggestion of their foibles. Some, however, have a saving grace. Once they stop resisting, they may actually take criticism to heart, taking direction, changing, and fixing the problem. And these types of perfectionists never stop growing.

With time, the self-defeating attributes of the perfectionist workaholic may self-mitigate. Why? Because they get tired. They become worn out and will burn out if they continue at their inhuman pace. You can wait for this to happen, but it will exact a high cost on the afflicted person, his or her subordinates, and the organization as a whole. So best to deal with it.

Failing Your Way to Success: Letting Your People Make Mistakes Without Destroying the Company

As we have seen in the previous section, learning to delegate takes on paramount importance as an organization grows in size and complexity. Some managers take naturally to this change, while others need to be pushed a little before they will let go. People who find it easy to delegate are secure enough in their abilities that they can survive the occasional failure, learn from it, and move on. Others, not just perfectionists, are convinced that to own up to even the smallest error is to place their head on the block. This is very common in developing countries, where well-compensated jobs are rare, management by intimidation is the norm, and mistakes are punished severely. You need to convince your staff that in your organization a certain amount of failure is forgiven, even encouraged. At the same time, some mistakes are so costly they could sink the organization. How do you know which is which?

Teaching through "permissible failure" works best with young, inexperienced employees. With this group, you need to remove the most severe consequences of failure: getting sacked. Some managers and organizations don't subscribe to this but instead believe in the "rank and yank" system of professional development. Usually these organizations are so big they can afford to attempt to teach these employees how to swim by throwing them into water over their heads and watching the outcome. This was GE CEO Jack Welch's technique. He allowed fear of failure to drive his young MBAs to the point where they discovered abilities they didn't know they had.

A resource-strapped, mission-driven organization probably can't afford that approach. Start with tasks that, if screwed up, won't cause much damage or can be easily repaired. If your new employees handle those without mishap, gradually give them more difficult assignments. As their responsibilities increase, provide more support and coaching, but only if they request it. Keep raising the stakes to the point where you begin to feel nervous. If you see them struggling, resist the temptation to take the ball away and do it for them. If they fail, ask them what they learned from the experience. If they give you a blank look, or worse, deny they failed at all, you have a problem; people who can't learn from, or admit to, their failures will not be an asset to your organization in the long run.

With older, more experienced employees, the process works differently. In these cases, most of the decisions will carry real consequences with substantial price tags. Here, you have to weigh in and provide direction. Ideally, you will achieve consensus with the employee on the way to effectively move forward. But what if you disagree and the employee insists on doing it his way? Now you have a real decision to make: overrule or give him his head, then stand back and cross your fingers.

If you decide to give him his head, you have to strike a deal, and if you are proven right, he must accept the consequences of his error. These results could be spelled out in advance and could be monetary fines or, in the worst case, dismissal.

Be sure your boss (or Board of Directors) knows that you have decided to structure a "teachable moment" for your employee, and that if it goes wrong, as you suspect it might, it's all part of your staff development program.

Sometimes what appears to be exactly the same decision in two different environments can produce totally different results. In 2004 FINCA decided to upgrade our core accounting systems in our affiliates. Our proprietary system, developed by our wholly owned software vendor, Micro Finance Solutions Incorporated (MFSI), was struggling to stay ahead of our rapid growth. Initially designed to take care of an operation that did hundreds of transactions per day, MFSI's product now had to support thousands of transactions daily on three continents. Before it exploded, we wanted to move to a more robust system. Our hope was to find a single vendor who could meet our needs globally. In this we were successful— sort of. Our tender produced four vendors, two of which were global and two of which were regional, one serving only Africa and the other Latin America. My CIO advocated one of the global systems, even though at the time it had no customers in the microfinance industry. My regional director for Africa had experience with the African system and loved it. My regional director for Latin America supported the Latin American system, even though the vendor had a shakier track record, because all his country directors preferred it. Only my regional director for Eurasia was willing to try the global vendor recommended by my CIO.

Like many generalist CEOs, I am hopelessly out of my depth in highly technical areas like choosing information systems. One of the few things IT people agree on is, if the subsidiaries have the same business model, avoid buying multiple systems to support it. I wanted to back my CIO on the global system, but going with the two "devil we know" regional systems seemed less risky. After much anguished dithering, I gave the regional directors their heads. We signed up for three different systems. The African vendor succeeded. The vendor in Latin America failed to deliver and we dumped him, but only after wasting three years and several hundred thousand dollars.

Why did the "give him his head" decision work in Africa but not in Latin America? Had I thought more about it, the reason was obvious. The risk of failure in Africa was minimal: my RD had personal experience with the vendor and knew he would deliver. My RD in Latin America, like me, was a technical neophyte. He merely followed the line of least resistance and caved in to what his country directors wanted.

And what of the third region, Eurasia? There, I am happy to report, we went with the global vendor and it proved to be the right choice. As I write this, we are preparing to install it in Latin America as well.[1]

Managing the Crossover Employee: From Riches to Rags

The greatest challenge for crossover employees, who enter the nonprofit world after time spent in the for-profit, private-sector ranks, is most likely the difficulty they will have adjusting to operating in a resource-poor environment. Many top managers are accustomed to hiring consultants to do the "real" work, which allows them to focus on the big picture and strategy. When they get to a nonprofit, they find there's barely enough resources to hire an adequate in-house staff.

---

1. We will explore the subject of making intelligent IT decisions in-depth when we follow my further adventures in IT land in Chapter 15.

Another big challenge is that while in many for-profit companies there is a "command culture" in which the boss makes all the decisions and the troops carry them out, in the nonprofit, all big decisions must be reached by consensus. You have to explain the "why" to the troops before they carry your instructions out. This drives managers from the private sector crazy. "Everything takes so long!" they moan. Yes, but in the end it's faster because when you try to rule by fiat your employees rebel, subvert, or otherwise figure out how not to comply. "Just fire them!" the manager exclaims. The problem is, it's hard to find qualified people in the field. If you "just fire them" you will spend a long time and a lot of money finding a replacement. Meanwhile, the wheels are falling off.

Another difficult aspect confronting the crossover employee is the proclivity of people in the nonprofit world to put the mission above the bottom line, even when it comes to making payroll. In FINCA, the field comes first, often to the consternation of the finance department, which is trying to manage dozens of grants and lines of credit to feed the growing portfolio in twenty-one countries while keeping enough cash at headquarters to make payroll.

For most crossovers, these are minor inconveniences compared to the upsides of working for a mission-driven organization.

Staying in Touch

My friend Darwin tells me that to stay in touch with what is really going on in the organization, managers can't just rely on what their direct reports tell them, but need to go two levels down. I'm sure he's right, but I go Darwin one better: I make an annual practice of meeting one-on-one with most or all of my headquarters employees, regardless of position. I tell them I am interested in hearing three things:

1. Any obstacles they are facing in their work that is preventing them from being as productive as they could be
2. Any problems they see in FINCA, either in their department or somewhere else, that for some reason no one is addressing
3. Any bright ideas they have for solving the issues identified in 1 and 2

I ask them to tell me if they want me to keep anything they say confidential. While it's a major investment of my time, I find it useful, as the rank and file tell me things I would not otherwise learn from my management team, things their bosses don't feel are important. The frontline staff often have useful suggestions as to how things could run better. And, of course, some take advantage of the meeting to complain. It's a great way to see if your young, up-and-coming staff are feeling sufficiently challenged and are likely to stick around.

More recently, I have begun extending this practice to the field, asking my country directors to give me access to their star credit officers for an hour or so conversation. I always find it an eye-opening, rich experience.

Remembering Why We're Here

There is an imaginary line that bisects our lives, above which we strive to connect with our "better angels" and below which we dwell in the everyday muck of trying to figure out how to pay the rent and make our car payments. The job of the nonprofit manager is to help bring the best out in people, to help them spend as much time above the line as possible. John Hatch, the Essential Visionary, was a master at this. The El Salvador program in its early days was a wonder to behold, with the highest staff morale of any organization on earth. John began each day bestowing rib-cracking hugs on every employee and asking how things were with their families. He lit a fire in his staff that for some has lasted to this day. He was able to do this because John is a person who almost never slips below the line. As one of his closest friends, I have rarely known him to indulge in feelings of self-pity or despair, even during times when he suffered unspeakable tragedy. Sadly, the Camelot John created in El Salvador during the early 1990s contained a female version of Mordred, who eventually exploited John's trusting nature and nearly destroyed the organization with a million-dollar fraud. This is the flip side of the nonprofit manager's brief: watch out for the villains in your organization, and stay one step ahead of them.

Figure out what motivates your employees, what their end game is. Take control of their narrative and reward them for their work. Just as I believe I am writing my own life, line by line, so can the nonprofit manager shape the narrative of his or her employees, helping them succeed.

Which provides the perfect segue to our next topic: leadership.

8

‖‖‖

LEADING THEM

Finding Your Inner Andre Previn

Driving home from work one day, I heard an interview on National Public Radio with master conductor Andre Previn. I can't reconstruct it verbatim, but it went something like this:

NPR: "Many people wonder, maestro. What is it you are actually doing up there when you are waving that baton?"

Maestro: "By the time opening night arrives, my work is actually over. In the weeks or months before, what I am trying to do is get these many gifted and talented people to play together. Any one of them could play a solo that would make you weep. But getting them to create something beautiful *together*, where they aren't playing over each other and canceling each other out—that is my job."

This resonated with me. While I had a superb first violin, viola, and cellist at FINCA, they sounded more like an orchestra warming up than one playing Vivaldi's Concerto in E Minor for Strings. I was managing them, but not leading them.

What makes an effective leader? Are they born or schooled? What are the traits you need to develop? Is an effective leader the same as a good leader? To begin answering these questions, let's first look at what it takes to be an effective leader.

In the swag box "Lineman for the County," we meet Al, a crusty old union boss who taught me part of what it means to be a leader, and how I later applied this knowledge to lead my way out of a crisis in El Salvador.

||||||||||||||||||||||||||||||||||||||||||||||||||||||||||||||||||

Lineman for the County

Al, the director of our program in the Dominican Republic, is a former lineman for a U.S. phone company. His face, red and cratered like a desert floor after a hard rain, turns the color of an heirloom tomato during lunch when his rum and coke regimen kicks in. Al takes it upon himself to design a training course for me. The first module is how to protect myself from hustlers like Al. He persuades me it's important for the unity of the Dominican labor movement to restructure a grant I have won for the *campesino* union so the funds pass through the confederation, controlled by Al's protégé, Rafael. I watch, helpless, as the funds are diverted to programs benefiting the urban unions. At a consolation lunch, over many rum and cokes, Al gives his young victim some advice:

"It doesn't matter how smart you are, Rupert. These people will only follow you if they think you can help them. And you can only help them if you genuinely care about them, *plus* you're tough and wily as I am."

Several years later, I move to El Salvador to finish the work of my assassinated boss, Mike, on the land reform program. My first job is to unite the squabbling factions of the democratic union movement. To do so, I must break with Mike's right-hand man, Pancho, who views one of the other union leaders, Marcos, as his lifelong rival. For several months Pancho and I keep up the pretense of business as usual, propping up the illusion we are still on the same team. Meanwhile, I channel more resources to Marcos, a more effective and less divisive leader. Marcos and I organize a nationwide demonstration, involving all the unions, pressuring the government to extend the land reform so that more landless *campesinos* can benefit. The democratic unions are united again, and Marcos and I are heroes. Pancho is seething with jealously. But Marcos has skeletons.

In days past, it is rumored, Marcos supplemented his meager union salary by working as an informant for Roberto D'Abuisson, leader of a death squad that assassinated many union leaders. Pancho uses this information to blow apart my still fragile coalition.

My worth to both AIFLD and the U.S. Embassy rests on my ability to keep the Salvadoran unions united and in support of the democratic process. I call a meeting of all the union leaders at the headquarters of the Democratic Confederation. On the way up the stairs I pass Pancho coming down, grinning. All the faces turn, expectantly, as I enter the room. I still don't know what I am going to say to them. That's when Al's words come back to me.

I tell them I have come to El Salvador at the risk of my life and that of my wife for one reason and one reason only: to continue the work of our martyred leader, Mike. I'm still committed to that, but if they aren't willing to put aside their petty agendas, I'm not going to keep risking my life for nothing. I will advise my boss, Wild Bill, to close the program, and my wife and I will return to Washington.

It is a big gamble. The savvier leaders know I am bluffing. Wild Bill will simply replace me with someone else, and the program will go on. But he might replace me with a time-serving jerk who isn't as committed as I am. They've all heard the story how Wild Bill asked for volunteers to go to El Salvador after Mike's assassination and only two hands went up. Mine was one of them.

I leave them to talk it over. After an hour, Chemita, my Salvadoran attorney and right-hand man, comes for me. He's smiling.

Effective Leaders

Effective leaders possess three traits:

1. Destination
2. Credibility
3. Toughness

Destination is obvious in the sense that no one will follow those who don't know where they're going; it is similar to having a vision, but not exactly the same thing. Both Hatch and Yunus have described their vision as "a world without poverty." However, even if one suspects, as I do, that millions who have benefited from microfinance over the past four decades have bootstrapped themselves out of poverty, few believe that small loans alone could accomplish that noble vision for *all* of humanity. A destination is a place you can actually get to. After a while, the followers of the Visionary need to know where she's taking them and when they can expect to get there. If the Visionary can't provide this information, she will be replaced by someone who can.

In addition to being able to articulate a clear destination, leaders must have the credibility that they can get the organization to reach its planned goal. The easiest way to establish this credibility is by having done it before, either in the current organization or in a previous one.

Credibility is not static, either. What makes you a credible leader for one phase of the organization's growth may not work during another phase. In my case, my experience as a credit officer in the Peace Corps, plus my management experience in the union movement, gave me the "content cred" to last me through the first decade of FINCA's development. But after the organization began to resemble a refugee camp for recovering commercial bankers, I realized I needed to go back to school and learn the basics of banking. (I can hear you laughing up there, Dad.) Fortunately, there was an excellent program offered by the American Bankers' Association, the Stonier Graduate School of Banking, which required me to spend only one week in a classroom, and I could do the rest of the class work online. I won't claim it turned me into a legitimate banker, but I did acquire the lexicon and ability to decipher a balance sheet and assess the health of a financial institution.

Finally, since there will be many contretemps and people who will be trying to stop you along the way, you need toughness. This may be the most difficult part, since you want to believe you have paid your dues and deserve some respite. But you need to stay tough, because the challenges never end. FINCA is at a stage today where I spend much of my time trying to prevent governments from destroying or stealing what we have built.

Take two very different leaders, both of whom we can agree were effective: Mahatma Gandhi and Joseph Stalin. Both had a destination. Gandhi's was an India free of colonial rule. Stalin's was a Russia ruled by the proletariat—and the legitimate representative of the prols: Uncle Joe. Gandhi's credibility derived from his ability to paralyze the British colonial structure by mobilizing millions of Indians in peaceful demonstrations. Stalin established his "street cred" by slaughtering millions of Russians and Georgians who resisted his efforts to collectivize agriculture. Both ultimately arrived at their destination and took the whole country with them.

Stalin and Gandhi were effective leaders, but were they both good leaders? I think we can agree we would prefer Gandhi over Stalin as our model for a good leader. For one, Gandhi found a way to achieve his goal without killing people. He also possessed what I would argue are the two key attributes of a good leader: he was self-sacrificing, and he cared about his followers. His self-sacrifice was a large part of his credibility. To be an effective leader of a nonprofit you need to care about your clients and your employees, as we heard from Brother Al at the beginning of this chapter.

I ask myself on a daily basis whether I am a good, effective leader of FINCA. I have promised myself that if the day comes when I cannot answer that question in the affirmative, I will step down and pass the torch to my successor. It's not enough to have been a good, effective leader in the past. To continue to be effective, you need to periodically check your personal DCT—destination, credibility, and toughness. If you arrived at your last destination, are you clear about the next one? Have you articulated it to your staff and achieved their buy-in? Do you still care enough about the organization and your employees to make the personal sacrifices required to get there?

Lousy Leaders

Before we leave the subject of what it means to be a good and effective versus a bad but effective leader, indulge me while I vent one of my greatest frustrations: the lousy leader. This is the person who gets elected to a position of authority and, instead of using his power to do good, does bad. If he's the leader of an entire country, he could improve the lives of millions of people but chooses instead to enrich himself and his cronies. You might, without being far off the mark, put the majority of the presidents of developing countries in this category.

When I first visited Uganda, I asked my taxi driver if he was glad to have seen the back of Idi Amin. His answer astonished me. "This guy Obote is much worse." After I had been in the country a while, I understood it was split along strictly tribal lines. If you were from Amin's tribe, you had prospered under his rule. If not, you suffered. This unveiled for me a fundamental truth about many leaders of developing countries and why the countries they rule never progress. These lousy leaders don't view their constituency as the entire population of the country but only that segment represented by their tribe. To the extent they deliver on providing benefits to their tribe, they are good leaders and will remain in power. If they take actions that benefit their rival tribe, they will be perceived as weak, stupid, and ineffective.

These tribal-based lousy leaders would argue they are only being practical; the rival tribe would behave in the same way if they were to enter into power: screw their enemies and plunder the nation's wealth for their tribe. They're right.

As a friend of mine from the Middle East once put it: "These aren't really countries; they're more like companies." What he meant was, the people who "led" them viewed their position more as an opportunity for private gain for themselves, their families, and their tribe than as a public trust.

We don't need to pick exclusively on the developing countries to find lousy leaders. Consider the case of a recent vice president of the United States, who, when asked to defend the tax breaks proposed by his administration, offered up not an economic rationale but the growled justification "It's our due."

Who was the "our" he was referring to? Not the majority of Americans who took home a few extra dollars in their biweekly paychecks.

The day may dawn when selfish, lousy leaders are a thing of the past, but for now they are very much with us, and their ranks are swelling, not diminishing. This makes it more comfortable to be a lousy leader—witness how none of the African leaders felt capable of censuring Mugabe; they all lived in houses of glass.

If I have inspired you to emulate the other, Gandhi school of leadership, then I will have accomplished much of what I set out to do by writing this book.

What if you are not in a position to lead, and, to make matters worse, are trapped in an organization with subpar leadership? What if you have leaders who have turned the organization into little more than a vehicle for their self-promotion, or worse, self-enrichment? Do you suffer in silence? Fortunately, there is another type of leader in organizations, one who "leads from the middle." These are the people who are just doing their jobs, but doing them exceptionally well and in such a way they build an internal following of admirers who recognize their contribution. If your organization has a worthy mission, even if you are poorly or suboptimally led, you can be effective and fulfilled by learning to lead from the middle. And who knows? Perhaps one day someone on the Board of Directors will notice and nominate you for the top job.

Talk Is Cheap: Simple Praise as a Motivator

If you're like me, you still have every trophy or plaque that was bestowed on you, maybe not in a special showcase but at least in a dark closet or storage room somewhere. Why? We can't bear to part with those first tangible expressions of the fact someone recognized we were good at something.

Even though trophies may not be acceptable as a substitute for monetary rewards, they are an invaluable weapon in your arsenal of motivators. It is also true that they probably work better the farther down the hierarchy you travel, simply because those who toil in your boiler room probably assume you never notice how hard or well they are working for you. Don't make that mistake. My friend Darwin enjoys pointing out that the most important employee in any restaurant is the lowest paid: the person who cleans the restrooms. If that person doesn't do a good job, the customers will never return.

As FINCA has grown from hundreds to thousands of employees, it has become more difficult for me to get out to meet with my staff, but whenever I do, I make sure they know how grateful I am for the wonderful work they are performing. If it is a special occasion, such as an anniversary, we recognize our employees for their years of service with an escalating system of rewards, starting with a silver pin to commemorate their having survived their first year with the organization and moving up to a weekend at a spa for those who have made it to the fifteen-year mark. This may seem like a lot of trouble, or a waste of money, but if you have ever witnessed the pride on the faces of your employees as they come forward to receive their plaque or anniversary gift to the applause and cheers of their coworkers, you will appreciate the importance of these tributes.

Group recognition is also a powerful motivational tool and one that has the added advantage of fostering another dynamic you want in your organization: teamwork. In FINCA, I pioneered the concept of the Teamwork Piggy, wherein at each monthly staff meeting, I challenge my staff to come up with three examples of collaboration between departments or individuals who have gone beyond their usual duties to help out another person or department for the "greater good" of the organization. Examples usually include things like helping the capital markets group assemble the performance information they need from the field to close a deal, or people mobilizing to manage a crisis, like the earthquake in Haiti or the political upheaval in Kyrgyzstan, which required us to evacuate people while still keeping the operation running.

The Teamwork Piggy (abetted by my ventriloquist squealing, which sounds suspiciously like a pig being dragged to a Guatemalan market) is the sole arbiter of whether an example qualifies as teamwork. If three such cases are approved, the Piggy receives a quarter, euro, or pound coin (depending on the prevailing exchange rate). When he reaches a certain threshold amount, it results in a staff appreciation event, such as a tour boat ride on the Potomac or a trip to the racetrack. All new employees are initiated into this ritual by having a veteran staffer introduce them to the Piggy (a black ceramic piggy bank with the FINCA logo) with the explanatory narrative, which goes something like this: "As a barnyard animal, the pig has long been associated with pejorative traits such as slovenliness, rudeness, but above all, selfishness. The FINCA Teamwork Piggy rejects those stereotypes. A model of civility and selflessness, the FTP graciously stands aside to let the other pigs have first shot at the trough and even makes way for them to be the first to board the truck to the slaughterhouse. As such, we at FINCA have elevated him to the position of decider when it comes to determining whether teamwork has occurred."

Another of my creations, the Golden Tree Award, recognizes FINCA programs that have surpassed the 50,000-client milestone. Client outreach is one of the most important measures of the degree to which a country program is achieving the mission. When I introduced this recognition award, only a few FINCA programs had exceeded even the 25,000-client mark. Within a year of announcing it, three programs—Ecuador, Mexico, and Azerbaijan—had qualified for the Golden Tree. A few years later, I was obliged to create another milestone award in order to keep up with two of my fastest-growing programs, in Mexico and Kyrgyzstan, both of which achieved 100,000-client Platinum status. It is easy to envisage the day when I will be forced to consult anew with my periodic table of elements to come up with a 200,000-client award.

Recognition is a great tool for reinforcing the mission. Decide what indicators best reflect progress or "move the needle" and design an award around their achievement. Any pretext you can invent to honor your front-line troops and build morale while maintaining momentum is a worthy one. It reminds everyone that you are paying attention and you care.

Indulge me in one final testament to the power of praise, and its flip side, the dampening effect of failing to recognize effort and achievement. My fifth-grade teacher, Ben Murphy, was a former journalist and the man responsible for first putting my pen in motion, back in 1959. He introduced me to the world of creative writing, and at the end of the year he presented me with a cheap, gold-painted plastic trophy in recognition of a number of short stories I had written. (Yes, I still have it.) The following year, I proudly presented my sixth-grade teacher, Mr. McKeon, with a short story I had written over the summer. He received it with a perplexed look, since he hadn't made any assignments as yet. A week later, he returned it to me with a red check mark at the top. I searched eagerly through it for comments, finding none.

Thirteen years passed before I wrote again.

Wear the Gold Hat for Her: Reducing Office Stress Through Releasing Your Inner Ham

As we have noted, mission-driven organizations, just like for-profits, can become stressful places to work. The mission attracts passionate, dedicated people who take themselves too seriously at times. You need to reduce the atmospherics occasionally. One way to do this is to encourage people to behave like lunatics, beginning with yourself. In my case, I have taken a barely discernable talent for music and reinvented myself as a rock star once a month, performing some hopelessly outdated '60s ballad to kick off each staff meeting.[1] An unexpected bonus was that my atrocious singing and guitar playing flushed out a number of authentic musicians and sing-

---

1. I actually initiated this practice long before Ricky Gervais and "The Office" came on the scene.

ers within my staff who now share the stage with me. In the early days, I used to charge each department to come up with a sketch for the holiday season party. Some were absolutely brilliant ("The Sound of FINCA" featured a take-off on the von Trapp family with the entire finance department dressed in nuns' habits), and all took the piss out of management in one way or another.

Conflict resolution consultants discovered long ago the effectiveness of role-playing as a means of surfacing staff issues, but it's much more fun, not to mention cheaper, if you can establish your own internal Monty Python unit. And the biggest payoff: word will get out that your organization is a fun place to work. Recruiting just got easier.

PART 3

||||||||||||||||||||||||||||||||||||||||||||||||||||||||||||||||||||||||||

MONEY DOES GROW ON TREES, BUT YOU HAVE TO PLANT THEM FIRST

How will you finance your noble mission? Whether your mission is as ambitious as pulling millions of people out of poverty or saving the world from being slowly cooked to death by greenhouse gases, or as modest as feeding homeless people in your neighborhood, you will need to develop a reliable income stream. Where will you find the resources to accomplish this, let alone meet the monthly payroll for your hardworking colleagues, pay the rent, and keep the lights on?

When John Hatch announced to me he was leaving our consulting firm to start a foundation, he promised me the process of raising the money to implement his Big Idea would take several months.

Several months.

How about several years?

Building FINCA's revenue stream was neither quick nor easy. Conceptually it may sound simple, but in fact it was a long, hard road. To be honest, the struggle continues to this day. I would like to report that after twenty-five years FINCA has amassed huge financial reserves so that our annual budgets are funded years in advance, or that we have a large endowment and are living off the interest and dividends. Fact is, we are still surviving month to month, scraping by on our meager budget of $180 million. The reason for this is that we have 750,000 clients to service and 7,000 employees in twenty-one countries on our payroll. That costs money.

In this section, we will explore the mysteries of how one mission-driven organization, FINCA, built reliable sources of income that over time have had a major impact on the lives of millions of low-income microentrepreneurs. I will argue that all nonprofits, regardless of whether they are large, medium-size, or start-ups, need to develop three pillars of support: private, public, and internal. Each of these pillars has its own rules of engagement and must be approached differently. If you crack their codes, however, you can create a reliable and substantial income stream and get to that magical place all nonprofit CEOs dream of: focusing on the mission and not having to worry about money.

9

THE PRIVATE PILLAR

Brother, Can You Spare a Dime?

The private sector pillar has the potential to be by far the largest source of funding—if you can figure out how to tap it. In 2006 the U.S. private sector donated $295 billion to charity. Most of this ($223 billion) was contributed by individuals, and the balance by corporations, bequests, and foundations. An astounding 80 percent of American households made annual donations of a thousand dollars on average. While a third of this went to religious organizations, the majority financed secular activities like education, health, and social welfare. Philanthropic giving is bigger in the United States than in Europe and other countries, in part because the tax system encourages it. U.S. citizens can deduct 100 percent of their contributions to qualifying nonprofits. Another factor is that Americans tend to view helping those less fortunate as their personal responsibility rather than the job of the government, as is the case in European countries. This makes the private sector pillar a very "target rich" environment.

On the downside, the private sector pillar can be the hardest to build and the slowest to grow. If you are a start-up, until you build a name for yourself you need to convince and enroll donors one at a time. Many donors, even those with substantial wealth, may give you a "tryout," making a modest donation and seeing if they get a prompt thank-you letter together with a report on how it was used. If you pass the test, the reward may be substantial. More than once, FINCA has received a fifty-dollar donation from someone procured through direct mail who then wrote a check for thousands of dollars years later.

For a long time, it may feel like every dollar you raise from the private sector has to be plowed back into investing in fund-raising to finance next year's budget. Don't despair. Be patient. Properly nurtured, the private sector pillar can become your largest and most reliable source of funding. If you create "brand loyalty," your private supporters will remain with you through good times and lean, unlike public sector support, which can be fickle and political. The loyalty, or lack thereof, of your supporters can also be a useful reality check on your mission. Is Main Street staying with you as you go through each stage of your growth, changing the way you execute your mission?

You need to diversify within this private pillar, creating income streams from major, medium, and small donors, foundations, corporations, and grassroots organizations like religious organizations and Rotary Clubs. And just as start-up tech companies need an "angel investor" to provide the initial seed capital, nonprofits should try to find their own angel: a wealthy individual or company that pays the bills during the early days before the donations, grants, and other income cover the operating costs.

In Part 2 we saw how FINCA's first chair, the Carpenter, subsidized our start-up costs once he realized his younger brother, the Visionary, was onto the "real thing." I was not executive director at the time, but Mr. Bean confided in me that the Carpenter's contributions during that first critical year amounted to many hundreds of thousands of dollars.

If you can find an angel, by all means do so. Where would you find such a person? Start with your family and friends. Chances are you know or are related to someone who has made it big and has the wherewithal to be your organization's angel. Whether they are willing to share their abundance with you in order to get your mission jump-started is another question, but it can't hurt to ask. On the first approach, don't ask for money. Ask for advice. Successful people *love* being asked how they did it, what the secrets are behind their success. Tell them your idea and then solicit their thoughts on how to turn your vision into a reality. Let the idea pop into their head: "Hmm, this sounds interesting. Might be worth throwing a few bucks at it and see what happens."

If your prospective angel doesn't ask to contribute, however, you have to be proactive. When you speak with her, be prepared with a first-year budget, if not on paper then at least in your head. Offer to match her contribution from other sources. If your angel does decide to stake you, make your success her success. Treat her like your partner, and, remember, the way to hook her is to take her to see your program in action.

If you aren't able to hook her, perhaps there is a deeper problem. Did you fail in getting her on board because your mission wasn't compelling enough, or because you just didn't sell it properly? Maybe the mission looked good to your potential angel, but when she looked at *you* she didn't see the person who could pull it off—a good investment, in other words. If it's the latter, that's a problem that can be solved in other ways, such as by building a team that plays to the Visionary's (your) strengths and shores up the weaknesses. But let's address the salesmanship issue first.

Fear of Fund-Raising: How to Overcome Your Guilt and Enjoy Asking People for Money

Feel uncomfortable asking people for money? Hate writing grant proposals?

You're not alone. But if you're the head of a nonprofit, or even just work in one, my advice is this: Get over it. In a nonprofit, especially a start-up, fund-raising is everyone's job. Most people who claim they can't ask people for money have never really tried. It's a mind-set and a skill, and just like other competencies it needs to be developed.

A successful fund-raiser quickly becomes a hero and one of the most visible people in a mission-driven organization. It can be the shortest route to the top. In a downturn, the fund-raising team will be spared any layoffs because to do so will only exacerbate the organization's financial woes. Even if all you do is introduce potential donors to your development people, you are fund-raising.

How do you get over that dread of asking people to part with their hard-earned jack and make a contribution to your cause? First, make sure you feel good enough about your mission yourself to really sell it. Then, put your money where your mouth is. Make a contribution yourself. This will inoculate you against a question that often comes up when you ask someone else for money: "How much do *you* give each year?"

Second, make sure you have no qualms about the way the finances of your organization are handled, and be sure you know exactly how much of each contribution goes to administration and fund-raising and how much goes to the mission. If this question does come up, make sure you answer it forthrightly. Mission-related costs don't have to mean they don't include anyone's salary, just that if they do, the people involved are in the field executing programs and not fund-raising or counting the beans. In FINCA, we take great pride in the fact that our administrative and fund-raising costs together comprise less than 7 percent of our total costs, while 93 percent of expenditures support the mission.

Third, figure out what it is you're selling. By this I don't mean chicken noodle soup if it's a Feed the Homeless operation. I'm talking about the larger idea that will hook the heart of your potential donor. If I ran a soup kitchen, I would tell people my mission was to make sure the least-fortunate members of our society have a place they can go to get a proper meal instead of having to forage in garbage cans.

Finally, turn your inhibition about taking people's money on its head and view it not as taking but as giving them something. What are you giving them? In FINCA's case, we give them the opportunity to help solve one of the world's thorniest problems: poverty. As one major donor to FINCA, an early retiree from Silicon Valley in his midthirties, put it: "I want the work FINCA does done. I can't do it myself, but I'm happy to provide you the resources so you can do it."

There is also evidence that giving makes people feel good and may even be mildly addictive. Charity Navigator reports that psychologists have identified something they call "helper's high," induced by endorphins that produce "a very mild version of the sensations people get from drugs like morphine and heroin."[1]

Once you have achieved this psychological breakthrough, asking people for money doesn't make you uncomfortable; it becomes enjoyable.

Now let's talk tactics. First, start with the small fry before you try to hook a big fish. Practice selling your mission to a stranger on a train or airplane. See what lights them up and gets them to ask the next question. See what parts of your message seem to confuse them and need reworking.

---

1. From Arthur C. Brooks, "A Nation of Givers," *The American*, March 31, 2008.

Smelt your mission down to one sentence, then build it out to a paragraph and beyond. Layer it as you would for a press conference where a pesky, skeptical reporter keeps asking the next annoying question.

Finally, there is the overwhelming question: how much do you ask for?

Vartan Gregorian, former president of Brown University and current head of the Carnegie Foundation, shared one of the secrets of his amazing fund-raising success, first with the New York City Public Library and then at my alma mater, Brown University. When approaching a major donor, he always asks the person for twice as much as he thinks they are capable of contributing. He claims that donors, far from feeling offended, are flattered you would think them wealthy enough to make a gift of that size.

Beyond Angels: The Importance of Grassroots Networks

You could go about acquiring your donors one by one indefinitely, but that probably is not the most efficient way. A better strategy is to penetrate networks of people who would potentially be attracted to your mission, find an entry point, then get yourself invited to one of their meetings where you can pitch your mission.

There are many service clubs in the United States, some of which are global, like the Rotarians, who are always looking for noble causes to fund. You probably know a Rotarian or two, since they have clubs in every major town and city in the world. See if you can get your friend to put you on the menu at their next monthly luncheon meeting. Rotary and many other service clubs are structured into regional, national, and global foundations, which have their own pots of money they use to match the gifts of their local chapters. Once you gain admittance to these private clubs, the rewards can be substantial. But beware: they all have their own internal politics, and if you run afoul of them, it can all come crashing down (see the swag box "Of Rubber Chickens and Rotarians" in Chapter 10).

To be effective at cracking networks, you need a skill set, starting with public speaking. Like asking people for money, speaking in front of an audience, especially a large one, is for many people a terrifying prospect. There are any number of seminars or workshops catering to people who seek training on public speaking.

I have grown to love it rather than dread it. Do I still get nervous? Yes. But I use the nervousness to my advantage. While I always know the basics of what I want to say, I purposely leave holes in my notes in order to leave room for spontaneity and creativity, much like the improv comedian who has to make it up on the wing. I almost always draw my opening monologue based on something that has happened to me during the past twenty-four hours.

I acquired my public speaking experience in the union movement, where passion was not only a desirable element in public speaking but a sine qua non. If you didn't have the ability to incite the rank and file, to whip them into a lather of indignation and rage at their oppressors, sending them out into the streets and marching on the capital, then you didn't last as a leader. Unless you are consummate actor, you can't fake this kind of passion. People sense when you are being sincere and when you aren't. If you have been drawn to your mission for the right reasons, you have it. Trust me.

When I'm in the green room, I play a narrative in my head that goes something like this: "This is not about you. You are just the messenger, and, one way or another, you need to get the message to the ears of these good people. They don't care a damn about you, anyway. They just want to hear what you are there to tell them, so get on with it."

The Sacred Trust: Never Take Grants for Granted

Fund-raising consultants make much of the fact that a $100,000 gift requires a lot less effort than a thousand $100 donations. This is true, but don't disparage those small contributions. Treat all donations, of whatever size, with the utmost respect. Remember the theory of relativity: a $10 contribution from a small donor may be a higher percentage of that person's wealth than $1 million from a major donor. I am always humbled when I receive a check for $10 together with a letter apologizing for the small size of the donation, adding: "It's all we can afford this year." Once, we received a $100,000 check from a parent who said that he had been saving it for his son but was afraid his son would spend it on drugs so he preferred to give to FINCA where he could be sure it would be put to good use. Moments like that really drive home the vast responsibility we assume when entrusted with other people's money.

Direct Mail: Pennies (and Dollars) from Heaven

One of the most attractive things about direct mail to a manager like me is that it can be outsourced almost 100 percent and takes very little time away from your primary job of executing the mission. Direct mail is a good option for a nonprofit that has an established track record and a certain level of name recognition, but it should not be attempted without expert advice. The initial investment in buying lists from similar organizations has to be carefully calibrated against the returns from the initial "prospecting" mailings and subsequent solicitations. The beauty of direct mail is that you can attract loyal donors who, while they may make small annual contributions, stay with you year after year and over time qualify as medium-size or even major donors. There are also those amazing cases where a "small" donor includes your organization in his or her estate, which can result in a bequest in the amount of hundreds of thousands of dollars. At FINCA, we have done the math, and even without those windfalls the return on direct mail is more than 300 percent.

To calculate your return on investment in direct mail, divide your donors into classes, which correspond to your acquisition (also known as prospecting) mailings. Your hit rate from this will naturally be small (1 percent is considered excellent) since most of these donors will have never heard of you, and those who do respond do so because your literature is compelling and resonates with them. For this reason, spend time polishing your message and doing a few test mailings to small samples of the list you have purchased.

Plan to do two or three acquisition mailings per year, if you can afford it. Probably you will lose money on these, but in its initial acquisition mailings FINCA actually made a small net margin.

Then comes the fun part. Four times a year, you send out an "appeal" mailing to all the donors you attracted through the acquisitions. Here your response rate will be much higher. Why four times a year? No one knows, but best practice in the direct mail trade has demonstrated this is optimal. To be certain, a percentage of your donors will be really annoyed that you pester them four times a year, but you can attempt to deal with these through tagging them for only one mailing per year.

Not only will the response rate be much higher on these appeal mailings, but the return will be also. The math is simple: your mailing costs are lower because you are sending out far fewer mailings, and your return is much higher because a larger percentage of the recipients are sending you checks. Keep track of your direct-mail classifications diligently, who responds with a check faithfully every quarter, biannually, or yearly, and who may drop off for a year or two (a "lapsed donor") but then responds to a "recovery" communication. These classes are the people who are responsible for providing you with a 300 percent return on your direct-mail investment.

The other reason you need to track your classes and your returns on each mailing is that you cannot count on your direct-mail consultant to always do so. Direct-mail consultants make their money selling you lists and communication strategies, so for them, the more mailings the merrier. Make sure these fresh acquisition mailings, which are probably growing larger every year (FINCA's most recent acquisition mailing went out to more than a million potential donors) are not subject to rapidly diminishing returns. In addition to tracking your returns on each class, also track the return on your total annual investment [Total Revenues / (Acquisition Costs + Appeal Costs + Consulting Costs)].

Hunting the Elusive Genuine Fund-Raiser: She May Look and Quack Like a Duck, but She May Be a Charlatan

After a certain point, you may realize you are spending so much time on fund-raising that you are neglecting the whole reason you started this organization: to execute the mission. Congratulations! You have reached the point where you need to hire a professional fund-raiser.

Where do you find one? The problem is, fund-raisers are not like CPAs, lawyers, or doctors. They don't go to fund-raising school, and they don't get a Ph.D. in fund-raising with a concentration in major donors. The profession has come a long way, however, from the days when it was like the financial planning profession in the sense that anyone could call himself or herself a financial planner and get away with it. What has changed is the proliferation of organizations that certify members of what I call the "soft professions" that don't require years of higher education, training, and a license, and in which malpractice doesn't result in the client being dead or the practitioner going to jail. Today there is a Certified Financial Planner Board of

Standards to try to introduce an element of quality control and avoid those cases where the financial planner turns out to have been planning to run off with the client's assets. There is even, believe it or not, a National Commission for Certifying Agencies (NCCA), which is the accrediting arm of the National Organization for Competency Assurance (NOCA), which will tell you, presumably, whether the certification is for real.

You can't be too careful, in other words. You might begin your search at the website of an organization called the Certified Fund Raising Executive International Credentialing Board (CFRE International), which, for $150, will give you access to its database of some five thousand certified fund-raisers in the United States, United Kingdom, New Zealand, and Australia. One positive is that to even qualify to take the exam you need to have a minimum of five years of experience as a compensated employee in the fund-raising department of a nonprofit, or as a consultant to the industry.[2]

But that is a pretty small pond to draw from. It's also clear from the website that it is mainly targeting candidates (fund-raisers) for its certification program, not necessarily prospective employers looking to hire their graduates. Does the fact that you have hired a certified fund-raising executive protect you from making a bad hire, someone you will invest in but who won't raise a dime? Of course not. It's just one tool for reducing the odds of making a mistake. The reality is, many of the best fund-raisers are too busy raising millions of dollars for their foundations to find the time to be tested and recertified every three years by the CFRE board.

If you're running a start-up, the difficulty of your search is compounded by the fact that you don't have a lot of money to pay fund-raisers until they, well, raise a lot of money. This makes you especially vulnerable to a prevalent species inhabiting the world of uncertified, self-proclaimed fund-raisers: *Argentus Subitus Charlatanus* (ASC).

ASCs are difficult to detect until they are actually in the job, by which time you may have already wasted thousands of dollars paying their salaries and expenses. They are good salespeople. During the interview, they know all the answers you want to hear. You warn them you don't have a

---

2. The FAQ page on the website does add the qualifier that this requirement is in effect "right now," suggesting that in the future it may be relaxed, presumably to swell the ranks of potential applicants.

big budget, either to finance a fund-raising campaign or even to pay their salary. Not a problem, they say. Raising money for your brilliant idea will be easy. They sound convincing. They tell you they will be the best investment you ever made.

FINCA ran into such a person when we first decided to hire a professional fund-raiser. The swag box "Promises, Promises" describes FINCA's accident-prone search for a "real" fund-raiser, which, in its early stages, generated many hard lessons but no revenues.

||||||||||||||||||||||||||||||||||||||||||||||||||||||||||||||||

Promises, Promises

John, our beloved founder and the Essential Visionary for FINCA, meets a woman named Carmelita who persuades him she can raise millions for our organization. As a board, we should insist on interviewing other candidates, but John is convinced Carmelita is our savior and the two of them begin targeting prospects among the New York business community. After several months without raising a dime, John informs the board that Carmelita will be moving back to the Southwest to work from there. We rejoice, silently.

Back on her home turf, Carmelita still struggles to gain her footing. She organizes a prospective donor tour to La Paz, Bolivia, to usher in the Harmonic Convergence, a propitious alignment of heavenly bodies purported to herald a time of "renaissance and planetary quickening." She persuades John to have FINCA serve as a local sponsor for the Hands Across America celebration, which she claims will raise our visibility and lead to a flood of donations. She has FINCA sponsor a rock concert on a New Mexican Native American reservation.

The Hands don't quite make it across the Arizona desert, and the Native Americans refuse to allow the musicians onto the reservation until Carmelita comes up with twenty-five thousand dollars in cash. John, in South America at the time, returns to find that Carmelita, having drained FINCA's meager coffers long ago, charged all these expenses to his personal American Express card.

||||||||||||||||||||||||||||||||||||||||||||||||||||||||||||||||

Disillusioned by his experience with a "professional" fund-raiser, John reclaimed the role for himself, spending the next two years trying to raise money from whomever he stumbled into as he commuted back and forth between the States and Latin America, nursing along his pilot projects. He was not entirely unsuccessful. He raised money from the Inter-American Foundation, the Food Industry Crusade Against Hunger, and several Rotary Clubs. Once, in 1987, we thought we had hit the jackpot. A dog track owner in Florida called our small Tucson office, saying he had heard of FINCA and wanted to drop a million dollars on us. On his way to meet us in Arizona, he was held over in Dallas on business, but he said he would see us on Monday.

When Monday arrived—Black Monday, as it turned out—the stock market dropped 22.6 percent. We never heard from him again.

With our pilot projects gaining steam, and our do-it-yourself fund-raising campaign flagging, we were ready to give the professionals another try. John encountered a Virginia-based fund-raising consultant—let's call him Larry—who thought FINCA had a killer idea, for which fund-raising should be a slam dunk. In return for a $100,000 retainer, he promised to raise $1 million the first year, a return of 1,000 percent. This time, determined to do it right, we checked his references. The first former client we spoke to told us, "Larry didn't raise a dime." John insisted we hire him anyway. The board caved. Furthering our folly, we agreed to move into some recently freed-up space in the office Larry was leasing. A year later, several thousand dollars poorer, Larry had not raised a dime.

How did smart, otherwise sensible people fall into this trap, not once but twice? By failing to see the obvious field marks of *Argentus Subitus Charlatanus*; by allowing our eagerness to solve our problem, persuading us to take shortcuts and ignore red flags. With Carmelita, we should have said, hold on, let's see who else is out there. We might still have gone with her, but at least we would have felt we'd given ourselves a chance to compare. Second, if a reference comes back negative, for God's sake heed it. I have never ignored a bad reference, either on a hire or on a vendor, and had it turn out well.

Ultimately, we should ask ourselves what the cost of our fund-raising mistakes were. There was the money we wasted on their salaries and spent chasing their blind leads, but as painful as that was, it obscures the true cost: the years we wasted. Then again, maybe we weren't ready for success.

Maybe our programs were not sufficiently fire-tested that they could have survived a huge influx of funding. Maybe the money would have killed us.

Yeah, right.

You'll be glad to know we finally did hire a real fund-raiser. "So Glad We Got the Real Thing" describes the trajectory of Sofia, who realized my vision of creating a "fund-raising machine" at FINCA.

|||||||||||||||||||||||||||||||||||||||||||||||||||||||||||||||||||||||

So Glad We Got the Real Thing

In what seems like divine intervention, Sofia, a seasoned fund-raiser from the wildlife sector, picks up one of our brochures someone had left on the Washington Metro. The cover features a picture of one of our Peruvian clients with a basket of tomatoes on a straw mat, smiling up at the camera. Sofia is from Peru. She calls and asks for an interview. Sofia tells us during the interview she couldn't sleep the night after she read the brochure. It seems like her dream job.

We hire Sofia as interim director of development.

Over the next six months, Sofia tears into the assignment. The first year, she raises three hundred thousand dollars. Every year after, she ups her total by at least 25 percent. She methodically builds each segment: major donors, foundations, corporations, direct mail, and a sponsorship program with service clubs. Where once we had months where we raised nearly nothing in private contributions, by 2008 our monthly take never slips below five hundred thousand dollars and on average nets over a million.

We have a fund-raising machine.

What are the qualities that make Sofia so successful? For one, she can tell the story. She has grown up in Peru, not exactly in poverty—her father worked in the mines—but she knows how the vast majority of the population lives. She cleverly uses these credentials when she asks for money from wealthy Americans.

Sofia is a real manager. I let her gradually build up her department with "content experts" in the different segments of the private pillar. Sofia's other positives are that she is proactive and researches potential

new fund-raising tools on her own initiative. When I bring a new opportunity to her attention, she's on it. She also grows with the requirements
of the job.

‖‖‖

Now, what if you are not looking for a fund-raiser, but you are on the
other side of the table, seeking a position as a fund-raiser in a nonprofit? If
you have five or more years of experience, CFRE might be a good option.
While no substitute for hands-on experience, the "fund-raising competencies" covered by the exam look solid. If you are just starting out—an aspiring fund-raiser—your best path is to join the organization at the ground
floor, probably as a volunteer. Acquire the poverty experience so you can
tell the story. Then let the development director know you are interested
in working in fund-raising. Ask her how you can get some basic training
in fund-raising skills, either inside or outside the organization. Once you
have that, get permission to try out your newly acquired skills on your
friends and family. From there, graduate to strangers on planes and trains.
If you have any success, I guarantee that the development director will
take notice.

10

||||||||||||||||||||||||||||||||||||||||||||||||||||||||||||||||||||||

PRIVATE PILLAR PITFALLS

Sponsorship Programs and Dealing with Donors

At this point you are over your fear of fund-raising or you have landed the perfect person to go out there and start raking it in, a veritable fund-raising machine. The direct-mail program is producing results and you're ready to build lasting relationships with donors worldwide. So, what's next and what could go wrong? Let's take a look at some of the issues you may encounter moving forward dealing with potential partners and invaluable donors.

Grants That End Up Costing You Money: The Dismal Economics of Sponsorship Programs

Sponsor a child! Sponsor a family! Receive an adorable picture of the grinning recipient of your generosity (who knows, it might even be the actual beneficiary), or even a monthly letter. And for as little as two dollars a month! It seems too good to be true.

It is. These programs are quickly overcome by the "hidden" costs of reporting on thousands of individual stories. That is why most, if not all, sponsorship programs have abandoned the one-to-one, donor-to-child model in favor of one whose narrative goes like this: "When you sponsor a child, Rescue the Hungry Kids Foundation (fictitious) will use your monthly sponsorship donations, combined with donations from sponsors of other children in your child's community, to support community-wide programs in the areas of health, education, nutrition, and clean water, which will help your child escape from poverty."

The sponsorship organizations did not come to this revised model without some hard knocks along the way. In March of 1998, an article in *The Chicago Tribune* revealed that a number of child sponsorship programs essentially failed to deliver the promised resources to the end beneficiaries and in some cases even accepted money from donors after "their" children had died. In the microfinance industry, Kiva, an organization that raises funds in a peer-to-peer sponsorship model, is the latest to be accused of misrepresenting how its programs actually enable microloans to low-income microentrepreneurs.

In the previous chapter we talked about how service clubs, religious organizations, and other social networks can be a cost-effective way to raise money, providing access to thousands of potential donors and economies of scale in "retail fund-raising." The swag box "Of Rubber Chickens and Rotarians: The Rise and Fall of a Beautiful Relationship" relates the story of FINCA's experience with Rotary, a service club network, and a sponsorship program that raised a lot of money initially but ended in disaster.

‖‖

Of Rubber Chickens and Rotarians: The Rise and Fall of a Beautiful Relationship

As entrepreneurs and businesspeople themselves, Rotarians instantly "get" the FINCA methodology of self-help loans. Better still, there is a program of matching grants run by the International Rotary Foundation. If a local Rotary Club in San Francisco raises five thousand dollars to sponsor a village bank in Sololá, Guatemala, the foundation will match it with an equal amount, so FINCA will get a total of ten grand! In order to make the deal more attractive, John promises the Rotarians that 100 percent of the money will go to loan capital and zero to overhead. This leaves nothing to cover the operating costs of the country programs, much less any of the costs of the FINCA U.S. operation, so I decide to try to renegotiate the deal.

I call up the president of a Rotary Club in Northern California and try to persuade him to let us use 5 percent of the money for administrative costs. He refuses, saying that the deal he signed up for allocates 100 percent of their donation to loan capital. Undeterred, I sally forth, addressing larger and larger gatherings of Rotarians. The fund-raising model couldn't be working better and shows the power of leveraging a major social network. Rotary Clubs in the United States have "sister clubs" in cities and towns all over Latin America and Africa, and we have developed a number of champions within Rotary who spread the word that the FINCA program has the potential to be huge.

But as the total proceeds from Rotary approach $1 million, the first strains appear in the relationship. Our allies in the Rotary Foundation tell us the avalanche of grant requests coming from clubs who want to fund FINCA is in danger of crowding out other worthy Rotary projects, such as their popular scholarship program. Worse, the director of our Mexico program, already struggling to cover his overhead from the interest income on the loans and reeling from an overnight devaluation of the peso by 50 percent, dips into the restricted Rotary loan capital account to pay his administrative costs. FINCA discovers the diversion of funds, informs the Rotary Foundation, and replaces the money in the restricted account, "curing" the breach. The Rotary president sends us a letter that seems to indicate he's OK with this, but the president-elect of the Rotary Foundation demands a return of all the diverted funds. The financial situation of FINCA Mexico is such that this will require us to pull the capital out of the village banks, killing the program.

We send a delegation to the headquarters of the Rotary Foundation in Evanston, Illinois, who receive a cordial reception, plead our case, and return to Washington, D.C., to await the verdict. A few days later we are told that the decision of the Rotary Foundation president-elect would stand. We take it up at the next FINCA board meeting, and the consensus is that we had nothing to gain by writing a check to Rotary for a problem we had already righted, a check that would put the FINCA Mexico program in jeopardy.

||||||||||||||||||||||||||||||||||||||||||||||||||||||||||||||||||||||||

We were puzzled as to exactly why, with all the support FINCA had among the rank-and-file Rotarians, both in the United States and abroad, we couldn't salvage the situation. I regret we could not find a way to revitalize the FINCA-Rotary relationship. I miss those guys and their genuine commitment to the mission of helping poor entrepreneurs. Perhaps I was too stubborn and should have somehow complied with the Rotary Foundation president's demand, even if it meant sacrificing FINCA Mexico.[1]

Are sponsorship programs a lost cause? Perhaps not. What has changed the game is technology. If ways can be found to automate the reporting process so it's not so expensive and labor intensive to provide information to donors on individual clients and their businesses, the economics could turn viable. Mobile phones with photo capability could be used to take pictures of grinning clients outside their market stalls; those pictures could be immediately uploaded as an attachment to an e-mail to a donor in Boise, Idaho. The repayment history of the village bank could be uploaded to a donor-accessible database where Rotarians could mine it to their heart's content to ensure that their initial donation was still turning over in perpetuity. The key is to keep driving down those transaction costs until the numbers work. Kiva is working on this type of solution, as is FINCA. So stay tuned.

The Big Game: A Field Guide to the Different Species of Major Donors

In the early development of your organization, securing major donors for a potentially long-lasting relationship is key to growing and nurturing the private pillar. Of course all major donors are different, and you will find that even those who appear to be a perfect fit or a dream come true may come with instructions marked "special handling." Being familiar with the types of donors you will encounter and how to steward them will help you engineer a mutually beneficial and satisfactory relationship.

---

1. The good news is that as I write this, thanks to the efforts of our board members in FINCA Canada, the Rotary Foundation has opened the door to negotiations toward the goal of restoring FINCA to its former status as an eligible partner in its worthy projects worldwide.

Donorus Perfectus

Perfect donors do exist, but they are as rare as the Ivory Billed Woodpecker of the Louisiana Bayou. Here are their field marks:

- **Song:** A mellifluous "You decide what to do with my donation. You know best what your needs are."
- **Wing bars:** Solid gold
- **Flight pattern:** Unrestricted, climbing ever higher into the sky, year after year

If you land a *Donorus Perfectus*, treasure her. Don't take her for granted, treating her like an ATM. Find out whether she is a "high-touch" donor who wants to receive a phone call once a month and get an update on what's going on with your organization, or whether she wants to just write a check and be left alone. Don't be afraid to simply ask her how often she wants you to communicate with her. Customize your stewardship program to her preferences.

Sometimes even *Donorus Perfectus* will want you to apply her gift to a specific purpose, but the difference is, she will ask you what your highest priority is and let you spend it on that. Many donors and foundations claim to understand the need for a mission-driven organization to spend money—sometimes substantial money—on things like more qualified financial managers or systems, but they may have a difficult time feeling so good about such investments as compared to donations that will go directly to those in need.

Strings Attached: Donations with Strings You Can and Can't See

Regarding the more common species, most major donations come with strings. When they come with strings you can see, they are called "restricted." They require you to spend the money for a certain purpose. Most large foundation grants are restricted and often involve certain themes (child survival, women's empowerment, and so on) that may change from year to year. To land these kinds of restricted theme grants, you may need to modify your programs in some way in order to qualify.

You will need to decide whether or not it is worth your while to take this detour from your mission, just to secure the funding.

Recently, a new species of philanthropist has arisen: the "invisible strings" donor. This species of philanthropist may be willing to make a major donation to your cause, but he also wants to have a lot of say about how you use it, beyond simply restricting it to a specific purpose. He sees it more as an investment than a grant. Many of these New Age donors are young entrepreneurs who have made a fortune in the software business, or they could just be old money: highly successful businessmen. These invisible-strings donors at first seem too good to be true and have field markings identical or similar to those of *Donorus Perfectus*. As successful, wealthy individuals who have made a pile in the private sector, they clearly could provide the resources you need in abundance. But there are important differences between them and *Donorus Perfectus*.

The swag box "Too Good to Be True" relates the story of Benevolent Barry, a major donor who at first seemed heaven-sent but ended up putting us through hell.

▐▐

To Good to Be True

In 1994 John comes back from a conference with exciting news. He has met a wealthy businessman, Benevolent Barry, who is enamored with the FINCA mission and wants to see if it could be scaled up, not with public, but with private funds.

We choose the FINCA program that will be the recipient of Benevolent Barry's initial gift of a million dollars. We set our A team on it. Benevolent Barry provides a project manager from his side, Bonnie, to work with the FINCA team. In recognition of his major gift, we put Barry on our board. Everyone, with one exception, is wildly enthusiastic about the project. Our local Guatemala director, Carla, feels uneasy about taking on a new partner and being pushed to grow rapidly, but her complaints go unheard.

While the project plan is not a big hit with Carla, the establishment of a Project Management Unit is less so. She hates the idea of having two advisors checking on how she is spending the money and second-guessing her decisions. Carla falls behind on the implementation plan. The quarterly progress meetings grow contentious.

We inform Carla that we need to add some new members to her board, which currently consists of her close friends and relatives, the new members being representatives of FINCA International and Benevolent Barry. We force her to sign an agreement committing to make these changes. A few days later, Carla informs me that, unfortunately, the board of FINCA Guatemala has not accepted the agreement negotiated in Washington, D.C. I tell Benevolent Barry that if we work together, maybe we can find a legal solution to this bad news.

Benevolent Barry takes unilateral action to try to save the situation. He dispatches Bonnie to see if she can persuade Carla to break with FINCA and work directly with him. I warn Barry that it won't work; Carla will simply exploit the rift between us. As I predict, Bonnie's mission fails. It only makes Benevolent Barry angrier. He pulls the plug on the project and resigns from the board.

▌▐

In retrospect, it's difficult to see how both FINCA and Benevolent Barry could have been so naïve as to entrust our money to Carla without making sure we had the governance issue covered. Barry pinned the blame on FINCA, and perhaps rightly so, but it was a monumental due-diligence failure on both our parts. To be fair to both of us, there is a "political correctness" aspect surrounding the foreign aid industry that says that we must not be paternalistic or distrusting of our colleagues from developing countries, but rather should empower them to take over our aid-funded projects as soon as possible. Ironically, we would never dream of using this approach in the United States or Europe; we assume that whoever puts up the money has the control. This attitude, plus the perception on the part of many in developing countries that foreign aid is a murky quid pro quo for past transgressions from the colonial era, or worse, current compensation for geopolitical favors, attracts an inordinate number of crooks and opportunists.

We learned a number of other hard lessons in the Guatemala fiasco. One was that Benevolent Barry didn't see himself as a donor who made a major gift and then stepped back while FINCA managed it; he saw himself as an investor and partner. As someone who had achieved great success building and running his own businesses, Barry wanted to be hands-on, especially when his own money was at stake.

Second, while Barry loved FINCA's mission, he didn't necessarily love our organization. He was only interested in our organization insofar as it advanced the Guatemala project. He accepted a position on our board to watch over his "investment." This distinguished him from our other board members, who were concerned with the long-term success of FINCA as an organization and were more willing to tolerate our mistakes and learning curve.

Landing a major "strings attached" donor early in your organization's existence can be a great advantage, but it can also be damaging. Here are four ways to increase your odds of it being the former rather than the latter.

- Make sure you have control over the key risk factors, especially on the governance side. Ask yourself: If something goes wrong, will I have the authority to fix it?
- Make sure your organization is geared up to handle the "big money" and has the systems and staff to manage it. Persuade your donor to allow you to spend part of it on a pre-audit of your systems and staff before you begin to scale up. If you aren't ready, ask for more time to build your capacity. If the donor won't agree, difficult as it may be, take a pass.
- Though it may seem like a good idea at the time, don't offer your major donor a seat on your board, right out of the gate. Take some time to get to know each other. Giving money does not necessarily qualify someone as a board member. Also, if a donation is tied to a certain project, remember that the donor's priority will be his project, not your organization.
- Don't sign up for formal partnerships until your organization is developed to the point that it is prepared to manage them. If you do, make sure you have an escape clause if things go south. FINCA survived the Guatemala fiasco in part because our general counsel insisted on including a "best efforts" qualifier in the performance clause.

Angry Donor Management: Time-Tested Ways to Drive Away (and Recover) Your Donors

Just as there are many ways of attracting donors from the private sector, there are multiple ways to alienate and lose them as well. The easiest way is to fail to acknowledge their contribution. The second most common way is to oversolicit them, especially by mail. The most often heard complaint from oversolicited donors is that you are wasting part of their donation on postage and paper. Pay attention to these complaints. If you don't, your lack of responsiveness will eventually result in the dreaded "Please take me off your mailing list; I no longer want to contribute to your organization" letter. Usually this only comes after the donor has made multiple attempts to contact you. It means people on the front desk or your fund-raising team are not doing their job. You need to investigate what went wrong, and correct it. The best way to do this is to call the donors directly, make an abject apology, thank them for their past support, and ask them who they contacted, when, and through what means. You might even be able to salvage them as a donor.

Another way to alienate a major donor is to become too complacent and take their contributions for granted. This is a perennial danger with major donors who have contributed over a long period of time and who seem to no longer need the care and feeding—stewardship—they required as a new contributor. The temptation is to focus on new business. FINCA lost a major donor this way, who complained that, after ten years of increasing donations, FINCA had begun to "treat me like an ATM." In another case, one of our longtime board members and contributors, when she suffered a financial setback, complained she felt "dissed" by our development director, whom she described as "like a cigarette boat, leaving me in her wake." Fortunately, I was able to repair the relationship, and a year later, this board member generated a multimillion-dollar gift through one of her corporate contacts. There is an expression in the capital markets that says, "money goes where it is best treated." The same is true of donors. Make sure someone in the organization is checking the pulse of your major donors on a regular basis, to make sure they still feel appreciated. Better yet, do it yourself.

The good news is that with proper attention and care, many angry donors can be mollified and recovered. The ultimate recovery challenge is the Professional Angry Donor, or PAD. Some donors, I am convinced, contribute small amounts to a number of organizations in the hope that when they see the annual report, they can find a basis for attacking the management for not making good use of their funds. Others cruise the Web, landing on websites of foundations and then striking up conversations with their supporters or employees, questioning the authenticity of their claims and/or the motives of their founders.

The swag box "How Can You Look at Yourself in the Mirror?" describes an exchange I had with a PAD.

|||||||||||||||||||||||||||||||||||||||||||||||||||||||||||||||||||||||||||||||||||

How Can You Look at Yourself in the Mirror?

The publication of FINCA's annual report, which contains all the pertinent financial information as well as stories of our clients, always generates a substantial increase in donations as people are reminded of the good work we are doing. But not all the reactions are positive. One year, I receive a letter from a small donor who has analyzed our financial statements and reached the conclusion that only a small percentage of his and other contributions go to the program. Most, he has discovered, go to administrative costs. "How can you look at yourself in the mirror?" he asks me in outraged disbelief.

First, I ask Development to give me a complete giving history on this donor. As I suspected, he made one fifty-dollar "test" donation the previous year. Possible Professional Angry Donor. Then I go back over the income statement in the annual report, trying to figure out what has triggered this over-the-top reaction. Immediately, I see the problem. The financial statement in the annual report is unconsolidated and includes only the loans that FINCA headquarters made to the affiliates (a relatively small number) and not the loans the affiliates made to the clients (big number, roughly one hundred times the loans from FINCA HQ).

How can I mollify this PAD?

I write to the donor, explaining the misunderstanding. I thank him for bringing it to my attention. In the future, we will be sure to include both the consolidated and unconsolidated financial statements in order to provide a more complete picture of our operations.

Then comes the clincher. I write a personal check for fifty dollars, made out to the PAD. I send it off and await his response.

I never hear from the person again. Nor does the check appear on my bank statement.

||||||||||||||||||||||||||||||||||||||||||||||||||||||||||||||||||||||||||||||

Dreadful Dinners and Fund-Raisers That Aren't

Just mention the words "special events" and watch as staff and donors alike reach for their Blackberrys and put a fake entry in their calendars to make sure they're doing something else on that date. People hate going to them. Foundations hate organizing them. Most of them lose money. So why do they keep happening?

Nonprofits put on Dreadful Dinners for a variety of reasons. While most are lucky just to break even, some actually do make money, and they can even be enjoyable if the organization sponsoring them is creative, well-organized, and knowledgeable about such things. FINCA recently put on an event in New York City to celebrate our twenty-fifth anniversary and honor the contributions of Natalie Portman and Soledad Hurst, one of our longtime board members and major donors. We brought two of our clients, from Haiti and Kyrgyzstan, to tell their inspiring stories of how FINCA loans had helped them escape poverty. It was a huge public relations and financial success, raising more than a million dollars and treating the more than five hundred guests to a magical, memorable evening. It was also a hell of a lot of work and took months of staff and advisory board members' time.

If you do hold a DD, make sure you have a compelling keynote speaker as well as a celebrity or two on hand to pose for pictures with your guests. Warning: Please do not attempt a DD without a celebrity.

In some cases, as in the United Kingdom, people won't give unless they get something in return. This is because in the UK a larger portion of people's taxes go to support social services than in the United States, where nonprofits are active in every social sector including health, education, and even feeding the indigent. In the UK, people can rightly argue "I already gave" because they see this as the role of government. Nor do donors receive any favorable tax treatment for their contributions in the

UK—although the charity gets a matching grant from the government! The Brits will, however, attend a dinner or some other related event.

There are variations on the Dreadful Dinner theme. One is the auction. Some people think this is a lot of fun, but personally I find it to be a hell of a lot of work for very little return. FINCA attempted two of these, with mixed results. In the first, we gathered items from each of the twenty-one countries we work in. Talk about a logistical nightmare! We supplemented these with "celebrity items," which we hoped would ignite fierce (and for us, lucrative) bidding wars, like a baseball signed by Cal Ripken Jr. and a screenplay by Alan Alda of an Emmy Award–winning episode of *M.A.S.H.* If I tell you I still have the baseball you will understand what the problem is with these big-ticket items: nobody wants to shell out the big bucks. Your guests will trample each other to bid on the ten-dollar wampum key chain from the reservation in Oklahoma in the silent auction, but good luck unloading A-list actor Malcolm Cooter's *Still Life with Two Breadsticks and a Pineapple* for the minimum bid of fifteen hundred dollars.[2] (Oh, you didn't know he could paint? He can't.) To move them, you need an auctioneer who will "out" the deep-pocket donors and shame them into bidding against each other while everyone else hides around the punch bowl, cringing with embarrassment for the organizers.

A variation on the celebrity draw is the honoree approach. A former Advisory Board member of ours had his own theory on how to run these things, although he adamantly refused to take part if FINCA ever hosted one. (True to his word, he didn't even show when we had Queen Rania on the docket.) "You need to honor a villain," he advised me. "Find someone who has been discredited and needs to be publicly recognized for 'his contribution.' He will pay handsomely for the chance to resuscitate his reputation."

We never tried this, but it sounds intriguing. There can't be any shortage of villains hanging around Wall Street these days. And their pockets must be bulging with the proceeds of their dirty deeds.

Lastly, there are "friend raisers," an especially challenging variation on the Dreadful Dinner theme in which you are prohibited from making a

---

2. Don't try googling Malcolm Cooter. He doesn't exist. Or if he does, he isn't an A-list actor.

direct "ask" and must pursue your quarry post-event. "One Disenchanting Evening" describes a "friend raiser" in Northern California, where everything was going well until, having imbibed too much of the host's cabernet, I violated the prime directive: Tell the story; don't ask for money; let the people come to you.

▌▌▌

One Disenchanting Evening

After meeting with clients, talking to donors about FINCA's work is the second-best part of my job as CEO. In this case, the pleasure is double as I am headed to a soirée in Northern California, in the springtime, at the beautiful home of one of our major donors. "There's just one thing I need to tell you," says Bob, who works in our development department at FINCA. "Our host doesn't want you to ask for money."

"You mean it's a—"

"Yep. A friend raiser."

I promise Bob I will keep my "ask" in the holster. We arrive at our host's home, which is already beginning to fill with her neighbors. Our host introduces me to a young man, Richard, whom she identifies as the coordinator for foundations that wish to raise money in their community. Remember, Richard cautions me: "Don't ask, don't sell."

We have brought one of our staff from FINCA Guatemala for the occasion, a former client who became one of our best-performing credit officers. Ten years ago, after her husband died in a traffic accident, Isabela became the sole means of support for herself and her four children. She earned less than a dollar a day selling vegetables in the marketplace. Then she heard from a friend about an organization called FINCA who lent money to people like herself. She borrowed fifty dollars from FINCA, using the money to buy a small stove, which she used to make soup out of vegetables that went unsold at the end of market day. With successively larger loans, Isabela eventually opened her own restaurant, which she still operates with two of her daughters. Both of her sons have finished high school, and one has been accepted to college, she tells us with pride. She became a FINCA credit officer because she wanted to help other women like herself to break out of poverty.

As Isabela finishes her talk, several of the guests are visibly weeping.

Now it's my turn. Isabela's is going to be a hard act to follow. I tell our guests a little more about FINCA, how our methodology works, and then take a few questions. The women want to know how many of our clients are women and the men want to know what percentage of our donations are spent on overhead. I close with what I think is a clever joke. "If this were a different type of event, at this point I would ask you all for a contribution. But our host has warned me that this is a 'fund-raising-free zone,' so I will just conclude by saying that if this *were* a fund-raiser and you were interested in making a contribution, Bob here can give you all the details."

Our host invites everyone to mingle and enjoy another glass of wine. Richard, the gatekeeper, smiles and congratulates me on a great presentation. Someone even slips me a check on his way out. Things could not have gone better.

Or so I thought.

"Richard is furious with you," Bob tells me, as we walk to the car.

"What?" I am stunned.

"You asked for money."

"But it was a joke! I didn't really ask, did I?"

"You did."

Afterward, I talk to our host, and she confirms it. I am still in denial. I can't believe this can't be salvaged. Bob tells me he doesn't think so. Richard is really angry that I violated his protocol. I imagine him on a horse, wearing a serape and a cheroot clenched between his teeth.

"You'll never work in the Valley again, Scofield."

The moral of the story is, if someone tells you not to ask for money, don't.

██

11

‖‖

THE POWER OF THE OTHER PILLARS

Public and Internal

While it is possible to finance your mission exclusively from private sources—and some mission-driven organizations, in order to avoid restrictions placed on them if they did accept government grants, follow this strategy—there are two other potential sources of funding available to you, provided you are willing and able to develop them. The public pillar—availing yourself of government grants—requires a lot of work, initially, to establish yourself as a reliable partner in some area of interest to a government agency or other entity financed with taxpayer dollars. The internal pillar—generating an income stream from your beneficiaries or some other source either related or unrelated to your mission—will require all your ingenuity and creativity, but may be the shortest path to your own Financial Fourth of July (Independence Day). In any case, both of these pillars should be explored as an income diversification strategy because, as you will discover, all three pillars may grow and shrink over the life of your organization, depending on the vagaries of changing donor priorities, who holds the reins of power in government, and the fundamentals driving the robustness of your internal sources.

Have You Seen the Little Piggies, Feeding at the Trough?: Government Funding

If you can prove to the right people in the government that your mission is in the public interest, you can build a second pillar of support, funded by taxpayers like yourself. If you're wondering whether this is worth the effort, consider that in 2009, 49 percent of the total federal budget of $2.4 trillion went to contractors and grantees. As you may have already guessed, all of the top five contractors are from the defense industry. What you might not know is that almost all of the top one hundred grantees are states, usually for what is known as "funded mandates" in the health-care arena.

So, how did the nonprofits fare? They received less than one-half of 1 percent, a measly $959 million. What explains this Grand Canyon gulf between what the defense industry received and what organizations like FINCA were awarded? The defense industry would tell you that, though nonprofits do important things in the social sphere, they defend our nation's shores.

Another explanation is that they spend more money on lobbyists than nonprofits do. The top ten defense contractors spent $88 million on lobbying in 2009 and landed $133 *billion* in defense contracts. A total of $3.5 billion was invested in lobbying by all defense contractors, which produced a bonanza of $524 billion. Pretty sweet return on investment. By contrast, the total budget of the main international nonprofit lobbying organization, InterAction, was less than $5 million. You get what you pay for.

While the nonprofit slice of the pie is slim, however, it's worth competing for. And once you establish yourself as a viable recipient, you can develop a reliable income stream that will enable you to build your organization and advance your mission faster than if you depended on the private, "kindness of strangers" pillar alone. You also will have the satisfaction of knowing that at least some percentage of your tax dollars went to finance something you can feel good about, versus the black hole of entitlements and questionable military crusades.

What are the tools you need to play in this sandbox? First, you need grant-writing skills. The process begins with research. Locate the pots of money for which your organization is eligible. There is a whole industry devoted to helping you learn how to tap this resource, from telling you where the money is to helping you write successful proposals. Just search online for "government grants" and they will pop up like dandelions after a spring rain. But this isn't really the way you land them. Despite the lobbying efforts of the nonprofits, only a small percentage of grant funding is set aside—or "earmarked"—for nonprofits. The for-profit consulting firms are way ahead of you in that they are staffed to churn out hundreds of proposals every year. More important, they are plugged into the networks of the people who release the RFPs (requests for proposals). How does the nonprofit compete in this system when they are so hopelessly outgunned?

This is where the appeal of the mission comes in. Jaded members of Congress, constantly nipped at by greedy lobbyists seeking to position their client's snout at the trough, love to take an occasional break from their sordid existence to entertain someone with a real cause who is trying to do worthwhile work. All the more fun if they have a celebrity in tow who can pose with them for a picture to hang alongside the miscreants and brigands who clog their walls. Why not throw them a bone now and then?

The good news is that the same system that works for the power players can work for your mission-driven organization. You can lobby your funding into existence, if you learn how to play the game. It really is amazing, a real "only in America" story.

The swag box "The Big Money" describes how FINCA, Muhammad Yunus, and an antihunger citizens' group, Results, lobbied the Self-Sufficiency for the Poor Act of 1987 into being, creating a $100 million fund for microfinance.

██

The Big Money

In midwinter of 1987, FINCA connects with Sam Harris of the Results organization, a citizens' lobby whose mission is to mobilize political will to end world hunger. He has met Muhammad Yunus of the Grameen Bank, and he wants to work with FINCA to get a bill through Congress to get an earmark for microfinance.

Sam wants me to testify at a hearing on the microfinance earmark before the Senate Foreign Relations Committee. Testifying on the panel with me—or against me, as it turns out—is Marty Degata, a former USAID mission director I worked with in El Salvador during the war years of the early 1980s. Because AID automatically opposes earmarks, no matter how worthy the cause, poor Marty is in the unenviable position of having to oppose a bill called the Self-Sufficiency for the Poor Act whose purpose is to help hundreds of thousands of the poorest people on earth bootstrap themselves out of poverty.

"Training and technology frequently come into play only above a certain level of activity," I tell the panel. "The poorest of the poor can, through their own skill at survival, make astonishingly good use of even the smallest amount of capital without expensive training and technology. While that discovery threatens the livelihood of consultants such as myself, I cannot escape the conclusion that this type of project represents a superior investment—from the beneficiaries' point of view—than many of those much more expensive efforts with which I have been associated in the past."

Results creates an op-ed out of my testimony and has it published in five newspapers across the country.

Results has a very effective business model consisting of organizing citizen groups around the country who bombard their congressmen with calls and letters and face-to-face meetings, asking them to support the legislation, and who generate editorials in their local papers by educating journalists as to the merits of the bill. Meanwhile, in Washington, D.C., Sam goes about collecting cosponsors for the bill, which John Hatch has helped to write. Conservative Republicans love it because it's about the poor helping themselves, without handouts. Liberal Democrats love it because it addresses the problem of world poverty. After a few months, Sam and his cadre of citizens have signed up more than one hundred cosponsors in the House and more than half of the Senate. The bill does not pass as stand-alone legislation but its language—and $50 million—is incorporated into the Foreign Aid Appropriations Bill.

The speed with which the bill translates into resources for FINCA amazes me. A month later, John and I travel to El Salvador to meet with a USAID mission and sign a $10 million grant agreement.

The El Salvador grant allowed FINCA, for the first time, to roll out its village banking methodology on a large scale. Despite the fact that the country was in the middle of a civil war, Hatch and his team organized village banks throughout El Salvador. The Centro de Apoyo a la Microempresa (CAM) quickly became the largest microfinance program in Central America, with thirty thousand clients. AID loved the program, and when visitors from Washington visited the country (members of Congress, government representatives, and so on) visiting CAM was always at the top of their itinerary as living proof that our foreign assistance program was working and reaching the poorest of the poor. The project put FINCA on the map and elevated us to "playah" status alongside the best, most effective NGOs working in international economic development.

Buoyed by this success, we churned out other USAID proposals for other countries in Latin America and, eventually, Africa and the former Soviet Union countries, the so-called newly independent states. The love affair between AID and FINCA lasted more than ten years and brought in more than $50 million in grant funding. The second pillar allowed FINCA to eventually create a microfinance empire spanning twenty countries on four continents.

Did the story have a happy ending? Unfortunately, no. At this writing, not only FINCA but none of the major microfinance practitioners have received more than a handful of USAID grants in the past several years.[1] Yet, the money continues to be appropriated. So where is it going?

The swag box "Bandidos del Beltway" relates the sad story of how the microfinance industry failed to protect its gains and saw all its funding diverted to the Beltway Bandit consulting firms.

Bandidos del Beltway

Complacent with its newfound financial stability, FINCA and other microfinance practitioners are unaware of the dark forces moving to take control of "our" government funding for microfinance, which has

---

1. FINCA did land a sizable grant from AID for its Afghanistan program in 2003.

now doubled from $50 million to $100 million. The big international development consulting firms have quietly traveled the globe selling a new concept to the USAID missions. The microfinance movement has grown so large over the years—to more than ten thousand MFIs, according to some estimates—it would be impossible for the grossly understaffed USAID missions to sort out the Good from the Bad and Ugly. Why not give all the money to a project support office in each country, staffed by experts in the field who screen the proposals and make subgrants to the few and the worthy?

The missions love the idea.

The USAID missions continue to churn out RFPs like the one FINCA won in El Salvador way back in 1990. However, to its dismay, FINCA finds that by the time it responds with a proposal, the grant is already locked up by one of the major consulting firms. The design of the project is always the same: a big project support office, staffed by lots of expensive consultants who will put out a handful of tiny subgrants to the MFI practitioners who actually do the work.

One problem the Bandits have is finding people who will staff their in-country teams. They must be people with the experience and credibility in the field. Where could they find such people?

Over the years, many FINCA and other MFI employees have ended up working for the Bandits. FINCA is a double loser, watching the resources it lobbied into existence pirated away, plus losing several of its top employees. Occasionally, I approach one of our former employees and ask if he or she has tired of the consulting life and wants to get back into the real game. The response is always the same: "Thanks, but I don't want to work that hard ever again."

The real loser is the taxpayer. The business model of the consulting firm is different from that of the MFI. The consulting firm makes a 5 percent profit on its government contracts, but the real money is in the overhead, or indirect costs, which adds another 25 to 50 percent and covers the salaries and benefits of the home-office employees and owners of the company. Since the overhead is calculated as a percentage of the direct costs, the more money that goes to the overseas consultants' salaries, living expenses, and benefits, the higher the overhead.

FINCA tries to organize the other microfinance networks to combat this trend of giving all the AID resources to consulting firms versus directly to practitioners. But the microfinance networks are too busy competing with each other for the crumbs falling from the Beltway Bandits' voracious lips, and too disorganized to mount a counteroffensive.

▌▌▌

Let me hasten to add that the current state of affairs is completely the fault of those of us in the industry. We behaved like complacent fools and were parted from our gold. I will even admit that not all the work of the Beltway Bandits has been useless. The consulting firm Development Alternatives fielded a competent team that privatized a government bank in Tanzania and turned it into a very impressive microfinance bank. In a sweet reversal of fortune, both of the architects of this success later came to work for FINCA.

The days of the big money—at least from the government—are over. FINCA will have to fund its growth through some other means.

What will it be?

The Internal Sources Pillar: God Bless the Child That's Got His Own

Does your organization have the possibility of charging its beneficiaries for some or all of the services it provides? The very idea may seem like sacrilege in a mission-driven organization. After all, these people are poor, right?

C. K. Prahalad, in his landmark book *The Fortune at the Bottom of the Pyramid*, describes a number of cases where companies, some for-profit and other mission-driven, developed brilliant business models allowing them to provide products and services to a huge but previously ignored segment of the population with incomes so low they had been written off as potential customers. In Mexico, a building materials company called CEMEX devised a kind of "Home Depot for the poor" scheme in which poor people could make preinstallment payments of about fourteen dollars per week for a year and a half (totaling a thousand dollars) and in return receive the building materials *and* professional architectural and construction consulting to build their own house. By 2009 they had helped more than 260,000 low-income Mexicans build or improve their own houses. CEMEX recently launched a replica of the program in the Dominican

Republic. The program makes money, and the default rate on the in-kind loans of materials is less than 5 percent.

Another example of a company that managed to mix mission with business is the Avarind Eye Hospital, which over the past thirty years has treated 2.4 million poor patients, a full 20 percent of the blind people in India. Their model is simple: those who can, pay; those who can't, receive the care free. They manage this through a highly efficient division of labor in which the clinics are open twenty-four hours a day, which means the expensive equipment pays for itself three times as fast. High-salaried ophthalmologists do the surgery while lower-paid nurses and other staff handle the pre- and postoperative care.

Rethinking the Paradigm: Charge 'Em for the Mice, Charge for the Lice

How can you identify and build this third pillar? First, inventory all the services and products your organization provides and determine how much it costs to deliver them. Could all or part of that cost be defrayed through user fees? Perhaps you are afraid to even ask that question. What if you began to charge something for your services and all the beneficiaries went away? But if they could pay, and eventually gave you enough income to cover all your costs, you would have done a remarkable thing: taken a social service out of the realm of charity and into the marketplace. Moreover, you would have changed the relationship from one of dependency between a benefactor and a charity case to one of equals: a provider of services and a paying customer. The swag box "Mama May Have, Papa May Have" relates how FINCA's financial structure has evolved over the years, and how the third pillar has grown to the point where it constitutes more than 85 percent of the foundation's $180 million annual budget.

||||||||||||||||||||||||||||||||||||||||||||||||||||||||||||||||||||||||

Mama May Have, Papa May Have

Toward the end of the 1980s, we begin to realize that the token interest we charge on our loans of 3 percent per month is beginning to amount to real money. We experience it first in the diminished and less frequent pleas for money from our pilot projects in Central America, where our country directors are covering more and more of their operating costs with interest income from the rapidly growing loan portfolio. With less of the money FINCA International raises going to pay local salaries and expenses, more can go to loan capital—which makes the donors very happy. Plus, the loan portfolio can grow all the more rapidly.

We are trapped in a virtuous cycle.

This gets me thinking in another direction. Suppose the day arrives when both the government grants and the private money that currently support FINCA's headquarters costs dry up? How will FINCA International cover its costs of supervising the network?

I know it won't be an easy sell, but if I can get the affiliates to charge the clients an additional 1 percent fee, to be charged on every loan disbursed, and upstream that as an "affiliation fee" to FINCA International, perhaps one day it will grow into real money as have the other pillars. If it is to be paid by the clients themselves, it won't affect the finances of the country programs, so my country directors shouldn't complain. And it shouldn't be a heavy burden on the clients—just fifty cents on a fifty-dollar loan. There is another attractive feature. Unlike the government grants and the private donations, which come with strings, this is pure nonprofit gold: unrestricted income.

I am correct that it is a hard sell. USAID hates the idea, threatens to block it, but can't find a legal basis to do so. The local, autonomous boards of directors of the FINCA affiliates are appalled. How can money flow from a poor country to a rich country? It's not supposed to work that way! I make my case, explain that FINCA needs to strive for financial self-sufficiency at all levels. First and foremost, we need to make the clients self-sufficient; second, the affiliates; and finally, FINCA International itself. If we can achieve this, FINCA will be able to grow and continue to execute its mission into the indefinite future, regardless of how donations ebb and flow.

I eventually win over all the affiliate boards, with the exceptions of Costa Rica, Guatemala, and Peru.

Now FINCA has one of the most powerful financial models in the development community. It's a stool with three legs: government grants, private donations, and a robust stream of internally generated income with the potential to cover all the operating costs of both the field and—thanks to my controversial innovation, affiliation fees—the home office as well. And all are growing nicely.

The next step in constructing FINCA's internal pillar was to leverage its donated capital with borrowed funds, first from subsidized, below-market sources like program-related investments (PRIs), and eventually from commercial sources, like local banks in the countries where we operate. These sources, which now fund more than half of our loan portfolio, carry a market cost in terms of their interest rates, usually LIBOR[2] plus some markup in the hundreds of basis points.[3] This increases the cost of our loans to our clients, but we still earn a "spread" between them and the rate we charge our clients, so that we cover all our costs and generate a net margin, thereby adding to the girth of our internal pillar. We have another source of capital, client savings, which though it finances less than 5 percent of our loan portfolio at present, will grow dramatically in the future, as we transform more of our network of twenty-one country programs into regulated financial intermediaries, like commercial banks and finance companies. As in the case of our commercial borrowings, a growing deposit base will also nurture the expansion of the internal pillar.

Nor does it end there. At present, we are considering adding a fourth component to our capital structure (currently consisting of donated funds, commercial borrowings, and client savings): equity. How is this possible in a nonprofit? U.S. nonprofit law, as we have noted, is a wonderful creation in this regard, allowing a 501(c)(3) foundation to have any number of for-profit subsidiaries without jeopardizing its charitable status, as long as they advance the mission. This is surely the case with FINCA. In fact, through the power of leverage, one dollar donated to FINCA currently translates into at least four dollars in loans, assuming that we are able to borrow four times our capital. If we are able add client savings and investor capital to the formula, a dollar donated to FINCA can be leveraged more than ten times.

The point is, if you can find a financially sustainable business model to execute your mission, you can access the virtually unlimited resources of the capital markets, and your potential to serve your beneficiaries becomes, well, also unlimited.

---

2. The London Interbank Offered Rate (or LIBOR) is a daily reference rate based on the interest rates at which banks borrow unsecured funds from each other.
3. One hundred basis points equals 1 percent.

12

||||||||||||||||||||||||||||||||||||||||||||||||||||||||||||||||||||||||||||||

COMMUNICATION

From "Who?" to Wheaties

In the early days of a mission-driven organization's existence, it's difficult to justify spending precious resources on advertising and public relations where the return is neither immediate nor obvious. But if done correctly, it does eventually pay off.

Turning Your Name into a Household Word

Getting from "unknown" to "household word" status can be an expensive, agonizingly slow process or, for the fortunate few, can literally happen overnight and cost you nothing. In this media-crazed age, where "viral" communication can spread your name across the globe in a matter of seconds, you may get the publicity that turns you and your company temporarily into a household word, and then be forgotten by the end of the week, crowded out by the next hot story. Most organizations, even if they get that shot on Leno or Oprah, aren't skillful enough to capitalize on it. Some are. Women for Women, an organization run by my former deputy, received six million bucks in forty-eight hours following an appearance by their founder on Oprah. There is also the kind of overnight fame none of us wants, as the late Kenneth Lay of Enron and anyone else caught up in a scandal has discovered.

The first question you need to answer when designing your communication program is: communication to whom? Will you be targeting potential donors? Clients? Employees? All of the above? If we are talking about clients, then we are talking about a marketing program. If we are talking about employees, then we need an internal communications program. If it is potential donors and other people outside the organization we are trying to reach, then we are talking about an external (or PR) program. All are important, but without the external program, we have no money, and since this part of the book follows the one devoted to planting and nurturing the money tree, let's start with that.

My development director, Sofia, had been with FINCA only a few months when I added a small item to her job description: make FINCA a household word. At the time, FINCA was probably known to a few hundred people at best. The population of the United States at the time was just north of two hundred million.

My first question was, how did groups like CARE and Save the Children do it? Part of the trick is to be around a long time. Both organizations had been at it for many years, STC for ninety and CARE since 1945. They had considerable war chests to spend on advertising and publicity. At the time, FINCA was putting every available dollar into the pilot projects in the field. STC and CARE had celebrity spokespeople like Sally Struthers who went on television begging us to help "The Children." They also had high-priced PR firms helping them out. We had none of these.

We also had another problem: our name. Save the Children and Save the Whales, for example, mean something. Our acronym, FINCA, means "farm" in Spanish and in English it means nothing. Our full name, Foundation for International Community Assistance, sounds better, but it could also mean we did anything from donating goats to building latrines.[1] The problem was, while we had zero name recognition in the United States,

---

1. In fact, you need to be careful what you call yourself, as our imprecise moniker did generate a lot of "request mail" from individuals, cooperatives, and other grassroots organizations shopping for grants. There was one chap from India who, undeterred by my polite rejections, actually traveled to the United States to meet with me in the early '80s to ask us to finance a school in his village.

our programs in Mexico, Peru, and Central America had developed name recognition among our clients in those countries. They would resist any changes to the brand we had developed.

Communications Lesson One: If you are a start-up, think hard before you choose your name. You may be stuck with it a long time.

After much thought and debate, we decided not to change the FINCA name. We did, however, get some low-cost consulting from a PR firm that advised us to add a tag line. A tag line is a phrase succinct enough to appear alongside your name and logo that describes what you do. It seemed like a good compromise. Brainstorming at the organizational level did not prove fruitful, and it was actually my wife who made the breakthrough. Driving through upstate New York on a beautiful autumn afternoon, admiring the foliage, she said, out of the blue: "What was it that guy said who was the first man on the moon? Something like 'One small step for man, one giant step for mankind.' FINCA makes small loans so . . ."

"Small Loans, Big Changes."

Our tag line was born. We eventually translated it into Russian, Swahili, French, and Arabic. It has had a good run, about fifteen years. Now, with FINCA diversifying its financial services and doing more than just credit, our advisors tell us it's time for a change.

As our fund-raising operation grew, my development director persuaded me the time had come to hire someone to work in-house on our external communications. This was a hard sell. Communications didn't sound like fund-raising. Like advertising, it seemed like a way to spend a lot of money for a possibly, someday, maybe, indefinite return in the future. Sofia was adamant: if I still wanted to turn FINCA into a household word I had to start making the investment. Reluctantly, I agreed.

The search for the right director of communications was, like so many of our other searches at FINCA, an iterative process. The first few we hired were actually writers, not experts in the field of communications, but we didn't know the difference at the time. Writing good copy is only one part of the task of turning your company name into a household word. You need a campaign, consisting of advertising [especially free public service announcements (PSAs) if you can swing it], pitching stories to the media, doing special events, recruiting celebrity spokespersons, and taking advantage of the Web. These activities require a person who is upbeat, fun to work with, and, above all, aggressive enough to sell people on your organization and its message.

Despite my unwillingness to fund a full-on communications campaign, we were doing things to get our name out. Our direct-mail program had kicked into high gear; we were sending hundreds of thousands of letters out four times a year to potential supporters. Although our response rate was less than 1 percent, it didn't mean the other 99 percent of those mailings that elicited no response were a waste of money. Unless the recipients simply threw them away without reading them, we were creating awareness. Maybe the next time they saw our name they would actually make a contribution.

We also had our annual report, which was another opportunity to get "the FINCA story" out more and in depth. Just as with the FINCA story, your organization's story should be the compelling narrative that puts your mission into human terms people can connect with on an emotional level and that makes people want to contribute or become a part of your organization. In FINCA's case, it is the client story. The swag box "Client Story: Grandmother Provides Hope and Brighter Future for Her Orphaned Grandchildren" is an example of a compelling client story taken from our 2009 annual report.

▮▮

Client Story: Grandmother Provides Hope and Brighter Future for Her Orphaned Grandchildren

In Zambia, one of the poorest and least-developed countries on earth, sixty-three-year-old Mailesi Chankonse is raising three grandchildren on her own after their parents—all three of Mailesi's daughters and their husbands—succumbed to complications related to HIV/AIDS. Zambia suffers one of the world's highest HIV/AIDS prevalence rates, with 1.1 million people infected out of a total population of just under 12 million.

To support her grandson (age eight) and two granddaughters (ages two and five), Mailesi operates a market stall in downtown Lusaka's Bawleni market where she sells dried *Kapenta*, a popular Zambian fish. Knowing that she needed to increase her income so that she could afford the fees for her grandchildren to go to school, Mailesi joined FINCA Zambia's "Arising" Village Banking group four years ago. She took out a small loan to help her buy larger quantities of *Kapenta* at wholesale and to finance the expansion of her business.

Since joining the group, Mailesi has made all her loan payments on time, and her business has prospered. She currently has a loan of one million Zambian *kwacha* (US$200). Despite the challenges she faces, Mailesi is very proud that she can provide a home for her young family and that her two older grandchildren are attending school. She hopes they will all be able to gain an education and have a chance for a better future.

The FINCA story is where communications and fund-raising intersect. As one consultant we hired in the early days put it, your task is to "increase the number of people who can tell your story." The most effective—and, unfortunately, expensive—way to do this is to actually get them to the field. The next best thing is a video. FINCA has done a number of these. I costar with Natalie Portman in *Stories of Hope*, which profiles our clients in Mexico.[2] You can see it on YouTube. Directed and produced by award-winning Mexican documentarian Juan Carlos Rulfo, it lets the clients describe in their own words, uncoached, how FINCA changed their lives.

At what point, if ever, does it make sense for a nonprofit to hire a PR firm? My answer is, it depends on the firm, and it depends on your stage of development. FINCA availed itself of the services of three Washington-based firms, each at a different stage of FINCA's development. The first was very early on, in the late 1980s, before we even had an office. The law firm Arnold & Porter provided us with some pro bono assistance, including an introduction to the chairman of the Senate Banking Committee. It was too early in our development, and we did nothing with it.

A decade later, a member of our advisory board steered us to a different Washington-based PR firm, where his son worked. We put him on a retainer, and in return he taught us how to identify and map our audience (donors, policy makers, international development agencies, and so forth), shape our message, and pitch our story to the media. The media strategy was to identify an occasion, such as our anniversary, that might give a

---

2. Rumor has it I am up for a statue in the category of "Best Cameo in a Foreign Infomercial," but I'm not getting my hopes up.

journalist a reason to do an article on FINCA. We learned how very, very hard it is to put one past a reporter who instinctively is suspicious of your looking for a "puff piece." We did land a few stories during this period, although in what seemed like pure malice on the part of the journalists, FINCA's name was often left out of it. We learned that the media in general is not terribly interested in good news stories of any kind. More than once we were blown off the front page by some Act of Satan when we were certain we had a killer story.

In March of '98, President Bill and First Lady Hillary Clinton visited our program in Uganda. President Museveni wanted to take them to visit a sugarcane plantation, but Hillary insisted she wanted to see FINCA's program in Jinja, at the source of the Nile. Once he got there, Museveni had a pretty good time and especially enjoyed talking to the women. Bill was presented with a newborn baby and told its name was "Bill Clinton." The women danced up a storm and pulled Hillary and Mrs. Museveni onto the (dirt) floor with them. Surely, this was going to be the story that turned FINCA into a household word!

The next day, Arkansas made the headlines, but not in a story featuring its two most famous residents. Two kids, ages thirteen and eleven, stole their grandfather's hunting rifles and opened up on a middle school, killing five people and wounding ten others. Adios to the FINCA story.

Identifying Your Core Constituencies

The mapping exercise produced the realization that in order to truly become a household word, FINCA would have to spend A LOT of money. At least we would if we went about it in the traditional way a firm or product gets its name out. The conceptual breakthrough came in a throwaway line from our Advisory Board member's son, while we were playing golf at the Chevy Chase Country Club. "You know, Rupert, being a household word doesn't have to mean the whole population of the United States. It can just be with certain constituencies that are important to you."

Aha. So who were our "important constituencies"? We started with our direct-mail program and asked our consultant to profile the kinds of people who donate to FINCA. The answer came back that they were upper middle class, well educated. Not the type to react to a fly-covered child ad put out by a religious organization. They "got" that we were making the poor self-sufficient. They seemed to be of all political stripes.

Other constituents important to FINCA were the U.S. government, the international financial institutions like the World Bank, and a growing number of commercial banks that had begun lending to us. Corporations were also a constituency of growing importance to FINCA. Corporations tend to follow each other's lead, so that once you have a good reputation with one, acquiring new partners becomes much easier. If you are lucky, they will do a "loyalty program" for you and do your fund-raising. I have always looked with great envy upon British Airways' "Change for Good" program where they have collected coins from the passengers and donated the proceeds to UNICEF. It's a triple win. The employees love it, the company gets great press, and UNICEF gets its name mentioned on every one of the hundreds of thousands of flights BA takes every year. And it brings in real money. To date, they have raised more than 40 million pounds.

Back to the FINCA Household Word Campaign. Is it working? More and more strangers I speak to tell me "Oh, I know FINCA." Occasionally, one will even utter those words that gladden the heart of every nonprofit CEO: "Oh, you're the CEO of FINCA? I'm a contributor!" But here's my favorite: my nephew told me he met someone at a party who, when told his uncle was CEO of FINCA, "reacted as if I'd told him my uncle was Mick Jagger."

So we are getting there, but very, very slowly. The real problem with what I shall call the old-school communications strategy is that, like all other old-school advertising, it is difficult to tell whether it's working. A typical comment made by businesspeople with big promotional budgets is, "I know half of it works; I just don't know which half."

Companies called Yahoo, Google, and Microsoft have changed all that. If you put an ad on Google, they can trace who responds to it. They can help you target your potential customers. It was probably inevitable that some MFI would figure out how to use the Web and shake up the industry.

Overnight Sensation: How a Company Called Kiva Rocked Our World

Kiva is a Web-based, peer-to-peer microfinance lending program founded in November of 2005 by Matt and Jessica Flannery, a couple in their late twenties from the Bay Area. Matt was a software engineer employed by Tivo, the company that invented the digital video recorder (DVR), and Jessica was pursuing a career in microfinance in Africa. Jessica actually interned at FINCA's program in Uganda, which is where she got her hands-on experience with microfinance and her poverty experience.

Kiva's innovation was to harness the power of the Web to enhance the already great appeal of the sponsorship model. Pictures of microentrepreneurs seeking loans to finance their businesses are posted on Kiva's website, along with a brief description of their business idea and their personal information. Potential lenders can then choose to fund all or part of the client's loan, with a minimum contribution of twenty-five dollars. As "real" peer-to-peer lending programs have to be registered and regulated by the SEC, Kiva gets around this by intermediating not actual loans but what are in effect "reimbursable grants" (my term). A reimbursable grant acts like a loan in that the contributors can have their money back after the loan is repaid, if they choose. They can also choose to roll it over, either to their existing client or to a new one, which is what about 85 percent of them do. In effect, then, Kiva's "loan book" keeps growing. The fact that these loans are not really Kiva's assets, in the sense that they can go on its balance sheet, is another story, which we will explore in more detail later.

Has Kiva cracked the code on the dismal economics of sponsorship programs? From the stream of money pouring in, it would appear so, at least on the fund-raising side. In its brief five-year existence Kiva has raised enough money to fund more than $135 million in loans from almost half a million contributors. New lenders are logging on at the rate of more than 3,000 per week, or an annual rate of 160,000, dwarfing FINCA's sponsorship program even at its apogee. After twenty-five years, FINCA has about 100,000 contributors.

What is behind Kiva's phenomenal success? A look at the "Press Center" on their website tells the story. To look at their list of media hits is to make any nonprofit green with envy. All the biggies of print and TV are there: *Time, Fortune, The Wall Street Journal, The New York Times, USA Today,* ABC, *Good Morning America,* CNN, Fox, BBC—even Al Jazeera is there with a favorable story. The list is fourteen pages long and contains more than one hundred stories. But the most remarkable thing is not the magnitude of the coverage: every one of them is a *positive* story.

How did Kiva do it? With a multimillion-dollar PR war chest and a hundred-person media team? As far as I can tell, they don't even have a communications director. So what is going on here?

The answer is, they built it and the media came. They created a killer model that the press just ate up. Unlike most of the time when it is the scent of blood in the water that draws the media, in this case it is the heart-warming microfinance story, the poor helping themselves, *plus* that of a New Age company using cutting-edge technology to make it happen. A story so compelling, in other words, that no one from Oprah to the *WSJ* could bear to be left out.

And boy, did it work. Less than a year after they opened their doors, those kids had yet to make their first million in loans when they were included in *The New York Times Magazine* "Year in Ideas" special edition and had a documentary on "Frontline/WORLD." As they stated on their website, "the resulting traffic explosion promptly crashes the Kiva website for three days. Once the website is back up, Kiva makes $250,000 in loans the week following." A year later, the cofounders strike media gold with a shot on Oprah *with former President Clinton!* Their lender list tops one hundred thousand. Nicholas Kristol of the *NYT* becomes a Kiva lender and goes to visit his entrepreneur client in Kabul, Afghanistan, certifying the operation as legitimate. In the next three days, $250,000 in new loans pours into Kiva's coffers. The kids can do no wrong.

Iceberg, Dead Ahead: Unforeseen Issues for Kiva and Other MFIs

If you know anything about how the media works, then you know that last statement is a setup. At this writing, Kiva has stumbled a bit. The media has swung into its "teardown cycle," and not just Kiva but all of microfinance is being accused of having oversold itself as a solution to poverty. Some MFIs are criticized for charging usurious interest rates and profiting at the expense of the poor. (To be honest, some are.) Kiva has been taken to task in the media and on the Web ("Live by the Web, die by the Web") as "feeding a misunderstanding" as to how it actually pairs lenders with borrowers.

The good news for Kiva is that this recent negative press doesn't appear to have affected the magnitude of its funding flows in the slightest. It still has an embarrassment-of-riches problem as many relief organizations had in the wake of the tsunami in India and others will undoubtedly have in placing the funding they raised in the aftermath of the Haitian earthquake, where one of every two American households made some kind of contribution.

Unlike FINCA, Kiva does not have its own network of MFIs it can rely on to make the actual loans. Kiva has some volunteers it has placed in countries around the world, but not nearly enough to place all the money it has been raising. Kiva's solution to this problem is to channel the money through existing microfinance practitioners to perform this task. Currently, it has 144 "field partners" in fifty-two countries. But because of the labor intensiveness and high cost of handling and reporting on these many small reimbursable grants, most large, strong MFIs like FINCA are not interested in Kiva's money. They have solved their capital problem in other ways—by raising their own grant money in large chunks or accessing the capital markets. As a result, Kiva must appeal to the "long tail"[3] of smaller MFIs, many of whom live hand to mouth and welcome any kind of money to keep their modest operations solvent.

And therein lies a problem.

Many of these long-tail MFIs are essentially family businesses, run by small social entrepreneurs who are not capable of growing them to scale and whose finances are less than transparent. While they fulfill a social mission, they are also a source of livelihood, and like some of FINCA's early programs, their portfolios aren't large enough for them to reach self-sufficiency. So they could be tempted to divert restricted loan capital to cover their operating costs. How would they accomplish this? Very easily. They simply go to a neighbor or coconspirator and ask if they can "borrow" his identity, send his picture along with an invented business to Kiva, and wait for the money to come. When it came time to pay back the loan—alas!—Kiva would be told the borrower had defaulted.

This "ghost borrower" problem is not confined to Kiva's model but is endemic to all MFIs, even those, like FINCA, with strong internal control systems. Kiva, however, is especially vulnerable, since, unlike FINCA, it has no field staff of its own and must rely on these long-tail MFIs to monitor and audit their loans. As a result, Kiva has been burned a number of times.

---

3. The term *long tail* refers to data points (in this case, the numerous smaller microfinance organizations) at the right end of a distribution curve.

To their credit, they are transparent about this problem and have tried to deal with it via a rating system in which an MFI gets from one to five stars, attempting to measure the field partner's "repayment reliability." The indicators that go into this are recent financial audits, organizational age and sustainability, reference checks with other funders, and on-site due diligence. The rating dictates how much a field partner can have in outstanding loans.

Going into the future, Kiva faces a major dilemma. With its small, U.S.-based staff, it can't possibly audit and monitor its field partners to the extent necessary to know whether a loan reported as in default was actually disbursed to a legitimate client and not repaid or the MFI created a "ghost" client and the money was actually diverted to other purposes. Its rating system may be effective as a means of winnowing out the fraudsters and weak performers *after* the money has been lost, but it can't prevent Kiva from being targeted in the future.

However, the proof of Kiva's success in building a great communications model for fund-raising is that other organizations are beginning to copy it. And at this writing, FINCA is contemplating another run at a sponsorship model, hoping that by employing the latest advances in technology, we may finally crack sponsorship's dismal economics.

Department of Celebrity Affairs: The Inexact Science of Attracting and Nurturing High-Profile Spokespeople

There can be a cheerful symmetry between an A-list celebrity's desire to "give back" after he has achieved a level of fame and fortune and your organization's need to raise its profile. In fact, finding the right cause to advocate is now a standard part of every talent management agency's strategy for marketing their celebrity clients. But do check the dentures on that pony. Make sure you are getting an upwardly mobile, derby-bound thoroughbred and not someone whose mug shot could appear on a regular basis in the "People" section of the morning paper. At the same time, should you be fortunate enough to land a celebrity spokesperson, make sure you never do anything to make her embarrassed to be associated with your organization.

But first let's ask the question: given there can be a fair amount of work involved in attracting and nurturing public figures, is it worth the effort?

First, you need to know what they can do for you. This boils down to four things:

- Give you money
- Act as a "donor magnet," persuading other people to contribute
- Create awareness and draw attention to your cause
- Open doors for you with decision makers who can help your organization

As far as the "give you money" part, some celebrities are very generous with their personal wealth, while others feel that by lending their name and fame to a cause they're already making a big contribution. Let's take megastars Angelina Jolie and Brad Pitt, or "Brangelina" as they have been christened by the tabloids, whose record of giving, like every other aspect of their lives, is very public. Angelina has adopted as her favorite charity the United Nations High Commissioner for Refugees (UNHCR). The vast majority of UNHCR's billion-dollar-plus budget comes from member countries, with the United States contributing more than $600 million, but they also take private contributions. Angelina was named an Ambassador of Goodwill in 2001. Since then, according to UNHCR's records, she personally donates about $40,000 a year to the agency, usually restricted to a program in a specific country. But she also gives big donations to other charities, including Doctors Without Borders, to whom her foundation made a $1 million contribution. In 2006 alone, Brad and Angie donated more than $8 million to various charities.

But where Ms. Jolie really excels is in the "create awareness" and "open doors " categories. Since 2001 she has made more than thirty trips (that's an average of three per year) traveling to twenty-four countries where UNHCR has programs. She received several awards for bringing attention to the problem of refugees, including the Citizen of the World Award from the United Nations Correspondents Association and the Global Humanitarian Award from the U.N. Association of the United States. She also chairs the Education Partnership for Children of Conflict, whose annual meetings bring together more than one hundred current and former heads of state, global CEOs, major philanthropists and foundation heads, and prominent members of the media.

Message: If you can, get Brangelina.

What are your odds of attracting a celeb like Brangelina, who hits on all four cylinders described above? Not good, unless your organization is very well known. The alternative is to find someone who is up-and-coming and become well known together. This takes a lot of work, and, to be honest, a healthy dose of luck. Above all, you need an employee who is "out there," a tireless networker constantly on the lookout for the right celebrity, and who, once they find one, can close the deal.

Remember, you want "little known," not "unknown." In our case, we were fortunate enough to engage a celebrity on the rise and a young queen. We met Queen Rania of Jordan when she was recently married to King Abdullah of Jordan and about to burst upon the world stage with her combination of brains, charm, and beauty. We met Natalie Portman when she was about to graduate to very well-known status as a result of being the lead actor in the *Star Wars* prequel.

How will you know if you have found the right celebrity spokesperson? She will steer Larry King away from talking about her latest boyfriend to talking about your organization. Portman, by virtue of her brains, beauty, and eloquence, is the ideal messenger for FINCA, especially with the younger generation. Whether on Oprah, "The View," or CNN, she always steers the interview to the subject of microfinance and FINCA. On Capitol Hill, she opens doors. People who would think twice about meeting with me alone accept immediately when I add: "If you don't mind, Natalie Portman will be joining us."

Finally, respect the privacy and professionalism of your celebrity representative. Don't ask your celeb to use his or her contacts to arrange an audition on "American Idol" for your karaoke-addicted brother-in-law, or do anything to make him or her feel anything but proud of being associated with your organization.

PART 4

NOT ROCKET SCIENCE: STRUCTURE, SYSTEMS, TECHNOLOGY, AND STRATEGY

Building and running an organization takes a lot of hard, tedious work, and if you try to cut corners, as a crooked contractor might, at some point the house falls down. This section answers the following questions:

- What is a business model, and how does it relate to a nonprofit?
- How do you structure your organization? Who does what and where?
- What are the critical systems you need to keep the wheels on and stay in control?
- What is the role of technology in your organization?
- How do you decide if the benefits or the investment are worth the cost?
- What is strategy, anyway?
- How do you make time for it?

13

‖‖‖

YOUR ORGANIZATION'S STRUCTURE AND BUSINESS AND FINANCIAL MODELS

You might think a term sounding as basic as a *business model* would enjoy a universal definition, or at least some degree of consensus. In fact, like many terms people use at cocktail parties to sound smart and knowledgeable, few people really know what they mean. When three prominent Swiss academics surveyed sixty-two members of the information systems community, they unearthed fifty-four different definitions.[1] They also learned that the wide use of the term *business model* is relatively recent and coincided, unsurprisingly, with the expansion and pop of the tech bubble. During a narrow window in the mid- to late 1990s, claiming to have developed a "killer business model" in the technology space was your ticket to a massive infusion of fool's gold. Venture capitalists would

---

1. Alexander Osterwalder, Yves Pigneur, and Christopher L. Tucci, "Clarifying Business Models: Origins, Present, and Future of the Concept," *Communications of the Association of Information Systems* 15 (March 2005).

listen, wide-eyed, as geeks competed for whose business model could burn the most cash over the longest period of time before breaking even.

Though there are many vague and dumbfounding definitions for the term, mine is a simple one: "Whaddaya gonna do and how ya gonna pay for it."

I can summarize FINCA's unique business model in one sentence. Warning: It sounds an awful lot like our mission statement. "FINCA provides value to low-income entrepreneurs through the provision of financial and nonfinancial services, which it funds through a combination of donations and internally generated user fees."

The power of this business model is that it allows FINCA to diversify its funding sources, which is an enormous advantage over the "donations only" or the "user-fee only" model. During times like the current economic downturn, when donations are hard to raise, the user fees we generate on our loan portfolio are keeping us going. Conversely, we would not be able to afford the quality of people we have on our payroll were it not for the stream of unrestricted donations that fill the gap between our operating expenses and what we generate from the portfolio.[2]

But let's dissect the term *business model* a little further, using a conceptual framework espoused by two business school professors, Henry Chesbrough of Berkeley and Richard Rosenbloom of Harvard.[3] Their construct consists of five components:

- **Value proposition.** By this they mean the customer's problem and the company's solution to it. Taking the case of FINCA, our clients' problem is gaining access to capital to start or grow a microenterprise and thereby generate income to feed, clothe, shelter, educate, and maintain the health of themselves and their families. Our solution is to provide them with that capital through our microloans.

---

2. At the time of this writing, I learned from my finance team that we have succeeded in covering 100 percent of our operating costs of the whole network, including headquarters, with user fees. This means all new donations can be put to our growth. Forgive me if I crow a bit, but this a remarkable achievement for a nonprofit.

3. H. Chesbrough and R. S. Rosenbloom, "The Role of the Business Model in Capturing Value from Innovation: Evidence from Xerox Corporation's Technology Spin-Off Companies," *Industrial and Corporate Change* 11(3) (2002), 529–55.

- **Market segment.** This is your beneficiary or client, defined as a demographic. In FINCA's case, we target the low-income microentrepreneurs who are able to utilize our loans *and pay them back.*
- **Value chain structure.** This is another one of those cocktail party terms coming into wide use recently, the meaning of which few people who use it actually understand. It posits that there is a "chain" of activities or products between the producer of a good or service and the end user (client). In order to succeed, a company needs to understand where it fits in the chain. In FINCA's case, its value chain begins with capital it mobilizes, either from donors or investors, and ends with the client receiving and repaying the loan. We define our position on the value chain as being a "retail lender," that is, we make the loans to the individual clients.
- **Revenue generation and margin.** This answers the question, how does the company generate its revenues? In the case of FINCA, it is through the interest on our loans and from donations. In other nonprofits, it might be from a combination of donations and user fees covering all or some of the costs of providing its services. A nonprofit can also generate revenue from other sources, completely unrelated to its mission, as long as it pays taxes on those revenues.
- **Competitive strategy.** This describes the unique approach the company uses to prevail over the other companies operating in the same space. In FINCA's case, we need two strategies: one to compete successfully for resources (donations and investor capital), and one to attract clients. Our strategy to compete for resources is to convince donors and investors that FINCA is the best answer to their "value proposition," which is helping get people out of poverty through self-help. Our competitive strategy with our clients varies from country to country but always involves providing good products and better service than the competition. Notice I did not say "better products." In most countries, microloans are now a commodity, meaning every provider has the same product. In Bolivia, the most competitive microfinance market in the world, all the MFIs have the same products and great service; otherwise they wouldn't survive. What do they compete on? Who has the best advertising.

Organizational Structure

Your business model, including your competitive strategy, should be the key determinant of your organizational structure. What are your options? They boil down to centralized, decentralized, or matrix. Financial types tend to favor centralization because it gives them a feeling (often misplaced) of being in control. Operational types and staff relish the freedom of decentralization and being empowered to make decisions quickly, based on realities in the field. Some organizations fudge the decentralization versus centralization issue by creating a "matrix" structure. And, yes, just like in the movie of the same name, people tend to get lost in matrix organizations.

Let's be clear about one thing: when we speak of an organizational design we are talking about where *decisions* are made, not just what box we put our employees in. In a highly decentralized organization, all the important decisions are made by people outside of headquarters. The best example of this would be post–Revolutionary War America, where the states had all the power and the central government, such as it was, had none. The best example of a highly centralized organization would be most (pick one) Central Asian republics, where no one but the president has any authority to make any decisions.

Wikipedia defines a matrix organization as "an organizational structure where the project manager and the functional managers share the responsibility of assigning priorities and for directing the work." The best example of a highly matrixed organization is the United Nations. At the UN, most of the functional managers—the heads of human resources, finance, information technology, and so on—are located either at UN headquarters in New York or in one of the capital cities in Europe, while the project managers, the people who actually do the work, are located in the field, which means a developing country. In theory, the project managers are supposed to pay attention to directives coming out of headquarters or from their relevant functional head, regarding big policy questions or standards. In reality, UN project managers have a lot of autonomy in making day-to-day decisions.

In my experience, any organizational design can work or not work, depending on the *people* you put into the respective boxes of your organizational chart. If you put someone who is not afraid to make decisions at the bottom of the pyramid in a highly centralized organization, she will still make decisions; she just won't tell the people at the top, who think *they* make those decisions. Conversely, if you have someone at the top of a highly decentralized organization who wants to make all the important calls and doesn't like to delegate, then people in the subsidiaries will feel disempowered and afraid to take any responsibility.

The message is this: people are more important than structure. If your organization is filled with hardworking, creative, innovative people, it will succeed no matter what boxes you put people in. People who lose sleep over which box they are in, or who are obsessed with what authority they have to make decisions, are usually the ones who can't make decisions and still haven't figured out what their job is or how to make themselves useful.

With that pithy thought behind us, let's talk boxes.

FINCA's original organizational structure, a loosely managed and governed network of independent affiliates, was in keeping with the politically correct vision of most Northern Hemisphere NGOs of the day, whose philosophy could be summarized as "Fund it, build it, and then turn it over to the locals." This school of development sprang from the hypothesis that the lack of strong institutions is the main reason countries remained underdeveloped. Build strong institutions, the reasoning went, train local people to run them, and you will eventually have a developed country like Switzerland or the United States.

Sometimes this worked. If the local people who inherited these institutions were good, effective leaders, the result could be a strong institution that provided good services to many people. The Federacion Nacional de Cooperativas de Ahorro y Credito (FENACOAC), also known as the National Credit Union Federation in Guatemala, is a well-run organization created in the '60s by a team of Guatemalans and Peace Corps volunteers (several of whom work for FINCA today). It survived the bloody civil war of the 1980s, and it is democratically run and ably led, a real success story.

Sadly, the FENACOAC story is more the exception than the rule. What often occurred was that once these institutions were built, they were appropriated by the local leadership and turned into their personal businesses. Even if there were many more FENACOACs, they would not be sufficient in and of themselves to turn Guatemala into Switzerland. Why? Because some of the most important institutions—for example, the justice system—remain weak, corrupt, or otherwise fatally dysfunctional. Other institutions essential to the functioning of a "real" (i.e., developed) country—the education and health-care systems and just about any other public good or service—are starved by corrupt taxation and public finance systems.

Does the right organizational structure change as an organization evolves? As Sarah Palin would say, "You betcha!" Why should this be the case? Sadly, it is very unlikely that the same business model—and especially the same competitive strategy—that allowed you to succeed in the early years of your existence will still work as other nonprofits copy your successes and develop innovations of their own to mitigate the weaknesses in your model.

FINCA began 100 percent decentralized, then evolved through a series of "new paradigms," leading to increasing centralization of ownership and control, but never to the point where it squelched its initial entrepreneurial spirit. It is now, in every sense, a matrix organization, but one which has a set of rules for resolving jurisdictional disputes. As CEO, my role in this structure is to serve as a kind of Supreme Court of one, who weighs in on those rare occasions when the management team members fail to reach consensus.

While the structure of FINCA evolved largely through trial and error and without a blueprint, on balance we managed to stumble upon the appropriate structure for the stage of development we were in. We lost several of our programs along the way, and with the benefit of hindsight I would have abandoned the totally decentralized, autonomous affiliate model much earlier and spared myself, our donors, and our employees a chaotic experience during 1994. In that year, three of our Central American programs were hijacked, defrauded, and mismanaged, triggering a move to a new paradigm in which FINCA Corporate had to claw back the authority for making decisions that it had bestowed on its country affiliates only a few years before. Then again, perhaps my habitual management style of "change through pain" saved us millions in consulting fees.

At this writing, FINCA is struggling to identify the "next generation" optimal organizational structure. If history is any guide, we will ultimately settle for the least suboptimal structure. This will be some form of a matrix structure, with most decision-making authority still residing with the regional and country directors but with a greater degree of standardization of policies in most functions than in the past. Most fun of all, it will be filled with exceptions and concessions to the personalities and management styles of the different members of my team. Some of our HQ vice presidents will be given more authority to make decisions in their areas than in the past. The VP of Finance will have a dotted line to all the country CFOs. This is largely an internal control mechanism, opening a line of communication from the country CFOs to the VP of Finance in the event the country CEO is behaving in a fraudulent, unethical, or otherwise detrimental manner to the affiliate. But not all of the other functional heads—Human Resources, Information Services, and so on—will have the same dual reporting line to their counterparts that the CFO of FINCA International does, nor the solid line that the COO has to the regional directors. They will have to accomplish their goals by negotiating the matrix structure.

The matrix structure can only succeed if the people who are outside the direct chain of command have enormous credibility, born of superior experience and mastery of the content of their specialty. If they aren't perceived in this light, and if the line managers don't believe they have any value added, they will surely be ignored. How do they establish this credibility? Not easily. They must pass the early tests and show clear results. Conversely, if they flunk the early test, they will probably never recover. A previous chief information officer at FINCA, having made all the regional directors travel to Mumbai for a presentation, botched a demo of a core banking system and never recovered his credibility. Regional and country directors at FINCA are very unforgiving of people who waste their time.

Guess What? Management by Committee Does Work

One innovation that evolved at FINCA, with no direction on my part, was the creation of a number of "bipartisan" strategic committees in the areas of product innovation, technology, and human resources. The first, in product innovation, was the brainchild of my development director, Sofia, who had grown intensely frustrated trying to get the attention of the regional and country directors to try out new products, services, and strategic alliances with companies wanting to access our huge network of clients. A lot of interesting things were happening in the "technology space," including electronic payments and cell phone banking, and FINCA was falling behind its competition. In Africa, we had done a successful strategic alliance with Johns Hopkins in AIDS education in Malawi, but there had been no effort to replicate this program in other HIV-stricken African countries. Sofia was often able to raise donations to pilot these endeavors, but the RDs and CDs, all former bankers, wanted to focus on their "knitting" (financial services) and not be bothered with these "distractions." They privately accused Sofia and her team of trying to force these projects on them just so she and her team could reach their fund-raising targets. Sofia broke the impasse by creating a Strategic Initiatives Committee, comprised of the regional directors and the strategic alliance people on her team, which vetted these opportunities as they surfaced and made "go" or "no go" decisions.

Our chief information officer faced a similar problem in the technology arena. Often when he wanted to make a major investment—say, in data security and protection—the RDs and CDs balked because of the cost, which would negatively affect their operating results. In the matrix structure, the RDs had control over these types of investment decisions. At the same time, things like preventing identity theft were essential investments that could not be considered optional in an organization of FINCA's size and complexity. The creation of a Strategic Technology Committee created a forum for debating the merits of these decisions in an open and transparent way and offered a mechanism for reaching consensus.

There is one more aspect that is crucial to making these committees work. If consensus can't be reached, then the decision is escalated to me as the CEO, and I break the impasse. Fortunately, this doesn't occur often. To ensure that it occurs very infrequently in your organization, you can drill down and make decisions on who has authority, and to what degree, over certain types of decisions. Hiring is a good example. If a country human resources manager is to be hired in Congo, does the HR director at HQ have the final word, or a veto over selection of the final candidate? You should map out all these types of decisions—in a matrix—and define the authorities. One consultant we hired wanted us to identify in each decision area who needed to be involved, informed, or consulted. We began the exercise but chucked it when, as occurs often with "consultancy" type tools, it didn't work for everything. We decided that the process we were using through the strategic committees qualified as "good enough."

A matrix organization is more difficult for people to negotiate, but I believe it's the structure of the future.

Some Structure Traps . . . and Solutions

One thing all large, geographically dispersed organizations struggle with is avoiding polarization between headquarters and the subsidiaries. (This is the famous "us versus them" problem.) The headquarters team, if it is not careful, can tend to focus on itself, especially if all the "chiefs" are located there. FINCA was guilty of this HQ-centric orientation during its first decade, and many of our field staff would argue it is still a problem. I would agree, but with the perspective of the past twenty-five years, I would add that it was much more serious in the early days. In our pioneer planning exercise, our facilitator consultant made use of something he called an "organizing board," which described all the departments and their functions, whose efforts were supposed to lead to something called "valuable products." I recall when we held our first country director conference in Guatemala, and I proudly showed this product, over which we at headquarters had toiled for many hours, to our field team. The reaction of our country directors was, "Hey, where are *we* in the organizing board?" It was true. We were so caught up in our efforts to sort out what we all did, we completely forgot the people who were doing the most important work of all: our team in the field.

We mitigated this problem in two ways. First, in a reorganization that took place about ten years ago, we eliminated one of the layers at headquarters—the program director, or COO position, and his staff—and began having the regional directors report directly to the CEO. But even more important, I put the regional directors on the management team, making them equals, in effect, with the heads of Finance, Human Resources, and Development.

Another aspect of the "layer" issue, and a common mistake nonprofits make, is to try to deal with performance issues in the operating units in the field by adding a layer of management on top of them. FINCA made this mistake for many years. We created regional hubs and staffed them with people whom we believed were a notch or two above our country directors. Even where this was the case (and it wasn't, in many instances), strong hub staff were almost never able to compensate for weak management at the country level. The reasons for this were twofold. First, the country teams rarely accepted advice from hub staff, whom they perceived as too removed from their day-to-day operating realities to have anything useful to say to them. Second, the country directors were essentially on their own most of the time, making all the key decisions, and if they were bad ones, by the time the hub became involved the damage was done.

A young organization can avoid this trap by sending its best people directly to the front lines. They will rise, in time, through the ranks, and by the time they do they will have acquired invaluable field perspective, which will never leave them. Conversely, if good people join at the HQ level and never spend substantial time in the field, they will be forever handicapped from developing a true understanding of the field.

Structuring the Management Team

Another thing CEOs agonize over is who to put on the top team and how to structure it. In the past, big corporations didn't sweat this too much and usually went for the troika: CEO, COO, and CFO. More recently, the other "chiefs" have begun to achieve parity, and you see flatter structures (particularly in matrix organizations) with chiefs of People, Information, Legal, Marketing, and so forth.

Attend any management team meeting at a nonprofit and you are likely to see more people than in a corporate boardroom. A nonprofit, with its need to manage by consensus, benefits from having a larger, more inclusive management team. At FINCA, I have a very large management team, consisting of ten people. Part of the reason for this is that my COO and CFO are among the more recent hires, and it is very difficult—inconceivable, in fact—that I would demote one of my "legacy" managers who has been with the organization for more than fifteen years. But the other reason is that it allows us to debate and resolve all the major issues face-to-face (or by telephone or video conference), make decisions together, and communicate more efficiently.

In the affiliates, we have not gone this far, but we have adopted the European "management board" model, wherein the CEO, CFO, and COO are *supposed to* participate as equals in the decision-making process. While the CEO does have a tie-breaking vote on all major decisions, the MB as a group is held accountable for the performance of the affiliate and is rewarded or sanctioned accordingly. I use the phrase "supposed to" because, when a strong CEO is in place, the other two chiefs tend to follow his or her lead.

Fifteen years later, we still have an organizing board somewhere in our files, though it has been years since anyone looked at it or tried to update it. Why? Because everyone is working so hard they don't have time to worry about what box they are in. We have created a pretty good meritocracy where people know that if they do a good job they (1) will be recognized for it, and (2) can move up the ladder. Building these internal ladders is probably the most important aspect of org development. If you get that right, you have created an effective organization.

Structuring Networks: Affiliates or Subsidiaries?

Before we leave the topic of structure, let's look at an issue that many nonprofits struggle with: how to structure your networks. The default impulse of many nonprofits of a certain size is to create autonomous, locally "owned" affiliates at the grassroots level and then organize these into regional, national, and global structures. The different levels of organization go by different names. In the trade union movement where I cut my teeth, the lowest level is called a local; the next up, a council; the national level, a federation; and the global level, a confederation.

The microfinance field has two types of networks. The first and most common, employed by Women's World Banking and Freedom from Hunger (and FINCA in its first iteration), is a loose confederation of independent, locally owned affiliates (NGOs). The second, utilized by present-day FINCA and Procredit Holdings, follows the structure of a global corporation with tightly controlled subsidiaries.

The choice you make regarding how to structure your nonprofit network has major implications for the degree of control you will have over what goes on at the local level, including both the mission and the way in which the resources you raise are invested. Having had experience with both forms, I highly favor the tightly controlled subsidiary model. It is the only form that gives you the ability to ensure adherence to the mission and to be truly accountable for how the funds are utilized. I also know myself, and although many in my organization believe I am a patient man, I could never go back to those days when all I could do was try to persuade the affiliates to do things, with no ability to enforce or otherwise ensure the implementation of my ideas, policies, and strategies.

If there are such clear advantages to the controlled subsidiary model, why would any nonprofit opt for the alternate structure? There are a number of reasons. First, the apex organization might not *want* the fiduciary responsibility of being held accountable for what goes on at the local affiliate. Kiva, for example, exercises zero control over the MFIs it funds, and so when things go south, as they did with Lift Above Poverty Organization (LAPO) in Nigeria, it can simply dissociate itself from the offending entity. Other networks, like ACCION, have occasionally dumped an affiliate they considered to be misbehaving and damaging their network brand. FINCA did this with one of our affiliates in Central America when it went rogue.

The act of disaffiliation can feel very liberating, but we should not deceive ourselves: it never leads to recovery of stolen or misused funds, and it rarely causes more than suppressed mirth on the part of the excommunicated party. Our disaffiliated entities continued on as the personal businesses of our former country directors, and they liked it just fine. One, in Peru, even continues to use the FINCA name. We haven't bothered to sue them over it. The world is a big place, and there are other countries where we can work. Besides, though their program remains small, it's a great example of how sometimes "small is beautiful." With their ability to focus on just a few thousand clients over the past twenty years, they have gone deep into the social side, investing heavily in training at the village bank level, encouraging their clients to leverage their community infrastructure and undertake numerous other economic and social projects.

Another advantage of the loosely affiliated network is, presumably, that more innovation may take place in such structures. I actually believe this was true in the early days of the microfinance movement, especially in organizations like Pancho Otero's Prodem in Bolivia, which broke much new ground. Today, I'm not so sure. I believe networks like Procredit and FINCA have learned how to constantly innovate while still keeping tight financial and operational control over their subsidiaries.

Another factor to take into account when making the structure decision is the attitude of the people you look to for your financing: donors and investors. Two decades ago, there was no question that donors preferred the loose affiliation, "local empowerment" model. FINCA definitely lost some funding opportunities because of our "control" model. And even today there are many who believe that local ownership, for all its problems, is still the way to go. In their view, international networks like FINCA don't add a lot of value and instead constitute a cost burden on the country operating units, which could be more agile and efficient if freed from the yoke of FINCA headquarters and the four hubs. To give this school its due, it took us many years to figure out how FINCA staff at HQ and the hubs could contribute more to the affiliates beyond merely ensuring control. Even today, our best country directors will say they don't rely much in the way of support or technical assistance on HQ or the hubs.

At the same time, I can state unequivocally that FINCA's donors, and especially our creditors, greatly appreciate having one point of contact for the whole FINCA network of twenty-one countries and "one throat to choke" in the event that things go wrong and need to be fixed. Our investors greatly value their ability to diversify their risk by spreading their investments over our twenty-one countries. They also appreciate FINCA HQ's ability to intervene and deploy additional resources when countries go into crisis mode, such as occurred in 2007 when a rogue manager tried to hijack one of our programs in Latin America.

A final point of which donors and investors should be aware is that not all nonprofit networks are legitimate. Some are set up to take credit for the work of the local affiliates and to position themselves to intercept funds that could be utilized more effectively at the local level. I recall being at a conference attended by the president of Procredit Holdings, Dr. Claus Peter Zeitinger, renowned for his outspokenness, when the head of one of these bogus networks made the mistake of trying to take credit for the accomplishments of one of International Projeckt Consult's programs in Latin America. C.P. gave him a public spanking.

14

‖‖

SYSTEMS

Give Me Liberty, or Give Me Systems!

Systems make you free, or so goes the conventional wisdom. To some, this may seem like a ruse to convince people to follow policies and procedures, most of which are equated with constraints. Still, if you *don't* have sound systems, preferably with a high degree of automation, you will spend an inordinate amount of time trying to figure out where the beans go and trying to stay in control. I can personally attest to the fact that, when the wheels come off, massive resources are consumed trying to rebuild the organization.

Entrepreneurs naturally resist a strong control environment with lots of rules because they feel having to comply with policies and procedures slows them down and constrains their creativity. That is a legitimate complaint. At the same time, if your organization is a total policy-free zone, where no one knows the rules and everyone improvises, you have chaos. The key is to strike a balance between creating an ossified bureaucracy where everyone is obsessed with process versus outcomes, and an organization with so few rules that no one knows where the lines are.

How do we do that?

In this chapter we first look at what constitutes the basics of a sound control environment, the importance of hiring people with the right skills, and a vision of what this entails. We also see how, once you think you have the right systems in place and the right people to manage them, you can become lulled into a dangerous state of complacency, setting you up for a major catastrophe. We also devote a section to one of my favorite themes: fraud. Finally, we look at the role technology plays and the devilishly complicated process of choosing the right automated accounting and management information system.

First, the Basics: Audits, Internal Controls, and Other False Senses of Security

The size, structure, and components of an internal control system depend on the size, structure, and complexity of the organization you are running. If you are a one-man operation, the only thing you need is a checkbook and an Excel-based bookkeeping system. If you are a far-flung global microfinance empire like FINCA, with some regulated subsidiaries, you need a frightening forest of systems and small armies of accountants, auditors, and compliance officers to satisfy the requirements of your many stakeholders: donors, board members, investors, and regulators. Don't worry, we aren't going to describe all these here; it would take a separate book to do so. We will, however, describe the basic structures, system, and staff any organization of scale needs to stay out of trouble.

The Accounting System

Accounting systems come in all shapes and sizes, with price tags ranging from under a hundred dollars to many millions. If you are as "bean-challenged" as I am, don't try to buy one yourself. Get a recommendation, or better yet find a cheap but honest accountant to do your books for you. Even if your organization is large and complicated, you can still outsource this function. The downside is, you literally entrust your survival to another firm if you do this, and it means you have to have faith they know what they're doing, can secure your data, and won't suddenly go out of business, vaporizing all your records in the process. Personally, I could never bring myself to outsource something as critical as our financial accounting and reporting system.

If you decide to buy an accounting system, make sure it's appropriately sized and configured to your organization's needs. Don't succumb to the "module effect," wherein the vendor promises that his system has applications that can handle everything from payroll to lubing and washing the company car. Just like the copy machine that can color copy double-sided, collate, fax, scan, and staple on the rare occasions it's not being repaired, a complicated accounting system can generate more work than it eliminates when it doesn't function properly. I bought something called Dac Easy Accounting when I ran my consulting firm, and I was two weeks into trying to set it up when I gave up and went back to my Excel spreadsheet. The setup stage of installing an accounting system is critical: if you get it wrong, you will end up with useless rubbish. The key is to understand every aspect of your operation thoroughly, including the kinds of reports you require, before you begin to set up the accounts. FINCA didn't do this when we purchased our first "real" system, and for years after we were forced to generate a lot of the reports we needed manually, defeating one of the main purposes of buying an expensive system: eliminating the potential for human error or deliberate manipulation of data to create opportunities for fraud.

Policies and Procedures

The setup phase of installing an accounting system is actually a great opportunity to address the second critical area of your internal control system: policies and procedures. The first question to ask is: do you have any? (No joke.) The second is: are they written down, as in a manual? If you don't have any, and you are reading this book, and you are in a position of responsibility, immediately close it and find the most experienced person you know to explain to you the enormous risks you are taking. Then hire a "rules person" to begin the long, tedious process of identifying and documenting what your policies are or should be in all your functional areas: accounting, administration, travel expenses, communications, plus the most policy-rich area of all, human resources. When you have all your policies written and documented, you can relax. You now have things under control, and nothing bad can happen, right?

Wrong. You have omitted perhaps the most critical step of all, and that is communicating those policies and procedures to your employees. If you forget to do this, then your policies and procedures are useless because employees cannot obey a rule of which they are unaware. It isn't enough to hand your new employees a big stack of manuals during orientation. If you want people to be aware of and follow your policies, make your employees participate in a training session about them. A side benefit of this is that you can locate any issues people have with them. You might even get suggestions on how to improve them, or identify areas where there is a "policy vacuum." I think we invented this term at FINCA because, at some point, after several years of operations, we realized we pretty much had major policy vacuums in every functional area. Which brings me to the final point: the hardest thing about getting your policies and procedures right is that in an evolving organization (and if an organization isn't evolving, it's dying), they are constantly changing. At FINCA, we have addressed this through the creation of a Policy Hopper, which holds employee suggestions for new policies or amendments to existing policies. When a proposed policy goes into the Hopper, we create a working group to examine its pros and cons and then make a recommendation to the management team. As CEO, I have the final word on approval or disapproval.

Internal Audit and Compliance

With your policies formulated, documented, and communicated, you now stand a fighting chance of keeping things under control. If every employee were forthright, honest, and conscientious, that's all you would need to do. But we know they aren't, including some of the best performers. So now we need a police force to make sure the policies and procedures are being followed. This can be one of the functions of internal audit or, if your organization is large enough, compliance officers. In the case of a large organization with both, the compliance officer's job is to make sure that the employees are following the policies, while the internal auditor's job is to make sure that the policies are the right ones and are effective. This subtle distinction is important, and the reason is that a good internal auditor can make the difference between whether critical weaknesses in an organization's internal control structure are spotted in time—that is, before you suffer a million-dollar fraud—or go undetected. Internal audits can also offer an opinion as to how efficient your operations are, but that is just icing on the cake. The real role of the internal auditor is to warn the captain of the *Titanic* there is an iceberg, dead ahead, and if he stays the present course the ship is going down.

External Audit

An *external audit*, as the term implies, is a report from an outside and independent firm that offers an opinion as to whether your financial statements accurately reflect the financial condition of your organization. The highest standard is when your organization obtains an unqualified opinion, meaning that there are no areas where the auditors could not obtain sufficient information from you to feel confident that your financial statements fully captured what was really going on in the company.

Many people believe that if an external auditor has signed off on your organization's financial statements with an unqualified opinion, then they have looked into every aspect of it and there is no danger they have missed a major fraud. (We will see just how wrong that assumption is in the section "Fraud: The Last One You'd Suspect," later in this chapter.) If you have ever signed a "management representation letter," in which you offer assurances that nothing bad is going on in the company across one hundred or more indices, you will appreciate the myriad ways your external auditors cover their risk of having missed something important. The best way to think of an external audit is as a legal crutch that investors, directors, and other stakeholders can use if things go south in a big way, resulting in lawsuits. In that unhappy event, at least all parties with some kind of fiduciary responsibility can say, "But they got a clean (unqualified) opinion!"

Message: External audits are essential, and sometimes even useful, but by no means a comforter to make you feel warm and secure on a snowy evening.

Corporate Culture (Including Tone at the Top)

The best safeguard against fraud in an organization is not any of the systems described above but rather the culture you create. If you succeed in making your employees feel proud of the organization and the mission they work for, they will protect it "against enemies foreign and domestic." That includes blowing the whistle on people they overhear plotting or in the act of robbing or harming the organization in some way. Conversely, the quickest way to bring about the demise of an organization is to create a hostile or indifferent labor force who thinks, "The company doesn't care

about me, so why should I care about the company?" People with this attitude will turn a blind eye to fraud or, in the worst case, eagerly participate.

In FINCA, the best-run programs have created a *mistica*, as the Latin
Americans say, where the employees view the company as their long-term
source of employment, income, and job satisfaction. Conversely, where we
have failed to create it, you can sense palpably that the employees have
one eye on the door and they devote at least part of their day to surfing the
Web, looking for fresh opportunities. That is a sad state of events and one
you need to address immediately and aggressively.

How do you do this?

Start with a written code of conduct in which you clearly spell out
what you and your organization stand for and your expectations regarding
employee behavior. Don't assume everyone shares your understanding of
the difference between right and wrong. In some cultures, it's perfectly
acceptable to solicit bribes in return for services rendered. When I was a
consultant for the UN in Somalia back in the late '80s (when it was still
a Failed State Waiting to Happen), I interviewed a credit officer for the
Somali Commercial and Savings Bank, asking him to describe the procedure he followed when taking a loan application. When he got to the end,
just before he disbursed the loan, he told me: "And then I ask the borrower
to give me a thousand shillings." He clearly felt there was nothing wrong
with this. In Tanzania, where the same practice of bribe-for-service is well
established, we have had to enforce a "no tea" policy, where our credit
officers are told they shouldn't even accept a cup of tea from prospective
borrowers in return for a loan.

In the code of conduct, you also have to emphasize that it is everyone's
job to stop fraud and corruption. While the internal auditor may be one
person, the other employees are many, and they see and hear things every
day. How they respond (or fail to) when they overhear a colleague plotting
to steal from the company can make or break your organization.

The key question, however, is, do your employees love their jobs, so
much so they would never allow anything bad to happen to the organization? The CEO and top management play a key role in creating this
mistica. I shared some of the tools I use, including first and foremost the
mission, in Chapter 8, "Leading Them." Absent good and effective leadership, the organization will need an incredibly powerful mission to keep the
best employees—defined as the ones with other options—coming to work
day after day.

Governance

The Board of Directors has a key role to play in maintaining a sound control environment. Its members communicate, through the CEO, the importance of these things by setting up committees—for example, the Audit Committee—to take deep dives into the key areas and make sure management is paying attention to the details. That said, they are limited in the role they can play. In a mission-driven organization, especially, these people are volunteers and generally don't devote a lot of time to this kind of oversight.[1] But they can emphasize which areas management needs to pay attention to and, via the Compensation Committee, reward or sanction certain types of behavior.

FINCA's chairman of the board, the Carpenter, sent a clear message from day one that we needed to punish fraud—which he characterized as "stealing money from our poor ladies"—ruthlessly. Our written policy is to punish fraud with incarceration of the offenders, regardless of the sum involved. Initially, some country directors protested that this wasn't cost effective where small amounts were involved and the costs of prosecution were steep. Our chairman's counter was that we needed to make an example of the small offenders so that the big crooks would get the message: you steal from FINCA's poor ladies, and you go to jail.

Risk Management

Risk management is a growing field these days, especially in financial institutions where the basic business model is to determine the amount of risk you are willing to take (with your depositors' money), price it accordingly, and then cross your fingers that you have guessed correctly. In the recent financial crisis, 90 percent of banks "misunderestimated" the default risk in subprime mortgages and as a result nearly crashed the global financial system. How could this happen, when banks spent billions of dollars on complicated statistical models to calibrate their risk and spew out different

---

1. FINCA is an exception. Our Audit Committee meets for an entire day before the board meeting, going over the status of the countries on the Watch List (a tool we have to monitor the problem countries), the interim financial statements, and reports from the internal auditor. During the global economic crisis, the AC met every month to monitor our liquidity situation.

scenarios describing the probability that something would go wrong, and the probable losses to the bank if it did? Because, at the end of the day, the models and the assumptions that went into them were only as good as the people who built them. Common sense should have told the bankers that "Ninja borrowers"—No Income, No Job—would not be able to pay off a mortgage, especially when the variable rate went from 5 percent to 15 percent. But, hey, the model said everything would be OK!

Risk management, if not deployed in lieu of common sense, is an important tool in creating a sound control environment. At FINCA, we do a top-down assessment by the management team of the risks we believe are out there, and we put this together with a bottom-up assessment undertaken by our country teams. We then incorporate this into our annual planning exercise. This risk assessment then becomes the basis for our "risk-based internal audit," in which the internal audit department examines the internal controls we have in place to manage the risks identified in the risk assessment. It sounds easy. It is in principle. In practice, however, it's easy to miss some large, elephantine risks and very hard to measure them. How, for example, would you have identified the catastrophic earthquake that struck Haiti and wiped out two-thirds of our loan portfolio, plus damaged several of our offices, much less quantified that risk? Or the savage civil war that broke out in southern Kyrgyzstan, which cost the lives of six clients and millions of dollars in lost loans? You have to try.

People

We have already said that financial people are different from you and me. They have a high tolerance for tasks and routines that put most of us to sleep. So you need to make sure that you pick the right people to operate the systems and controls that we described above. If you don't, then your best-laid plans will "gang aglay," as Robert Burns so eloquently put it.

I want my internal auditors to be suspicious by nature; the kind of people who may not have the hard evidence yet but just *sense* something about a person that tells them he's a crook. Never underestimate the ability of one strategically placed (or misplaced) employee, for example, the rogue traders in Barings and Societe General, to bring down the entire organization. If someone objects to the internal auditor poking into her business, be very suspicious. A classic ploy used by highly successful, but crooked, employees is to use the fact they are making a lot of money for the firm to intimidate the lowly internal control people out of doing their jobs. Top management will often support rogues against IC because rogues threaten to take their skills elsewhere if you don't get these pesky auditors off their backs.

Even if you trust your people completely, put in place a division of responsibility over the key functions having to do with money. Don't let the same person who approves an expenditure write the check. Why? So that it will take *two people* working in collusion to rob you.

The Cost of Being in Control

Implementing these systems costs money, so the first dilemma the mission-driven organization confronts is how to pay for it. We hate to spend money on things other than the mission, and donors who are willing to put their money toward this kind of overhead are rare. Still, you have to do it, so make sure that you attach a certain percentage of overhead to every donation or grant you take in and set that money aside for these essential systems. What is a reasonable level of investment? The answer is, it depends on your level of risk and how much you stand to lose if you don't make these investments. I wish I had all the millions back FINCA has lost to major fraud over the twenty-five years of our existence, not to mention the opportunity losses we suffered during the years it took to repair our programs, when we had to freeze the front end and stop growing. In retrospect, we could have invested one hundred times more money in prevention and still come out winners. The main thing you have to understand is that *they are out there, right now, studying your systems and controls, looking for the holes in them, biding their time, waiting for the right opportunity.* Perhaps they will steal a small amount and see if anyone notices. If they get caught, they will explain it as "an honest mistake." If no one does notice, the small amount will become a big amount.

And this brings us to one of my favorite topics: fraud.

Fraud: The Last One You'd Suspect

Nonprofits, because they are filled with well-intentioned, trusting people, are especially vulnerable to fraud. John, the Essential Visionary, took the revolutionary step of casting aside all the traditional banking controls and told his people to replace them with a simple principle: *trust the borrower*. For many years, amazingly, it worked. Why? Because the people FINCA was lending to were poor but honest and had no alternatives. We told them that this was going to be their only chance, and if they didn't pay us back, FINCA would redline not just them but their entire community forever.

Today if we made that threat, the clients would laugh in our faces. They would respond: "That's OK, FINCA, there are a dozen other MFIs who are happy to lend to us."

While our clients represent some risk of fraud, the major risk lies in our seven thousand employees. Sometimes, as in Kosovo, our employees collude with the clients to engineer a really major rip-off: eight hundred thousand euros, as it turned out. In El Salvador, a charming female manager whose branch appeared to be growing twice as fast as any of the others embezzled more than a million dollars by creating legions of "ghost clients" who went undetected, despite numerous audits and other monitoring visits to her branch.

Unfortunately, that wasn't the only time FINCA lost a million dollars on my watch. We did go many years before we suffered another fraud of that dimension, and we never again lost that kind of money in El Salvador. The theater of embezzlement shifted to Eurasia, where we lost several hundred thousand dollars first in Armenia, then in Kosovo, and most recently in Azerbaijan.

You need to learn from your frauds, but it's not as easy as you think. After El Salvador, we thought we had learned the lesson of the rapidly growing, too-good-to-be-true branch office. So when one of our branches in Kosovo serving the Roma community grew rapidly, and one credit officer was managing an impossibly large portfolio, we did what we should have done in El Salvador: audit every single loan to make sure it was real and not a "ghost borrower." The internal auditor reported back: nothing suspicious. A year later, the fraud broke to the surface, and we learned we had made five hundred ghost loans totaling eight hundred thousand euros, spirited away by three of the Roma's leaders. One went to Italy, one to Serbia, and the other to Albania. We confronted the internal auditor: How was it possible he missed this? Didn't he audit every loan? Well, yes, he did. He visited the Roma community and asked to speak to every single borrower to make sure they had received the loans. Turns out they had received them, but he didn't ask the next question: did you put the loan toward your business or give it to someone else? Also, in more than half the cases, it turned out he didn't actually speak to the borrower, but accepted the explanation of his neighbors that the borrower had gone to Montenegro on a business trip.

Obviously, our internal auditor either didn't have a good nose for sniffing out fraud or, possibly, he was part of the deception. This gets to another aspect of the people issue: be sure your internal control people really understand what their job is and, unlike our Kosovo auditor, don't simply go through the motions of conducting an investigation.

One final thought on fraud, in case, Dear Reader, I haven't given you enough over which to lose sleep. You will never know how much money is being embezzled, misappropriated, or otherwise misdirected in your organization, especially if it is a large pond. Not all fraud is obvious; some types go undetected. There is a difference between what I call dramatic fraud and subtle fraud; it's kind of like the difference between a blowout and a slow leak on a tire. El Salvador and Kosovo are examples of dramatic fraud, where, when we pried the lid off, we discovered a massive defalcation had occurred. Subtle fraud is rarely detected as such and is the result of a gradual siphoning off of the company's funds through less obvious means, such as falsification of receipts, collusion between vendors and your administrative staff, or unnecessary severance payments or other benefits paid to employees. You may be unaware you have created an enabling climate for subtle fraud, but your employees will know. Once they see others taking advantage, if you have not set the right tone, they will want to find a way to join in the feast.

How can you combat subtle fraud? Your tools are the same: aggressive internal audits, strong internal controls, and striking the right "tone at the top." But more than anything, don't fall into the trap of small thinking. Don't think, "Oh, it's only a few bucks being added onto the gasoline bill." Someone I interviewed for a job once in Africa described how his office manager routinely added 10 percent more to the fuel receipt each time he filled the tank of every car in the fleet, which over the period of a year amounted to five hundred thousand dollars. The internal auditor somehow never noticed that often the number of liters of petrol was more than the capacity of the tank.

15

STRATEGY

Getting Beyond "Everybody Go Long"

The early years of an organization are completely devoted to survival, getting past the statistical death rate for start-ups. If you have hit on a Big Idea, as FINCA did with its "killer village banking app," you can go far just by punching out replicas of that strategy as fast and as extensively as you can. At some point, however, the new kid on the block grows up, and the competition takes notice. This is the time to shift gears and develop a long-term plan that involves more than "everybody go long," that is, just doing more of the same.

The swag box "The Strategic Plan That Wasn't" describes how FINCA developed its first strategic plan, which was little more than a blueprint for building the organization, with some high-level targets thrown in.

The Strategic Plan That Wasn't

After our first decade of existence, FINCA is doing pretty well. We have seven programs up and running in Latin America and a beachhead in

Africa in Uganda. We have seventy-five thousand clients and $10 million in loans in circulation. Not bad, considering we did all this with no road map or plan. Poised on the threshold of our second decade, we hire a consultant to facilitate us through a strategic planning process.

First, our facilitator challenges us to envision where we want to be five years from now, in 2000. He calls this the "ideal scene." We set a high-level target: double our outreach to one hundred and fifty thousand clients over the next five years. How will we achieve that?

To begin with, we will need more money and more people. We will need at least another $10 million in loan capital, but probably more since our existing seventy-five thousand clients' businesses will grow and require more capital. We estimate how many more and what types of people we will need to hire, as well as what this will cost us. The facilitator takes us through a SWOT analysis, where we try to identify our strengths and weaknesses as an organization, as well as the external opportunities and threats that exist in our operating environment. We list as one of our strengths ourselves: a small but highly motivated, committed management team. Our list of weaknesses is long.

The facilitator points out that if we don't include projects in the plan to address our weaknesses, the chances of failure will be high. We identify the kinds of "institution building" projects we need to design and implement to eliminate or at least mitigate our weaknesses, so that we have a better chance of achieving our ambitious goal. We cost everything out. We arrive at a massive expense budget, which is about 4,000 percent higher than our current level of spending. We turn to our fundraiser. She smiles, shaking her head. No can do. What can you do? we ask. She commits to an annual growth rate in private donations of about 25 percent. We enter into a long, contentious debate regarding what a realistic income budget looks like, and how this "pie" will be divided among our different departments. The realization that we won't have nearly the financial resources we require to pull off the plan dawns slowly.

The first planning exercise ends in the production of FINCA's first Five-Year Strategic Plan, covering 1995–2000. There is nothing "strategic" about it. We are just going to do more of the same. To address the many weaknesses we have identified, we design a forest of projects. Every director seems to have two dozen or more. We realize we need a project planning tool to design and execute them. We choose Microsoft Project. The software forces us to design our projects in meticulous detail, budgeting out not only the financial resources required but also the level of human effort. We make the mistake of dropping the software on our managers with zero training, and everyone implements it in a different way.

Despite all these travails, however, five years later FINCA arrives at the threshold of the new millennium with exactly one hundred and fifty thousand clients. We did it! The plan worked!

||||||||||||||||||||||||||||||||||||||||||||||||||||||||||||||||

Can We Start Drinking Now? How to Tell Success from Failure in Plans

If you achieved your quantitative targets, your plan was a success, and you can break out the champagne, right? Not so fast, there, Jasper. Conversely, if you missed your numbers, the plan failed, correct? Not always.

Buoyed by our success and convinced of the magical power of the planning process, FINCA plunged into the second Five-Year Strategic Plan, which would take us to 2005. This time we hired a fancy consulting firm, one founded by the Futurist Alvin Toffler. We did some high-level brainstorming. We got trapped in the usual spin cycle of initially creating an ambitious plan and budget, only to have our development director tell us she couldn't raise that much money. We bought a simpler project planning tool, called Gateway, but still everyone moaned about all the time it took to enter the details: tasks, budgets, and responsibilities. We talked a lot about strategy, but we didn't really come up with anything "game changing." We set our high-level target at three hundred thousand clients, double our current outreach. After all the analysis and discussion, our "strategy" still boiled down to "Everybody go long."

Then 2005 arrived, and—lo!—we had surpassed our goal of three hundred thousand clients. The plan worked again!

Or did it? While we reached our outreach target, as I looked around the network I saw trouble spots. The quality of the portfolio in Africa was uneven. Malawi, South Africa, and Zambia had high arrears. We had a similar problem in Latin America, where countries like Ecuador and Mexico were doing very well but all the Central American countries were stagnating. What had changed? How come "Everybody go long" hadn't worked this time?

What changed was that FINCA now had competition. Microfinance was no longer the cloistered province of a handful of international financial NGOs but now an interesting market for "downscaling" commercial banks and thousands of mom-and-pop MFIs. Clearly, if FINCA remained on its present course, some of its programs would still be around in 2010, but the weaklings might not be.

It was clear our third strategic plan had to look different from its predecessors. We needed to think hard about what was working and what wasn't. The big theme I could see was that where we had strong, experienced managers with backgrounds in banking, the country programs were doing well. Conversely, where we had legacy NGO country directors, we were struggling.

My first conclusion was that we needed to invest heavily in upgrading our human resources and get more "bankers with a soul." Another theme I saw was that where we had transformed our financial NGOs into regulated, deposit-taking financial intermediaries, we were growing rapidly. So the second big strategy had to be transforming the rest of the financial NGOs into commercial banks and finance companies. Finally, we had to upgrade our management information system (MIS) so that we would have "one truth" instead of different versions of our basic financial and outreach data, depending on who assembled it and with what tool (more on FINCA's earlier experiences with management information systems and technology implementation later). If we could execute these three big strategies successfully over the next five years, I believed we would arrive at 2010 positioned not only to be one of the survivors, but one with a solid platform for the rapid growth, with quality, well into the future.

Now we had a truly "strategic" plan, which involved much more than just organic growth. For good measure, we set ourselves an ambitious goal of more than tripling our outreach: to one million clients.

As I write this, we are in the final year of our third strategic plan. How are we doing? Looking at the numbers, not so hot. We will seriously underperform on our main metric (one million clients). Instead of tripling the number of clients, we will be lucky to end the year at seven hundred and fifty thousand. One thing that derailed us was, of course, the global financial crisis. Latin America, in particular, was hammered by a perfect storm of weak local economies, ebbing remittance flows from the United States, and the discovery that many of our clients—like their cousins to the North—were overindebted. Only two of our Latin American programs, Mexico and Ecuador, made money in 2009.

Thankfully, there are signs that 2010 has been a much better year for FINCA in terms of both outreach and financial performance.

Once I discovered the difference between a plan that is truly strategic versus one that involves merely doing more of the same, I came to an unexpected realization: I enjoyed the planning process. What could be more fun than competing in a multidimensional chess game against worthy adversaries in a worthy cause, and working with some of the greatest people on earth, my colleagues at FINCA, while doing it?

Strategic Planning: A Few Tips to Make the Planning Process Less Like a Triple Root Canal Without Anesthesia

You should hire a professional facilitator to guide you through your initial planning exercise, since the discussions can at times grow spirited and you may need an impartial referee to pull the participants off each other. But be mindful that the planning retreat is just the beginning of the process; the follow-up—including the monitoring, implementation, and periodic evaluation of the pieces of the plan—is even more critical.

- Start the planning process with a "rain of ideas" from your staff and other stakeholders, including your beneficiaries, the people most affected by your mission. Answer the following questions: What is the high-level goal you want to have accomplished by the end of the period covered by the plan? How will you define success? What does your organization's SWOT (strengths, weaknesses, opportunities, and threats) analysis look like?
- Map out the factors, external and internal, that will either help you reach your objectives (strengths and opportunities) or constitute obstacles (weaknesses and threats).
- Divide the planning process into two big pieces. The first describes the goals and how you will achieve them, for example,

what resources you need, human and financial, and what programs you need to implement. The second describes the institutional infrastructure you need to put in place—systems, policies, and so on—to successfully execute the programs. To do the latter, refer to your SWOT analysis and see what weaknesses and threats need to be mitigated. Make sure that for every weakness cited you have a specific project to address it. Make sure that for every opportunity, you have a plan (within the overall plan) to take advantage of it.

- When you are starting out, choose a simple project planning tool. Microsoft Project may be too detailed and could be boycotted by your team. Some people will refuse to use it anyway. Make allowances for the fact that while some of your managers' jobs are "project heavy" (those who are in the process of building their departments) and lend themselves to a planning tool, others involve performing repetitive tasks and don't require a project planning tool.

- Give your managers some flexibility, but not when it comes to the data they are required to input for you to track their progress. Don't let them make you produce their progress reports by having to extract the information from their tool or by interviewing them.

- Train your managers so they will have a fighting chance at mastering the planning tool sufficiently that they won't tear their hair out in frustration when they try to use it.

- Map out the competitive environment within which your organization operates. Think of yourself as a fish on a coral reef, competing with other fish and predators for a limited supply of food, light, and oxygen. What can you do to set yourself ahead of the rest of the school, as well as outwit the predators trying to eat you? This is your strategy.

- Like everything else, your planning requirements will evolve as your organization grows. In the beginning, it will be project heavy as you build the infrastructure. Then it will be strategy-focused as you need to key in on the competition and figure out how you survive and thrive.

- The planning process will reveal things about your top team, including who is good at selling their projects and who isn't. If someone is a poor salesman, it doesn't follow that his project ideas are no good or a bad investment. You may need to overrule the rest of the pack occasionally to make sure a mission-critical project doesn't end up on the cutting-room floor just because the manager didn't make the case for it.

Strategy and Technology: If at First You Don't Succeed, Fail, Fail Again

Regardless of your organization's mission, status, or funding, the strategy you implement and the outcomes of your project planning will be informed by current and constantly evolving technologies. Technology is so important—and expensive—that it often merits its own stand-alone strategic plan. In the countries where FINCA operates through regulated financial institutions, many of the central banks require that we have a strategic plan for technology that describes our planned investments in the various IT systems we use to manage our operations.

To illustrate just how fast technology has evolved over the years, when I made my living as a consultant in the mid-1980s, one of my clients, the United Nations Capital Development Fund (UNCDF), advised me to buy something called a fax machine. "If you have a fax machine, we can turn around contracts in a day, and you'll get a lot more business," my contact advised me. A decade later, I was pitching a senior AID official for some business in Latin America. He offered to help me out and said that he would "send an e-mail" to one of his colleagues in Guatemala. I pretended to know what he was talking about. A decade after that, we were all tearing our hair out over the "watched pot" of dial-up. Today, we are connected twenty-four hours a day, walking around with Blue Teeth implanted in our temples, talking to ourselves. The velocity of technology development and the advantages it confers in terms of efficiency, price, and response time is truly transformative. The consequences of not keeping abreast of it are severe. The mission-driven organization needs to be "fully strapped" technology-wise, or it won't keep up.

After losing control over the money, a bungled accounting system conversion is the second highest cause of management mortality. This is because, after finance, technology is the generalist manager's greatest weakness. Indeed, travails similar to those experienced during the search to find "the CFO You Need" (described in "When Beans Bite Back," in Chapter 5) can be relived during your quest to hire a competent chief information officer or to engineer a successful system conversion. You will discover that where IT is concerned, everyone has an opinion, even the technically tone-deaf. No other issue has greater potential to divide your organization into competing camps.

FINCA itself has had a fifteen-year-long search for a more robust management information system (MIS), which began in the wake of the El Salvador fraud and continues to this day. We eventually got on a trajectory where our core IT systems limped along more or less apace with the rest of our development as an institution. But the trajectory was not that of a Saturn rocket, "breaking the surly bonds of earth," but more like that of a sputtering Yak 40 trying to clear the treeline. It also carries a number of important lessons for generalist managers as they struggle to survive in this perilous land where they neither speak the language, trust their guide, nor possesses a reliable road map.

The Small Company Problem: When All Else Fails, Improvise

The change in our luck came when, through one of our employees, we learned of the existence of a small Guatemalan company that had developed an automated accounting system for cooperatives and had adapted it for the growing microfinance market. The program, called Sistema de Informacion Electronica para Microfinancieras (SIEM), worked well and was affordable enough that we installed it in the seven FINCA programs in Latin America. As its client list grew, however, the vendor began to experience the typical problems of small, undercapitalized companies attempting to survive in the software space. The company's small staff was having trouble keeping up with all the requests for support. Miguel, the sole owner, was a brilliant software engineer but we had concerns about his management strategies. I could foresee the day when FINCA would be totally dependent on this small, dysfunctional company. I proposed a bold solution: that FINCA buy a controlling stake in the company, injecting enough capital that we could improve the product plus solve the support problem. Many on my staff and board opposed the idea, parroting the commonly held belief that nontechnical companies like ours "don't want to be in the software business." My rejoinder was, what is the alternative?

Stand by, watching, as the vendor flounders and takes FINCA down with it? I shouted down my colleagues and won over my board. Microfinance Solutions, Inc., or "Rupert's Folly," as it came to be known, was born.

Do You, the Investor, Take This Vendor, for Bad or Worse, till Death Do You Part?

The marriage was troubled from the start, and it illustrates the problems of partnerships where the interests of the parties are not fully aligned. The vendor, Miguel, was upset with the amount of the starting capital "wasted" on legal costs. He had a point: most of it was spent by FINCA's attorneys trying to put in legal remedies that would protect FINCA in the event the marriage ended in divorce.[1] Miguel was also unhappy that the main focus of MFSI was on the FINCA clients, versus trying to develop business with new clients. But there was another issue. As the rollout of the system spread beyond Latin America to Africa and Eurasia, major problems emerged. The installation in Azerbaijan took more than a year and a half, with the FINCA staff and software company each blaming each other for the delay. FINCA Azerbaijan's IT team claimed the SIEM was buggier than nightfall in a Bangladesh rice paddy. Miguel retorted that FINCA's IT people were incompetent. I found myself in the position of many generalist managers with zero technical background: the Monkey in the Middle, trying to sort out who was to blame, not trusting either party to give me the whole picture, and with no basis to render my judgment other than my intuition. At some point, I finally grasped that the kernel of the conflict was not technical at all, but financial. If the software was to blame, MFSI would have to correct the bugs on its dime. But if Miguel could convince me that it was FINCA's IT staff's fault, then FINCA would have to pay. Meanwhile, the problems weren't getting fixed.

When Things Grow Desperate, Reach for the Help Line

Eventually, I got smart and turned to one of my Advisory Board members with a background in software development and asked him to help me

---

1. Burning precious capital on contract lawyers may seem wasteful at the time, and based on remote, unduly pessimistic scenarios of future problems, but, as will be seen, in this case it was money wisely spent.

out. He traveled to Guatemala and met with Miguel. The truth came out: there was a design flaw in the software that kept generating random "out of balance" errors in the monthly financial statements, which had been driving the FINCA country CFOs crazy. It was a problem with the software program's "architecture" and could only be fixed by rebuilding the entire system.

After my Advisory Board member wrestled the gun from my head, I asked his advice as to what I should do. We had bought a lemon, and now two-thirds of FINCA's network of twenty countries depended on it. Above all, I wanted to know why the architecture wasn't designed properly in the first place? The answer was, Miguel was a software engineer, not a banker. He did the best he could, talking to FINCA's country directors and CFOs about what they wanted the system to do, but he was missing some "secret sauce" elements that only experts in banking software know.

Lesson: Don't believe software engineers when they tell you they can build a program to run anything. Writing code is only one of the skills required. There must also be a technical expert in the content involved.

The other thing I realized was I could no longer trust Miguel. If he kept something this important from me, what other things might he be hiding? His "the customer is always wrong" attitude now made perfect sense.

I filed for divorce. In the breakup process, I truly appreciated all the tiresome legal work that had gone into structuring the deal. Things like Tag Along, Drag Along rights. I fired Miguel and bought him out for three hundred thousand dollars. Now FINCA owned 100 percent of a company with broken software.

Cha-ching! Another million bucks on the fire.

Learning to Live with It

But wait: things were not as bleak as they seemed. The resourceful FINCA IT people, over the years, had learned to work around the SIEM's annoying defects. With Miguel gone, I put our newly hired CIO in charge of the MFSI, and he put the staff on a one-hundred-day crash program to fumigate the bugs in the SIEM and improve the technical support to the customers. It worked. The complaint level dropped off asymptotically. The Monkey in the Middle was able to move on to his next nightmare.

The lesson is, in time, resourceful IT people can learn to manage the buggiest software. So it's not always necessary to throw in the towel and give up.

We know from a previous section, "Failing Your Way to Success: Letting Your People Make Mistakes Without Destroying the Company," in Chapter 7, that FINCA eventually outgrew the SIEM and embarked on another round of conversions, this time to "real" core banking software. The search for the Holy Grail, a single global system, continues to this day, as does the learning process. Among the valuable and difficult lessons FINCA and I have learned in regards to technology implementation are:

- Treat the impending conversion the same way you would a crisis (because sooner or later it will become one). Put your best business and technical minds on it.
- Create a joint team, comprising technical, financial, and program people, to vet the major IT investment and strategy decisions. Fight all the battles *before* you make the investment, not in a second-guessing fest postinvestment.
- Trust your instincts. True, you are not a technology genius, and life is too short for you to master the details to the point where you can argue bandwidth with someone who has an advanced degree in computer science. But you do have some sense for a superior case when you hear one, and you can probably tell the difference between the person who knows his stuff and a charlatan.
- You also know performance management (see Chapter 6 if you've forgotten) and how to write goals in such a way that you can tell whether your CIO is "getting it done" or not. As with the CFO, set early tests that, if passed, tell you you might have made a good hire, and if failed, tell you it's time to cut your losses.
- Decide. Don't let the bickering go on indefinitely. Choose the horse you are going to ride, and then ride it until it stumbles, throws you off, or crosses the finish line. And as an Advisory Board member adds: "If the horse is dead, Rupert, get off."

Remember, there is not one right way. There are many paths, but unless you choose one, you aren't going anywhere. As a friend once consoled me: "All IT solutions are suboptimal. Just choose the least bad."

PART 5

||||||||||||||||||||||||||||||||||||||||||||||||||||||||||||||||||||

THRIVING
AND SURVIVING

In this final section we look at three areas that are often neglected or receive insufficient attention by nonprofits but that can mean the difference between success and irrelevance over the long term, and between your survival and early retirement as a manager.

Innovation, discussed in Chapter 16, is typically considered the province of for-profit companies, who must be constantly coming up with new products to retain their existing customers, attract new ones, and outwit their competition. I argue that it is equally important for the nonprofit to be constantly innovating, not only because the line between the commercial and nonprofit sectors is growing increasingly blurry but also because you owe it to your beneficiaries, donors, and employees to give them the best service possible.

Chapter 17, on governance, emphasizes the critical role a strong, feisty Board of Directors can play in your success. It provides advice on how to spot problem directors early and how to mitigate the damage they cause to you and the organization.

Chapter 18, "Humanitarians at the Gate," is for those who currently hold or aspire to the corner office, providing tips not only on how to cling to power but also on how to enjoy the daily challenge of being at the top of the food chain with no visible predators.

16

BUT IT USED TO WORK SO WELL!

The Time and Place for Innovation

With those vital but somewhat tedious essentials for success described in Part 4 behind us, let's look at that arch nemesis to systems, policies, standardization, and everything neat and orderly: innovation.

Nothing works forever. At the same time, change is risky. It is imperative to consider the following questions:

- What role does innovation play in your organization?
- Who is nominally in charge of it?
- Who actually does it?

Ideas, products, organizations, and people all have life cycles. When they are young, innovation is everything. If they enjoy early success, they may be tempted to stick with the existing winning formula until it goes stale and doesn't work anymore. Then they have to innovate again in order to remain competitive.

Is it possible to be too innovative? You betcha! As an organization grows, unless it achieves some level of standardization, it will fail to replicate its successful innovations and it will lose a lot of time and money on dead ends engineered by "false innovators." False innovators are those who execute the existing, winning formula poorly, claim it doesn't work anymore, then constantly change it in order to cover up their incompetence. By the time you recognize these people for what they are—a variation on the destroyer theme—they have broken your program.

The key to long-term success for an organization is to strike the right balance between innovation and standardization. This is not as simple as it sounds. First, you need to identify *what* things should be open to innovation, and then you need to identify *who* in the organization should be licensed to innovate. Some of the *whats* are no-brainers, like new products. Others are not so obvious. For example, you might think you don't want to encourage a lot of innovation in the area of internal controls, but to stay ahead of the fraudsters trying to subvert them, you need to do some tweaking every now and then to throw them off guard.

The question of who should be permitted to innovate is a tough one. For many people, this is what makes a job fun, and ideally you would want to create a culture where everyone is encouraged to invent better ways to do things, from the janitor on up. In practice, some people are better at it than others, and some (false innovators) will do harm if licensed to innovate. Requiring people to first master and adhere to the existing products, policies, and procedures before licensing them to innovate is one approach. Muhammad Yunus gave me some advice when I first took FINCA to Africa. The Ugandan bankers were telling me the village banking methodology would not work in Africa as it did in Latin America, saying I should change it. "Don't change anything," Yunus counseled. "Implement it exactly as you do in Latin America. If it doesn't work, then adapt it."

That said, you occasionally need to turn a blind eye to those rule breakers who come up with innovations that improve your products and services, lower your costs, and give you an edge on the competition. The swag box "Creative Destruction: Managing Without Manuals" describes FINCA's struggle to achieve an effective balance between standardization and innovation during the early days of the organization when everyone, even the client, was an innovator.

Creative Destruction: Managing Without Manuals

In the early days, everyone in FINCA, even the accountant, is an entrepreneur. The only manual in existence is *Como Organizar un Banco
Comunal (How to Create a Village Bank)*, authored by John Hatch and
his wife, Mimi, a retired schoolteacher who provides her husband with
the format for what becomes the ultimate lesson plan. The manual
describes how to organize and manage a village bank in loving detail,
from the first organizational meetings, to the disbursement of the loans
and their recording by the treasurer of the village bank, to the final
repayment.

How to Create a Village Bank offers no guidance, however, on the
organization of the back office, or the entity that will raise and manage the funds, hire and train the credit officers, and supervise the loans
once they are disbursed. Initially, there is no need for this since Hatch is
working through other organizations like CARE, Save the Children, and
Catholic Relief Services, leveraging their financial and human resources
to implement his Big Idea. The problem arises when FINCA starts to
trade for its own account: chartering, staffing, and financing local NGOs
under the FINCA banner. When it comes to figuring out how to structure and manage the FINCA affiliates, we offer no guidance to our four
pioneer country directors. As a result, the first FINCA affiliates are a
reflection of their organizational abilities—or, as it turns out, their lack
thereof. To compound the mess, as the programs grow in size and complexity, the country directors hire accountants and other managers who
are also expected to bring in their own systems. Systems and manuals
do begin to surface, but they are a hodgepodge of materials improvised
by the best people we can afford—and, needless to say, all different.

If the back office is in chaos, the front end, where the village banking
methodology is evolving, is a wondrous tropical rainforest of innovation. In Sasabe, a small Mexican pueblo just across the U.S.–Mexican
border in Arizona, the women of one of Hatch's village banks ask if they
can make use of the savings that have been piling up in the bank. They
want to put it to work in their microenterprises, just as they do with the
FINCA loan. They can track it just as they do the FINCA loans, via the
simple bookkeeping system Hatch has taught them. Go for it, he tells

them. Over the next several weeks, Hatch watches in amazement as the women lend out their savings to the members with the most rapidly growing businesses, charging them double the FINCA interest rate and using the proceeds to pay out an interest rate to the savers. The "internal account" is born. The village bank has become a real bank, putting net savers together with net borrowers and turbocharging the impact of the FINCA capital.

In Costa Rica, our director deploys her gifts as a community organizer to turn her village banks into much more than just a credit distribution network. She encourages them to organize joint projects, like a charcoal plant, which makes use of the stumps left by a rapacious lumber company. Other village banks, bordering on Costa Rica's pristine rain forest, create artisanal bed-and-breakfasts to capture the hordes of low-budget, backpacking tourists. More is possible in Costa Rica due to the investments the country has made in educating its citizens.

We described in Chapter 13, on structure, how FINCA gradually reined in its country directors from the point where they had 100 percent authority to innovate, to a structure with more control from the center and emphasis on standardization and replication of successful innovations. A key step in this evolution was the development of a FINCA operating system, consisting of standardized systems and policies governing all the basic components of our operations: accounting, finance, human resources, and even fund-raising. We still encourage innovation, but now within the boundaries described in an *Affiliate General Policies Manual*. Innovations must be authorized by the Strategic Initiatives Committee, piloted on a small scale initially, and, if successful, then replicated throughout the network.

Striking the Balance: Make It Your Own

So has FINCA gone too far in the direction of standardization, killing our entrepreneurial spirit? The evidence says no. Recent innovations have raised FINCA's game in markets as diverse as Kyrgyzstan, Uganda, and Mexico. For example, our country director in Kyrgyzstan hit on a new way to open branches, achieving a critical mass of customers using staff of the closest existing branch, so that when we made the investment in infrastructure we already were halfway to breaking even. This was simple but brilliant out-of-the-box thinking.

In Eurasia, our regional director retooled the group-lending methodology by first asking the clients what they liked least about the existing methodology—obligatory savings and long meetings—and responded by eliminating the savings requirement and shortening the length of the meetings. The number of group-lending clients grew rapidly.

A third example can be found with our country director in Guatemala, who created a set of innovative client training materials for illiterate or semiliterate clients that resulted in increased outreach and higher repayment rates.

The best country directors in FINCA have something in common: they have found ways to put their stamp on our programs, customize them in ways that "make them their own." I encourage all our country directors to do this when they take on a new assignment. Similar to the question I pose when I interview a prospective new employee, I ask them to look at the condition of the program on the day they take it over and then try to visualize how it will look three years hence, when they turn it over to their successor. What improvements will they have made that will forever carry their imprimatur? This will be their legacy.

How to Tell Good Innovation from Bad Innovation

There is probably no way to know, before you implement it, whether an innovation is going to work or not. Sometimes it works exactly as you had hoped, but there can be unexpected side effects that cause more damage than the positive impact from the innovation. In Africa, we were seeking a way to increase the productivity of our credit officers, who were able to reach only three hundred clients on average, versus four hundred to five hundred in Latin America and Eurasia. Someone hit on the brilliant idea of changing the frequency of the village bank meetings from every two weeks to once a month, which would immediately free up 50 percent more of the credit officers' time, enabling them (in theory, at least) to attend to twice as many village banks each month. Initially, the productivity climbed, although not by a factor of 100 percent. But the arrears also climbed, astronomically. It turned out that thirty days was too long between repayments. The "innovation" was abandoned.

Mitigating the Costs of Failed Innovations

There are a number of ways to avoid wasting time and resources on bad ideas, as well as the costs to the organization of failed innovations. Here are a few we have found over many years:

- Don't allow just anyone to innovate. Require aspiring innovators to have demonstrated their ability to abide by the existing policies and procedures before making their case for why something needs to be changed.
- If the innovation constitutes a significant change in the way the organization currently operates—introduction of a new product; a change in a time-honored process or procedure—require that the aspiring innovator make a written case for taking the organization's time and resources to experiment with the new approach or product. The analysis should include what the potential risks to the organization would be of the failure of the innovation.
- Regardless of how brilliant or promising the idea appears, run a pilot with limited resources and clients and in a limited market. Some of FINCA's biggest flops have been to roll out a new product on a program-wide scale before it was properly tested.

Innovation Without Borders: Losing Focus or Adding Value?

You could limit innovation to the core competencies of your organization, but that might be shortchanging your clients and limiting your impact. In the microfinance industry, there is a divergence occurring between organizations taking a "purist" financial services approach and those taking a "holistic" philosophy. Organizations of the holistic school tend to view their mission more broadly than simply financial inclusion and are open to deploying any available tools from both the social and economic sectors—including health, education, water, and sanitation, plus a host of interventions in the productive sphere—that might make their clients' microenterprises more profitable and improve their overall social and economic welfare. Hence organizations like Bangladesh Rural Action Committee (BRAC) have pioneered the BRAC chicken project, which provides technical assistance, feed, processing, and marketing services to its clients who raise poultry on a small scale.

FINCA has been less aggressive in pursuing outside-the-core-competency innovation, perhaps as a result of our geographic dispersion. Working in so many jurisdictions and cultures presents such myriad challenges that little time remains to experiment with interventions that may be perceived as time-consuming and risky, with no guarantee of major value added for our clients. Where we have pursued these initiatives, they tend to be tightly related to the credit operations, as in the launching of green-energy loan products in Uganda and payment card technology in Mexico, programs that both came about due to the forging of strategic alliances.

Using Strategic Alliances to Leverage Innovation

One way to mitigate the distraction factor of Innovation Without Borders is to pursue strategic alliances with other NGOs and private-sector companies who have expertise in the area in which you have chosen to innovate. In Malawi, FINCA partnered with Johns Hopkins Foundation for AIDS Research to provide AIDS education to our female clients. The project was a double win in that the women received advice on how to protect themselves from infection and FINCA found that the village banks participating in this training had more members (and clients for FINCA Malawi) and were more cohesive than the village banks that did not participate.

In Uganda, FINCA is partnering with Grameen Phone, one of Yunus's "home runs," a company launched in Bangladesh to finance mobile phone purchases by "cell phone ladies" who sell time to customers in their communities unable to afford their own phones. This alliance led to an innovation within an innovation, in that a principal use of our green energy loans went to financing solar-powered batteries, which have spawned microenterprises based on recharging mobile phones in rural areas off the grid.

Our payment card project in Mexico is the result of a strategic alliance with VISA. This is a dream alliance in that VISA is providing both the payment card technology and several hundred thousand dollars in grant funds to finance the pilot and subsequent rollout. It is already saving our clients thousands of dollars in transportation costs because they can access our loans through local ATMs rather than have to come to our branch offices to collect and cash paper checks. It also provides them with more security, a big factor in the current climate of violence in Mexico, as they can draw out the cash as they need it instead of in one lump sum.

GE, another of FINCA's strategic partners, is a company that takes partnerships with NGOs very seriously and appreciates the value they bring to the table in terms of deep knowledge of what GE perceives as an important future customer segment. I recently attended a conference in India sponsored by GE, in which the company invited representatives of NGOs working in the environment, health, and energy sectors to critique some of its product and marketing ideas in the "social investment" sphere. GE encouraged the NGO reps to be candid in pointing out any flaws they saw in GE's strategies, as in the case of a marketing plan GE had for selling high-end diagnostic equipment to down-market public hospitals. The NGO reps took them to task for a strategy that they believed would lead to massive unnecessary testing, the cost of which would fall on the low-income patients. I was impressed at the sporting way in which the GE staff took the criticism of a project in which they had obviously invested considerable time and money, but most of all that they would choose NGOs—often perceived as being highly critical of the private-sector approach to health care—as one of their focus groups.

What and Where to Innovate?: Identifying Other Market and Government Failures

The creators of microfinance didn't think of themselves as addressing a market failure. They thought of what they were trying to do as simply putting capital into the hands of poor people. But the market failure lens is a very useful way to look at what else needs to be done in a given country to unleash the productive power of the poor. At FINCA, I am challenging my staff to look harder at these areas and not merely think of ourselves as bankers. There is a compelling development case as well as a straight-up business reason for this. Whereas once petty traders in Latin America, Africa, or Asia could generate attractive returns to each dollar of credit obtained—sometimes percentage rates in the thousands, over the course of one month—today capital is less scarce and the marketplaces are crowded with thousands of petty traders who have access to microloans on attractive terms. This has driven margins down on these activities, which have low barriers to entry. As a result, a number of microfinance organizations, FINCA included, are asking ourselves how we can help our clients become more profitable, grow their businesses faster, and demand more of our products and services.

A similar case can be made for filling voids in the social sector. Here, however, the challenge is more daunting, as there are fewer examples of anyone, even social entrepreneurs, figuring out how to provide such services on a financially sustainable basis. An innovative company in the UK has come up with a brilliant model for rehabilitation of criminals. The problem addressed is the high rate of recidivism in paroled criminals, the majority of whom end up back in prison. Individuals and funds can invest in a company that works on preventing recidivism through counseling former convicts and helping them find and hold jobs. If the company achieves a certain success rate, then the investors obtain a certain level of return on their investment.

Here are some tips for managing and getting the most out of innovation and strategic alliances in a nonprofit:

- Innovation requires patience, and you shouldn't give up if the first attempt ends in failure. For example, the Mexican payment card project benefited from failed pilots in Guatemala and Nicaragua.
- Innovation Without Borders is probably going to take more time than innovation within your core competencies.
- Choosing the right partner in a strategic alliance cannot by itself guarantee success, but it certainly will increase the odds.
- Strategic alliances and partnerships work best if there is a 100 percent win-win, that is, both parties achieve their goals. For this reason, it is vital that both parties clearly articulate what those goals are, early in the process.

- Don't pursue strategic alliances with private companies if your real motive is to get a grant out of them. This will certainly backfire, and since Fortune 500 companies do talk to each other, word may get out that you are not a reliable partner.
- Less is more in strategic alliances. Don't enter into so many that you don't have the time and resources to make them work.

Something of Value

Another critical part of the innovation-standardization dilemma is the question of what *not* to change. You don't want to innovate away the mission. In the microfinance industry, you can become so caught up in the challenges of creating a sustainable financial institution you forget why you created it and whom you are trying to serve.

The swag box "A House of My Own" relates the story of FINCA Uganda client Nayima Umaru's climb out of poverty. Nayima stands as a reminder that whatever else may change in our organization, it can never become so like a bank that it turns down people like Nayima.

||||||||||||||||||||||||||||||||||||||||||||||||||||||||||||||||||||||

A House of My Own: Nayima's Story

I was born in Mombassa, Kenya. When I was fourteen, my father forced me into marriage. I had two children, both girls, by my first husband. Then he revealed to me that he had another wife, from Uganda. He said we must go live with her. But when we arrived, she did not accept me, and put me and my daughters out of her household.

I married for the second time. I had six more children, all girls. This made my second husband very unhappy because he wanted sons. He abandoned me as well. When he returned, a year later, he had become ill. I spent the little money I had saved caring for him. He died soon after, leaving me pregnant with twins.

I moved into a single room here in town with my ten children. The hardest part was taking the children out of school because I could no longer afford the fees. The only work I could get was cleaning houses of my extended family members. I fed my children with the leftovers from their tables. I could not afford soap, so I borrowed the "bubbles"—my employer's dishwater—to wash our clothes. Sometimes, I would go to the market with the other ladies and borrow a basket full of bananas and fried cassava and sell them by the roadside. But it was very little.

One day, I heard about a program called FINCA that made loans to poor women like me. A friend took me to a meeting of a FINCA village bank. I listened as the promoter described how we could get loans of fifty thousand shillings (US$50) to start a small business or microenterprise. To get the loan, the other women in the village bank had to agree to repay if the woman failed to repay. I knew this was my big chance. If I could earn more money, I could put my children back in school. But the other women in the village bank turned me down. They felt I was too poor. Also, because my father was not Ugandan, they felt I would run away with the money. I got on my knees. I begged them to give me a chance. But they refused. Then, the woman who had brought me to the meeting took pity on me. She convinced two of her friends to join her in saying, "If Nayima doesn't pay, we will pay for her." The other women accepted me. I was going to have my chance.

Once I got my first loan, I had another problem. I had no idea what I would do with the money. The three women from the village bank who had guaranteed my loan told me they were going to a nearby village that enjoyed a good crop of tomatoes. They would purchase them in quantity and sell them here in the Jinja market. They invited me to join them. We bought the tomatoes but then had a problem getting transport back to Jinja. We arrived home just as the market was closing, too late to sell anything. That night, instead of sleeping with my children, I slept with the tomatoes. The next day, when the market opened, I was the first one there. I sold everything, and at a good profit! I easily made the first weekly payment to FINCA and had enough left over to buy more tomatoes.

Over the next four months, I repeated this operation, many times, each time making a good profit. I received a second loan, this time of one hundred thousand shillings ($100). This time, all the ladies in the village bank were willing to guarantee my loan.

After three years of selling fruits and vegetables in the market, financed with ever larger loans from FINCA, I saved enough money to open a restaurant. At first, I had only a small stove, one table, and four plates. Then I was able to buy a refrigerator. Today, I have ten tables, a bigger gas stove, and a blender to make fruit drinks. My daughters all work here, except one, who is going to the university.

Now, the best news. All these years I have been living in this small room, behind the restaurant, saving for the day when I could buy land and build a proper house for my family. That day has come. Last month, I bought a piece of land in town. I am building a small house on it. A house of my own!

▌▌

There is a picture in my office of me, Natalie Portman, and Nayima sitting in a back room of her restaurant in Jinja, Uganda. After hearing Nayima's story, we stepped outside to a small patio where the light was better. A journalist from Reuters held a microphone out to Natalie.

"So, Queen Amidala, what is your impression?"

"My impression?" Natalie chose her words carefully, as if afraid she might muff her lines. "Sometimes I worry about things: personal relationships, my career . . ." She shook her head. "I don't have problems."

17

||||||||||||||||||||||||||||||||||||||||||||||||||||||||||||||||||||||||||||

GOVERNANCE
BY DUMMIES

Wise Counsel or Micromanagement
by the Ignorant?

Building an effective board takes almost as much work and time as building the rest of the organization. In the post-Enron world, finding people foolhardy enough to serve and expose themselves to the multiple risks and liabilities of board membership is an enormous challenge. This is true even of nonprofits. There are risks—to the mission and to you—of getting board members who are too intrusive. Often, straight-up business types don't understand or appreciate the Visionary/Founder continuing to play a major role in leading the organization, and they want to change him out for someone more malleable or management oriented. Witness how an intrusive board nearly destroyed Apple Computer by kicking its founding Visionary, Steve Jobs, out the door. Fortunately, they realized their error years later and brought him back to revive the company.

The ideal board member, like the perfect donor, is a selfless creature who has only the best interests of the organization at heart. Good luck finding twelve of these right out of the starting gate. Instead, look for people who have one or more of the qualities you seek in the ideal board member, and live with their shortcomings.

If one of the not-so-subliminal messages of Chapters 4 and 5, on recruiting, is that you have to pay a lot of attention to the people you bring into your organization as employees, then it is even more important that you are focused when considering candidates for your Board of Directors. Why? Because, in effect, you are interviewing your own bosses. Certainly this is the case if you are the CEO, but it goes for any of the top managers as well. And as anyone who has worked for someone else knows, a good boss can be a great teacher and mentor, and a bad boss . . . well, we all know what a bad boss can be.

Building an effective, cohesive board is even harder than building a great management team, and in the process you encounter many of the same challenges. But before we even go into the mechanics of that process, we must ask the question, is it worth it? Why not take the approach of Carla in Guatemala, or countless other nonprofit owner–CEOs, and stack your board with friends and relatives you know you can trust and control? There are three main reasons.

First, the law may require that you have independent, outside directors on your board. As yet, this hasn't reached the nonprofit sector the way it has the private sector under the Sarbanes-Oxley Act of 2002, but if the current trends in increasing transparency and government regulation of nonprofits continue, it's coming in the not-too-distant future.

Second, an engaged, combative board that understands it has real fiduciary responsibility is the best way to keep *you* out of trouble. If they know their butts are on the line should they allow you to do squirrelly things like lease bimbo-filled Lear jets to the Bahamas with company funds, then they are more likely to put a stop to it.

But the best reason for having a high-end board filled with objective heavy hitters is that they can help take your organization to a whole new level of performance. How? It depends, of course, on the profile of the people you bring on board.

When I look at prospective board members, I evaluate them in the context of the Big Five: (1) motive, (2) money, (3) networks, (4) wisdom, and (5) time.

Goes to Motive

People join nonprofit boards for many reasons. Most have healthy motivations, like wanting to give something back, whether that be their money, skills, or both. Others have a personal agenda that could reveal itself in time. Don't choose board members solely on the basis of their claim that they love your mission to death and just have to be a part of it. If your mission is compelling you will find many of those, and you need to be ruthless enough to ask yourself, and them, if what they have to contribute is of great value to the organization.

Having a personal agenda is not an automatic knockout factor. It just means you need to treat them as short-term board members who will decamp once they have achieved *their* goal, which could be something like adding your organization to their résumé.

Money: Tell It to the Birds and Bees

Some people believe there are board members so valuable they don't need to squeeze them for a contribution. The problem with this is the implicit message to the other board members: you other guys are not as valuable. Having some people pay the tuition and others be on "scholarship" can create ill will on the part of those who pay the full freight. You may have legacy board members who are unable to give at the same level as your more recently recruited heavy hitters, but avoid letting any new recruits off the hook. Make sure you are clear with them as to what their minimum annual contribution will be. Experienced board members will ask this question up front, but if they don't, put it early on your list and make eye contact when you say it. Make sure they know you are serious about collecting. Even then, your job is not done. I've known board members to make big contributions as a donor, only to stop giving altogether once they were on the board.

Networks

If connections and networks are among the things your prospective board members bring to the table, make sure they are truly willing to put their contacts at your disposal. Put them to an early test. If they come through, make sure you take full advantage of their contact, and thank both profusely for the assistance they have provided. There is nothing worse than "burning" board members by having them put their valuable contacts at your disposal and then having you duck the meeting.

Wisdom

Board members with deep experience in their area of expertise, or even at building and managing an organization in general, can be incredibly valuable in sharing their lessons learned and helping you avoid, or cure post facto, costly mistakes. Our chairman, the Carpenter, helped steer me through the El Salvador fraud crisis by showing me how to prepare a "case book" detailing (1) the history of what happened, (2) what we were doing to recover the money and prosecute the evildoers, and (3) what we were doing to plug the holes in our internal controls and other defenses.

On the other hand, beware of the ego factor. Some board members get incredibly offended if you ask them for their advice but don't take it. Worse, some will give you unsolicited advice and expect you to act on it. Ideal board members understand you have many priorities, and they don't take offense if you can't act immediately on their suggestions, however brilliant.

Time

Some board members may have networks and wisdom to offer, but if they are too busy to make them available, they aren't much use to you. In this regard, your best prospects might be those who are *recently* retired and need something to keep them busy. Notice the adverb. If your board members have been retired for too long and are considered out of the game, it's possible no one returns their phone calls since they believe the board members can't return any favors.

Beyond the Big Five

If your prospects don't offer at least two of the Big Five, I can't think of a good reason why you would want them on your board. If they tell you all they have to offer is "management oversight experience," run for the hills. This type of board member will keep you bogged down with protocol and processes until you want to scream. If they tell you they are between jobs right now or they have a consulting business (usually the same thing), your radar should put off a loud ping. They may perceive your organization as the solution to their employment problem. A common employment strategy is to get on the board of a struggling nonprofit, be hyperactive in the meetings, win over the chairman and a few other key members, and help them arrive at their "Hey, what about Bob?" moment. A former colleague of mine was booted out of the nonprofit he founded when someone he had put on his board persuaded the other chair members that he could do a better job.

Timing and Resources

When recruiting board members, try to find people at the right level for your organization's stage of development. When your organization is young, avoid the temptation to recruit heavy hitters and celebrities right out of the gate, even if you can (which is unlikely). You will frustrate them because you can't take advantage of what they have to offer. We had an Advisory Board member who was so amazingly well connected he dropped two dozen names during the introductory lunch. Not slouches, either, but people like the CEO of Time Warner and head of the International Monetary Fund. These were great contacts, but at the time, FINCA could not take advantage of them. After a year, the board member politely resigned.

To identify the kinds of people you want on the board at a given stage, make a list of what the organization needs in order to get to the next level. It might be access to certain types of technical expertise it cannot afford to buy in the marketplace. It might be a golden rolodex of people in positions of power who can open doors or help your organization when it gets in trouble. Once you have figured out what you are looking for in a board member, write a job description and profile, just as you would for hiring a new employee.

If your organization is young, recruit people who are willing to overlook your early mistakes and help you grow into the leader and the organization you strive to be.

First think of friends and family members who have made it and could be at a point in their lives where they are able and willing to help. They will be more reliable and less likely to have a personal agenda than outsiders are. If they are true friends, they will be the first to tell you when you have screwed up, and do so privately, as opposed to the outside board member who may openly admonish you during the board meeting itself.

But wait! Objection, Your Honor! Isn't that what Carla did in FINCA Guatemala? Stack the board with friends and relatives? That's true, but it "goes to motive." Carla's motive was to gain control of the foreign-donated assets provided to FINCA International and turn FINCA Guatemala into her personal business. The founding board of FINCA International was interested in developing a global foundation benefiting millions of low-income entrepreneurs, and the creation of a closely held, "insular" board was just a way station on that path. Since then, the board of FINCA International has been greatly expanded and diversified. More important, the mission as originally envisaged is being realized.

Just as when you make a bad employee hire and have to cut your losses, when you bring the wrong person onto your board there is a price to be paid. Some board members can be seriously disruptive, especially if they think management doesn't know what its doing and needs to be replaced. Even if all that happens and you discover you've hired a dud, it is incredibly awkward having to ask a board member to step down, especially an uncompensated board member of a nonprofit. If you bungle it, you might even lose some of the board members you don't want to see go, if they think they will be next.

In a rapidly growing organization, you can have another problem: getting the right mix of legacy and new board members. Once again, the similarity to the employee mix is striking. The legacy board members are the ones who got you to where you are today, but they may not be the ones to take you into the future. Still, you need those loyal members who have been through it all with you and whom you can count on in a crisis. At the same time, bringing heavy hitters onto a largely legacy board can leave the new recruits thinking, "I really don't fit in here."

You need balance.

Avoiding a Bad Hire

How do you avoid making a bad "hire" onto your board? Through the creation of a board "farm team," or Advisory Board, you can mitigate the risks of making costly mistakes for you and the organization. Giving your new board members a tryout on the Advisory Board will provide you with the opportunity to see if they hit on any, most, or all (lucky you) of the Big Five. Make sure the Advisory Board is more than a thinly disguised Triple-A league. Your new recruits will enter the organization with enormous enthusiasm, but if they don't hear from you on how they can contribute (other than their money), disillusion will set in. We made this mistake not once but twice in FINCA, focusing only on getting people with deep pockets, not thinking through how we could utilize other assets they had to offer. The majority of the members of our first two Advisory Boards, instead of being promoted to the Executive Board, resigned in frustration.

To avoid this happening, draw up a charter for the Advisory Board and write a plan for each member. At FINCA, the main function of our Advisory Board is to organize one or more successful fund-raising events each year. We also make sure that we have a project for each of the non-fund-raising members that takes advantage of their expertise. We put this right into our annual operating plan, assigning responsibility to one of our department heads.

Most of the people who have served on FINCA's board, and all of our current members, have been outstanding, and we are lucky to have worked with them. We have made a few mistakes, particularly among those we recruited in the early days. In these situations, we recruited them on the strength of one person's recommendation and failed to check references. Now our process is more careful. We follow the same steps we do when hiring a key employee: interviews, background checks, and reference checks.

It's not rocket science. It's not brain surgery. It's not even accounting.

Entitlement Board Seats

Another mistake you can make when building your board is to create "entitlement" board seats. In the old-paradigm days of FINCA, when the affiliates had autonomous boards dominated by local members, I had the "brilliant" idea of putting one representative of the board of each affiliate that surpassed the ten-thousand-client mark on the board of FINCA International. Over time, three in Latin America and two in Africa qualified. That meant five of the fifteen board seats of FINCA International were occupied by people who felt no obligation to make financial contributions.

They "already gave" by virtue of serving without compensation on the affiliate boards. I did this, in part, as a quid pro quo to get the affiliation agreements (and the affiliation fees) approved.

There were undeniable benefits to having the affiliates represented on the FINCA International board. They contributed to the discussions with local knowledge and a perspective that would otherwise have been missing. The optics and the diversity element were also big positives. We still greatly value these legacy affiliate representatives, of whom three of the five have remained on the board of FINCA International and continue to provide valuable insights, contacts, and strategic contributions. One has risen to a prominent position within her government. But had we carried this policy to its natural conclusion, the local representatives would have eventually filled every board seat, leaving no room for fresh recruits who might bring important networks, skills, and major gifts of their own.

Board Games

Whether you serve on or at the pleasure of a board, you need to know the dynamics that can make the experience mutually satisfying and healthy for an organization as opposed to an exercise in frustration.

Let's take the perspective of management first.

The CEO's Solemn Oath: Be Prepared

To survive in the job, CEOs need to spot challenges and threats to the organization well before the board does. They also need to bring solutions. CEOs should never go into board meetings without knowing exactly how they want it to turn out after having lined up the support they need from the chair and other key members to win approval of important resolutions. If you leave these things to chance, chances are you won't like the outcome.

Engagement with the full board is brief and periodic, but intense. To avoid micromanagement and second-guessing by the board, CEOs need to shape the agenda in advance so the board deliberates on the issues the CEOs see as vital to their strategy and make sure the board arrives at the "right" decisions. This doesn't mean that you have to have all the solutions and strategies going into the meeting, just that you need to have *at least one* proposal for each, for the board's consideration. Failing that, if you really are clueless, at least frame the problem and issues in such a way as to guide the debate. This will increase the odds that you come away with the guidance and direction you need to navigate through the problem. The worst case is when the board imposes a solution or strategy you know instinctively won't work.

One consolation: the CEO having all the answers can actually take the fun out of being a board member. So don't feel you have to have things 100 percent figured out, down to the smallest details.

My recommended rite of board preparation goes something like this:

Two weeks before each board meeting, step back and ask yourself and your team: "How are things going?" Start with the financials. Are they black or red? Are they trending up or down? Your chief financial officer should know this. If not, make a note to get a new one after the board meeting, and perform the analysis yourself. Nothing scares the board more than questions without answers regarding your finances.

Next, survey the condition of your mission-critical programs. Do you like what you see? Are things going according to plan? Are you meeting the performance targets you set at the beginning of the year? Don't fudge or provide partial information, reporting only on those indicators that are pointing north and having the ones that aren't going well mysteriously disappear from the board book. The savvy board members will begin to lose trust in you and your team.

Finally, take a look down the road. What challenges do you see on the horizon that could derail the good progress you are making? Which are under or beyond your control? The board will be impressed if something bad happens and you predicted it. Conversely, they will be negatively impressed if it does and you didn't.

At FINCA, I bring the whole management team together at least a week before the meeting and we all rehearse our presentations, trying to antici-pate all the questions that might arise. Here it helps to know your board members; who can be counted on to ask the tough questions or challenge your chosen strategies.

Finally, whatever you do, get the materials out at least one week before the meeting. Nothing pisses a board off more than getting ten pounds of documents dumped on them the day of the board meeting.

Mea Culpa

If you have messed up, admit it. The board most likely already knows you've made a mistake. Take a look around the table after you utter those terrible words "I screwed up," and see how few people make eye contact. Yep, they were already thinking that, and now it's out in the open. A fair-minded board will give you some time to fix things *as long as they see you are not in denial*. When I had my triple meltdown in Latin America during my *annus horribilis* in 1994, the only reason I survived was that Chairman Bob saw something in me that told him I had the ability to put things right, if given the time.

The Special Relationship

If CEOs' contact with the full board is at best four times a year, their contact with the chairman must be far more frequent. This relationship is key to keeping the organization on course. When things go south, this is your first phone call. Don't let the chairman hear bad news from someone else. It should also be your first call when you have something to celebrate. You should consult with the chairman several weeks before every board meeting, or at least before the board materials go out to the rest of the board, and agree on the agenda.

I have been extremely fortunate in having had the Carpenter as my chairman. He hits on every one of the Big Five qualities you want in a board member. His motives for being involved in FINCA have always been completely selfless. His financial contributions were key to getting us through our lean years and to self-sufficiency. His networks in the Kansas City philanthropic community brought us one of our most valuable board members. His vast experience dealing with every conceivable situation, from a roaring, Force Ten crisis to petty board politics makes him an *inagotable* font of wisdom.[1] Finally, despite the demands on his time as CEO of an innovative cereal ingredient and health and wellness company, he has devoted innumerable hours to FINCA, all pro bono. If you can find a Carpenter of your own, consider yourself blessed.

---

1. *Inagotable* translates roughly to "inexhaustible," but the connotation in Spanish is more nuanced.

Board and Management Team Relationships

You should encourage your board to develop relationships with the members of your management team. This will evolve naturally through their participation in meetings of the board committees, which should include, at the minimum, Audit, Nominating, and Compensation. At FINCA, we also have a Technology Committee and a Social Audit Committee.

Don't, however, allow ambitious staff members to use this interface to drive a wedge between you and the chairman or the other board members. One of my CFOs tried to forge a relationship with a board member to sow doubts about my abilities, and for a time succeeded. Fortunately, my duplicitous CFO supplied misinformation that, once I became aware of it, was easily refuted. The problem is, if the informant's accusations are scary enough, the board member hearing them might go straight to the rest of the board before doing a reality check with you. Then you are fighting an invisible dragon. In this case, my longstanding relationship with our treasurer caused him to first talk to me.

Despite the risk cited above, never try to bar your management team from developing healthy relationships with the board members, as our high-performance psychotic Donaldo attempted to do. Just make sure your management team members report back on relevant content of their discussions with your board members and that they are not using these opportunities to advance their personal ambitions and agendas at your expense. Notice the qualifier. It is not realistic to suppose they won't take the opportunity to showcase their talents, and that's fine. What's not fine is when it becomes a detriment to you.

Games CEOs Play: When the Jimmy Choo Is on the Other Foot

While as CEO I report to the board of FINCA International, I am also on the boards of many of the affiliates. In the latter capacity, I have seen all the strategies of CEOs that don't work, frustrate board members, and cause them to lose confidence in management. Foremost among these is the BBB strategy: Bury the Board with B.S. When Gloria saw her ship going down in Honduras, she would dump ten tons of irrelevant documents on the board members, usually the day of the meeting itself. Then she would try to railroad through certain decisions, especially salary increases for herself and the staff. Meanwhile, the real burning issues, like the fact that we had millions of Honduran pesos in our transitory accounts we couldn't account for, passed without discussion.

In Latin America, Donaldo employed the "take my ball and go home" strategy. When his proposal to sell a majority stake in FINCA didn't fly with the board, he told us: "Then I don't know what else to do." He challenged the board to come up with a better strategy. As board members, we all had the same thought: If we have to come up with the strategy, what do we need him for?

Other FINCA CEOs have employed the Chicken Little strategy with the board members at one time or another. It goes like this: "If you don't approve these raises for my top management, everyone is going to quit." We protest that under this management team we are losing thirty thousand dollars a month. Why would we reward them with raises? "Because if we don't, they will all go to the competition." And have you analyzed the financial impact of these increases on the bottom line? "There's no time. You have to approve them today." Notice that if we don't approve the raises and the top management quits, we the board members are now to blame, not the CEO. Don't let yourself be blackmailed. Start working on finding a replacement.

Keep an Adversary on the Board

A board that is too supportive, too unquestioning of the CEO, can be a dangerous thing. The corporate world is replete with examples of this lethal groupthink, where elephantine problems go unnoticed in an environment of jolly CEO-led rosy scenarios until the roof caves in. Someone needs to say not only does the emperor have no clothes, but he looks really bad naked. Better to have one or two disgruntled members who don't buy your approach and are constantly critical. They will highlight your Achilles' heel before it trips you up. The swag box "Critical Carlos" describes one FINCA board member, Carlos, who attacked management's performance mercilessly in Latin America, even when things appeared to be going well.

Critical Carlos

Carlos, FINCA International's board member from Ecuador, disagrees with nearly everything management does in Latin America. Not a board meeting goes by without his questioning the wisdom of my personnel decisions or the overall strategy. In the past our performance in Latin America has been indefensible, but since I hired a new regional director, things have begun to improve. "I am really worried about Latin America," Carlos keeps repeating. "I think we have the wrong team."

What is going on? Carlos once filled in as country director of FINCA Ecuador, so he feels he has inside knowledge of what it takes to run a FINCA program. He also serves on the board of FINCA Ecuador and is fiercely proud of the program, considering it the best-performing affiliate in the network. He constantly holds it up as the gold standard to which the other Latin American affiliates should aspire.

On a substantive level, Carlos doesn't agree with all the policies of FINCA International. He thinks board members should be compensated, while our policy is that they serve pro bono. He worries about the liability he assumes as a local board member of FINCA Ecuador and the fact that he is outnumbered on the board by the FINCA International representatives. He would like to see more decision-making authority vested in the affiliates.

"Why do you put up with him?" my colleagues want to know. I explain that Carlos has a lot of support from other board members and to remove him would appear an obvious effort on my part to crush dissent. But the real reason is I'm using Carlos to keep the pressure on my team in Latin America to perform. And there is something else I can't quite put my finger on. Instinct tells me there is a chance he could be seeing something no one else does.

Two years after Carlos disrupts my board presentations with his own jaundiced analysis, Latin America crashes and burns. The regional director resigns. I did have the wrong team.

Carlos was really annoying. He was also really right.

For Prospective Board Members: Risks and Rewards

Since you probably will serve on a board at some point in your career, including that of your own organization, you need to understand what you are getting into. Three changes in the nonprofit sector have raised the stakes for people contemplating serving as board members. The first is a growing trend toward increased scrutiny of nonprofits, by both the government and the media, a response in part to abuse of the form by politically motivated groups who have used them to mobilize funding and/or the electorate along partisan lines. The second is the increased exposure of board members themselves to legal risk as a result of misbehavior on the part of the board and/or management. Finally, as nonprofits increasingly resemble their for-profit cousins in seriousness of mission, size, and complexity, serving on a nonprofit board can mean a real commitment of time and energy.

Despite these changes, the personal liability incurred by nonprofit board members does not (yet) approach the level of exposure associated with for-profit boards. This is because nonprofit board members do not have "fiduciary responsibility" for the funds managed by the nonprofit. This is a legal term meaning, in essence, your ass is on the line if something goes wrong; you may be criminally liable and your personal assets at risk. Instead, nonprofit board members have three duties: care, loyalty, and obedience. Care means staying sufficiently well informed to make good, prudent decisions and be able to exercise management oversight. Loyalty means putting the foundation's interests above your own (no self-dealing). Obedience means staying faithful to the organization's mission.[2]

If a board member of a nonprofit exercises these three duties, he or she can probably not be sued, but it is still advisable to buy directors and officers insurance to cover both the board and top management. One has to hope that litigation in nonprofits never flourishes as it has in the for-profit sector. If it does, there won't be any resources left for the mission.

In terms of what you actually have to worry about as a board member, one of the greatest risks you run is failing to ensure your CEO doesn't do anything illegal. If, for example, the CEO of a cash-strapped nonprofit decides a good way to conserve cash is to fail to submit payroll taxes, or to

2. From *Essentials About Your Board of Directors*, by Joanne Fritz, About.com Guide.

pay penalties on these, the board members can be sued by the IRS. As a board member, you should at the minimum ensure that the nonprofit has directors and officers (D&O) insurance and will indemnify you (make you whole) for any transgressions on the part of management of which you were unaware.

One might think that, in return for this increased "quid" on the obligation and liability side, there might be an offsetting "quo" in terms of a change in the hallowed tradition of pro bono service on the part of board members in the charitable sector. Not so. At this writing, only 2 percent of nonprofits pay their board members. Watchdog groups who rate charities ding them if they have more than one compensated board member.

Fortunately, FINCA is still able to find both international and local board members willing to serve pro bono. Why? Because people continue to feel privileged and honored to be associated with our mission.

One Final Word on Money: What Should Social Entrepreneurs Earn?

If you are on the board, either as CEO, as chair, or in some other capacity, part of your responsibility is to make decisions on employee compensation. Obviously, if it is *your* compensation at issue, you will need to excuse yourself from the deliberation, which will normally take place within a compensation committee: a subcommittee of the board charged with determining compensation levels for the top management and often "benchmark" raises for the rest of the staff.

Let me take this topic head-on because it's something all of us in the nonprofit field skate around and are very nervous about. I will start with myself. In 2009, I earned $290,000. I have a good benefits package, which includes health insurance, life insurance, a retirement program, and a car FINCA leases on my behalf. It's not particularly brave of me to "out" myself in this regard, since you can find it on FINCA's 990 on our website anyway. Is that a lot of money? It is to me. I never thought I could make a living at this work, let alone a decent living. This income places me in the top 5 percent of all Americans. I could add a number of caveats like (1) I worked for FINCA for nothing for the first several years, and at much lower compensation for many years following that, (2) most of my classmates at Brown are far richer than I am now, or (3) I am now in my sixth decade and so will have only a few more years before FINCA puts me out to pasture—but it's a lot of money. Is it too much money? Not according to "industry standards," which are scrupulously researched by FINCA's compensation committee with information provided to them by compensation experts who look at the earnings of CEOs of nonprofits of comparable size. According to those, I am actually below the median for a CEO managing an organization the size of FINCA.

Charity Navigator, a watchdog organization that has given FINCA its highest, four-star rating in three of the past four years,[3] has this to say about CEO compensation:

> *While there are certainly some charities that overpay their leaders, Charity Navigator's data shows that those organizations are the minority. Among the charities we've evaluated, the average CEO salary is roughly $164,000. Before you make any judgments about salaries higher or lower than this average, we encourage you to look at CEO compensation as a percentage of total expenses. A charity CEO compensation of $200,000 for an organization spending $20 million per year (1%) probably seems much more reasonable than the same salary for a $1 million organization (20% of expenses for one person).*
>
> *These charities are complex organizations, with multi-million dollar budgets, hundreds of employees, and thousands of constituents. These leaders could inevitably make much more running similarly sized for-profit firms. Furthermore, when making your decision it is important to consider that it takes a certain level of professionalism to effectively run a charity and charities must offer a competitive salary if they want to attract and retain that level of leadership.[4]*

For the record, in 2007 my total comp (salary and benefits, all in) was 0.52 percent of FINCA's total expenses.

Still, considering who FINCA works with, the poorest people on earth, I must admit I am not entirely comfortable earning at this level. That is

---

3. Owing to an accounting technicality, which shifted the focus from our consolidated (containing the whole operation, including field programs) to our stand-alone (just headquarters) financial statements, our rating was cut from 4 to 2 stars in 2008.
4. Reprinted with the permission of Charity Navigator, www.charitynavigator.org, America's leading independent charity evaluator.

why, over the years, I have plowed back a good chunk of my income into FINCA and other causes.

The field of microfinance is also unique in that it straddles the non-profit and for-profit world. Some, like my friends at Compartamos in Mexico, think it's perfectly OK to approach the problem of poverty with a straight-up profit-maximizing model. They argue that this will guarantee that the industry is never underresourced. They argue that if you can get rich helping the poor—the two co-CEOs each have $50 million in the bank to prove it—this will attract more talented people to the industry.

My position is that the jury is still out on which of these models—profit maximizing versus subsidize the poor—will ultimately do more to lift people out of poverty. In the meantime, if you are out to make money as a social entrepreneur, you should be transparent about it and certainly reveal that this is your intention if you are soliciting donations from the general public. FINCA is following a middle road, where we are seeking a "triple win": a fair return to social investors, market compensation for our employees, but endeavoring to leave the clients with the lion's share of the wealth they create as a result of our services.[5]

We live in interesting times, in a society that rewards its court jesters and gladiators (talk-show hosts, comedians, and sports stars) far more than the people who grow our food or look after our health. Let's not even talk about the Wall Street execs who raked in billions and in return destroyed the global financial system. What if, instead, we rewarded our best and brightest with a per capita bounty on every person they pulled out of poverty? What if our best entrepreneurial minds focused and were rewarded on that? How long would it take to turn that pyramid on its head, with the top five billion all earning more than twenty thousand dollars per year, and only a few million earning less than a dollar a day?

Well, maybe someday.

---

5. Also known as "impact investors," social investors are people and funds that accept a lower financial return in combination with a high "social return," which is defined as the economic and social benefits perceived by the beneficiaries of the investee's mission. In FINCA's case, this would be the increased income and social welfare of our loan clients. Recently, major efforts have been made to measure this and put a quantitative value on it. FINCA is considered a leader in the industry in the "social performance" field.

18

||||||||||||||||||||||||||||||||||||||||||||||||||||||||||||||||||||||||||

HUMANITARIANS AT THE GATE

Surviving and Thriving in the Treacherous World of the Modern Nonprofit

In a sense, this whole book is a survival guide for anyone who joins the ranks of a modern nonprofit. In this chapter, we offer some survival tips, whether you are in middle management, clawing your way upward, or have already reached the dizzy heights at the top of the food chain with no visible predators. We start with crisis management, then offer up a goody bag of advice on situations that are certain to come up at some point during the voyage as you circumnavigate the globe in quest of your own personal Moby Dick. These will range from tips on surviving the terrorist-infested waters of failed states to neutralizing a hostile colleague intent on doing you in, to avoiding the dangers of early success, and, finally, despite all the excitement that comes with that coveted corner office, to getting a good night's sleep.

Perfect Storms: When the Sea Was Calm, All Ships Showed Equal Mastership at Floating

Crises sort out the strong from the weak, the capable from the incompetent. Sometimes managers themselves don't know to which category they belong until they're in the midst of a Force Ten gale. CEOs who don't get out in front of a crisis quickly invite meddling from both the board and other members of the management team. Manage it successfully, and you emerge with a new level of confidence and support from your top team and board. Bungle it and everyone begins to ask, "Is the boss up to this job?"

"Hello, Tanzania? Is Anyone There?" describes a crisis I faced in Tanzania, when the employees deported the regional director and took his team hostage after he fired their boss. Resolving it required me to draw on all my experience and skills at crisis management.

<hr />

Hello, Tanzania? Is Anyone There?

After years of early success, FINCA Africa is not in good shape. Our six country programs are all fraying at the edges, and the current regional director seems unable to turn it around. I replace him with someone new, a tough-minded former commercial banker who has come to FINCA, in his own words, to "recover my soul."

From the new regional director's first encounter with his team, it is clear his style is very different from that of his predecessor. He tells our country director from South Africa that his plan and budget are from "Disneyland," and when he refuses to approve several million dollars in loans requested by the director from Tanzania, he makes her cry. He has been on the job less than a month when he informs me that he wants to fire this director. I am shocked, as I consider her one of the stronger members of the Africa team. He tells me she is a good field person but has serious deficiencies as a financial manager. Worse, she's refusing to take direction. Reluctantly, I give him the OK to let her go. I ask him to consult Gwen, our HR director, to make sure there is a smooth transition.

Over the weekend, I get a call from Sandy, our internal auditor, who is based in Dar Es Salaam, Tanzania. He tells me that our entire regional team has been deported, and the HR director of FINCA Tanzania is in jail. Our regional director is somewhere mid-Atlantic and can't be reached.

"What the hell happened?" I ask.

He explains that the regional director fired the Tanzania director, then told the rest of her team that if they didn't get their act together, they would be next. I'm afraid to ask the next question.

"Who is in charge of FINCA Tanzania now?"

"Nobody."

The decapitated local management team is in total disarray. I call the CFO and beg him to take over as interim director. He refuses, telling me that he is going to resign. There is no one below him who can do the job.

I have just become the acting country director of FINCA Tanzania, and Sandy tells me that the rest of the staff is demanding to talk to me. They have declared themselves on strike and won't go back to work until their demands are met.

After a heated call with the leader of the strike, Temeke, I decide I need to go to Tanzania to deal with the insurrection. I assemble my crisis team.

"What do we tell our creditors and the donors?" my CFO asks.

This is always a hard decision. You have to be totally transparent, but without alarming them so much they pull all their loans.

"Tell them that we tried to change out our director, and the staff reacted really badly. And that I'm going to Tanzania to resolve the situation."

Despite the gravity of the situation, I find myself smiling. I take a perverse delight in a crisis I know is going to take all my skill and diplomacy to defuse. I arrive in Dar Es Salaam two days later, after no sleep in the thrombosis section of British Airways, and go straight to the office.

The first floor is deserted and suffused with an eerie silence. Sandy and I go into the hot, sunny backyard of the building, and there they are, all one hundred of the employees. I walk among them and shake their hands. No one is smiling.

The meeting begins. The staff has a number of demands—foremost among them is that I fire the current regional director. I tell them I will not, but I agree to their backup demand that, for the time being, he will not return to FINCA Tanzania and that I will supervise the program. It's a big concession, but I sense if I don't agree to this we will lose control over the program.

Then I make a demand of my own: they must return to work.

"How can we?" Temeke exclaims. "If you have fired the Tanzania director, our leader, then we will all be next!"

The others nod, expressions grim. Now that I have met him face-to-face, I realize Temeke is no ordinary rabble-rouser. The man is intelligent and charismatic, and he obviously has the support of the entire staff. He clearly has been in charge here all along. Our entire $6 million loan portfolio is in his hands. If I am to outwit him, I will have to draw on all my experience with strong, wily union leaders.

It emerges that, in addition to firing the Tanzania director, the regional director has eliminated the incentive program that was responsible for more than 50 percent of the field staff's compensation, essentially meaning that in one week, their pay was cut by more than half. I agree to their demand that the old system be reinstated. Grudgingly, they agree to go back to work.

That night, I finally get in touch with our regional director and tell him that I will be managing Tanzania for the time being, while he will continue to take care of the other five programs. He is something of a folk hero in Tanzania, having managed a privatized government bank and turned it highly profitable within the space of four years. He has the admiration of many higher-ups in the government. And now I have to tell him he can't go back. He's not happy, and I get the feeling he may bail on me. The country directors of the other five African countries tell me that, despite his crusty style, the regional director is the guy who can turn Africa around, and they beg me not to lose him over this.

Reluctantly, our regional director agrees to stay on in his diminished capacity as regional director of Africa-minus-Tanzania. I am two for three. Now I have to see if I can keep the lenders on board.

I am able to, but I have to put FINCA International on the hook as a guarantor of FINCA Tanzania's loans. If things go south, FINCA International will owe millions of dollars. My board will not be pleased.

I coronate Sandy, who has emerged as the principal hero of the crisis, as my representative in Tanzania and return to Washington. The road to full recovery of the program will be long and fraught with challenges, but at least now we have a fighting chance.

The Tanzania story had a happy ending, but it took time. We weeded out the ringleaders of the strike, one by one, although the process took a year.[1] Our regional director returned from exile and after a lot of hard work eventually repositioned the program as one of the best in the network.

The key to crisis management is assembling the right team quickly and then moving decisively, inside and outside the organization. The right team means only the people you absolutely need, who can be pulled off their day jobs for the duration of the crisis. This is harder than you might think. Everyone wants to be a part of a life-threatening event because (1) it's exciting, (2) it's a chance to be a hero, and (3) heads may roll, creating upward mobility. Essential members of the team are the CEO, the CFO, the HR director, the general counsel, and the communications director. Why these guys? I have never known a crisis that didn't have personnel, financial, legal, and PR dimensions. When you come to the execution of the plan, they can all delegate to their subalterns, but you want them involved in the development of the strategy. Depending on the nature of the crisis, others may need to be involved.

Once you have assembled your team, you need to develop your strategy and your action plan. If there is disagreement within your team as to the way forward, you need to make a ruling quickly, but agree that if Plan A fails you will default to Plan B.

Equally important are the internal and external communication plans. Inevitably, there will be differences of opinion on what messages to put out and to whom. Do we tell the staff and the donors everything, at the risk of sowing panic? Putting out anything less than the full story risks blowing your credibility when the full, gory facts do come out, as they will. A good scandal spreads like wildfire through the outback after a severe drought. If you don't get your "one truth" out there early, a dozen twisted versions will beat you to it.

The most important part of crisis management comes after you have survived it. Sit down with your team and force yourselves to analyze what

---

1. Note to my union brothers and sisters: these guys, it turned out, were ripping us off. They were not champions of the working class.

happened and how it could have been avoided. Commit your lessons learned to paper. Keep a crisis book that becomes required reading for your managers and new hires.

A Deadly Enemy Is Your Best Teacher: What Doesn't Kill You Makes You Stronger

You can't do good work in the world without making mortal enemies. This is because, if you are being effective, you are upsetting the status quo. You can learn much from a determined adversary and grow stronger with each slain enemy, armed with the wisdom and skills you'll need to prevail in the next encounter.

Your Physical Survival

The most dangerous enemy is the one who will actually kill you if you get in his way. I learned this the hard way with my dear friend, mentor, and colleague Mike Hammer. To our minds we were creating a more just society and saving El Salvador from the communist insurgency. To the Salvadoran ruling class we were interfering in their "internal affairs" and stealing their land. They proved they were capable of murder to stop us.

If you are an idealistic person wanting to engage the world, you don't want to be cowed in hiding in a gated community where you can't interface with your beneficiaries, but neither should you trust fate or even God to protect you from the bad guys. The world has changed in the thirty-five years since I was a Peace Corps volunteer, and not for the better. In those days, I could go anywhere in the poor rural and urban barrios of Guatemala and not worry about being robbed, assaulted, or kidnapped. There was a kind of aura around Americans, and a belief, according to some, that if you harmed an American the CIA would immediately deploy a team of assassins and take you out.

Today, all that has changed. I learned this for myself in Santo Domingo in 1990 when a pair of "Dominican York" crack addicts threw me over a sea wall and robbed me, but not before filleting my forearms with their switchblades. Go into any Latin American city today and you will find a police-free zone where gangs rule and have life-and-death power over anyone who enters.

Don't think for a minute that the all-powerful diplomatic community can protect you from this kind of mortal adversary, or that your enemies will be dissuaded from moving against you because they fear the consequences of killing a foreigner. Hundreds of aid workers are killed every year in foreign lands, and the perpetrators are never brought to justice, or if they are, they buy their way out of prison quickly. In countries like Afghanistan there is a new kind of threat: Islamic extremists specifically targeting aid workers. Insurgencies used to leave aid workers alone, but Al-Qaeda recognizes that winning over the local population with development projects is a viable way to win popular support, and therefore a threat to their objective of establishing their new, global caliphate. It's a strategy they use themselves.

What steps can you take to avoid becoming a victim?

First, understand what you are getting into. Ask yourself if you believe so fervently in your mission that you are willing to die for it. Don't do it for the 100 percent danger pay. If the attack comes, it will give you no comfort to know you're dying with a fat bank account.

Second, protect yourself. There are two schools on how to accomplish this. The first is the "keep a low profile" school. This says you shouldn't hire a big security team of *pistoleros* with armored cars and drive around looking like you are someone important and worth kidnapping. This approach has some merit, but it also has its limits, as a group of ten Americans, Germans, and Afghans from the International Assistance Mission discovered just two days before I wrote these lines. They had the bad luck to encounter a group of Taliban who claimed to believe they were foreign spies and working to convert Afghans to Christianity. One of the team, Tom Little, had been working in Afghanistan since 1976, always moving around unarmed, without security. Tragically, his luck finally ran out.

The second school, to which I subscribe, says you need to take steps to protect yourself. This doesn't mean relying on poorly paid guards employed by a local security service. Your mercenaries will throw their AKs down at the first sign of trouble, or worse, could be bribed to set you up. It means becoming a "hard target," which requires learning to handle a weapon yourself, learning evasive driving action if you are ambushed, and varying your routine so that no one trying to kill you can build a plan around it.

Third, listen to the locals. They will have a higher threshold of fear than you as a foreigner, so if they tell you don't go somewhere, don't. They can also serve as a more effective source of intelligence than the diplomatic community, as they go places the foreigners can't. We tend to think there is a clear demarcation between the Good Guys and the Bad Guys, but in fact the lines are often blurred, especially in the poor communities, where everyone is just trying to survive.

Finally, use the mission. Your best protection is the vast majority of good people who populate developing countries, who, if they believe you are trying to help them, will take care of you. If they believe you are sincere, even your enemies may cut you some slack, or at least give you a heads-up when it's time to go. When I was working in El Salvador, after Hammer's murder, I often received death threats, but some of them were more benign than others. One of my favorites: "We know you think you're doing something good for our country, but please leave before we have to kill you."

The Enemy Within

The second kind of enemy doesn't threaten your physical security but can derail your plans or even your whole career if you don't learn to protect yourself. This enemy inhabits organizations and, for whatever reason, has decided that you are an impediment to his achieving his objectives. Perhaps he wants your job. Perhaps he is content to be your chief advisor, but on the condition you tap him for succession, and he may have concluded you aren't willing to do that. Some variations on the enemy within will seek to prove their worth to you by creating problems for you and then offering to solve them. The enemy within's weapons of choice are innuendo, half truths, character assassination, and manipulation of the simpleminded.

Pancho, whom we've met several times before, was the master of this kind of internecine combat. Pancho taught me more about defending myself than anyone. What made him such a formidable adversary? For one, he was professionally trained in intelligence-gathering techniques. He was also a master of another technique used by this type of adversary: the credible lie. People are often willing to believe the worst about others. Salvadorans are so susceptible to this they invented a word for it: *chambre,* which translates roughly as "malicious gossip." Pancho's *chambre* always contained a kernel of verifiable truth, which made it more difficult to dispel.

Pancho was as likeable as he was deadly. Somehow, with little or no resources, he was able to get people to do his bidding. He was brilliant and had a great sense of humor. At the same time, he knew everyone's pressure points and how to use these against them. He was especially adept at manipulating the gringos and getting money out of them.

How could I prevail against such a formidable adversary?

First, I had to understand his objective. Pancho's goal, in this case, was to take out his archrival, Marcos, and supplant him as my proxy within the Salvadoran trade union movement, the guy through which I realized my employer's agenda. This put him in direct opposition to my agenda, which was to get all the democratic union leaders to put aside their rivalries and unite around support for the land reform program.

Second, I had to trick Pancho into revealing his strategy. To do this, I played the fool, getting him to underestimate me. In this case, Pancho's strategy was simple: he manipulated the leader of the union where he enjoyed the most support, who also happened to be the most simpleminded and dependent on Pancho to hold his position, and got him to do his dirty work. Pancho cleverly made it appear as if it was this leader's decision to refuse to participate in any initiative that included Marcos, not a *movida* on Pancho's part.[2]

Third, in keeping with the advice of the Mafia dons, I kept my friends close but my enemy closer. I made Pancho believe I still trusted him, that we were still on the same side, as long as possible.

This only worked for a time. Once Pancho figured out I had been playing him instead of vice versa, the gloves came off. This led to the incident described in the swag box "Lineman for the County" in Chapter 8, where I had to switch tactics, dragging our dispute out into the sunlight. I forced people to take sides. I rewarded those who chose to support me and threatened to punish those who opposed me. I used my power.

Also, since I couldn't be everywhere, I recruited allies to make my case for me. My main resource in this ground war was Chemita, who enjoyed close to equal stature as Pancho with the other union leaders and could disable his lies as fast as Pancho manufactured them.

---

2. *Movida* is Salvadoran slang for an underhanded maneuver designed to do in an adversary.

The most important thing to learn from the enemy within is that, if you allow him to win, take even one trick, he will only grow stronger. People naturally gravitate to the person who delivers the results they seek. You need to make sure that person is you.

Finally, if you detect a *movida* within the ranks, don't make the mistake of thinking that you can rise above it, take the high road, and it will go away of its own accord. If you aren't willing to get down in the mud and deal with the threat, you better have an agent, a deputy, who will take care of it for you.

Balancing the Loyalty-Competence Trade-Off: When It Comes Down to Dealin' Friends

One of the most difficult decisions CEOs face is when people in their inner circle are no longer able to pull their weight. These people may have contributed years of their lives helping to build the organization. Now, either because they failed to upgrade their skills as the requirements of their position changed or because changes elsewhere in the management team have placed new demands on their level of performance, they are struggling. Stronger, more recent additions to your team grumble that so-and-so constitutes a drag on the whole organization's performance. At the same time, if you let one of your old-time loyalists go, who will you confide in when you feel there is no one around you can trust? Not only that, who will have your back if some of the newcomers end up to just be out for themselves?

Longtime loyalists cannot be dispatched with the same celerity as you would a more recent hire whom you dismiss for performance reasons. You owe it to them to exhaust every resource, leaving no stone unturned, in attempts to keep them on the team. It's not just that you owe them for all the times they saved your ass when the organization was in crisis. In a high-performance organization, team members cannot rest on their laurels; everyone has to earn his keep on a daily basis. But how you treat your longtime, loyal employees says a lot about you as a leader and about the culture of your organization. You can't just kick them to the curb and think: "Oh, they'll be fine."

First, try hiring an executive coach. These coaches can be a great resource and help you focus on solving the specific problem that is holding your loyalist back. Usually they are industrial psychologists accustomed to dealing with top team members who are experiencing problems either performing their duties or fitting in with the rest of the team. The coaches' methodology is to first interview the boss (you) and peer colleagues to get a view as to where the team member is falling short, and theories as to why. Then they work on the team member herself. As one coach put it, the problem is often like the answer to the classic question: "How many psychiatrists does it take to change a light bulb?" Only one, but the bulb has to want to change.

You should let team members choose their own coaches, but subject to your approval. The most important question you should ask coaches is their success rate. Be prepared: they may recommend, after their best efforts, that you terminate your loyalists.

If that is the case, you still shouldn't give up. Think about what attributes your loyalists possess that can still be of value to the organization, perhaps in a different role. Tell them you don't want to lose them, but they have to accept a new position, maybe even a demotion. Tell them you realize they could easily get a similar position with a smaller, less driven organization, but you would really prefer they stay with you.

If they won't work with you, you have no choice but to do the hard thing and let them go. You can't make the organization suffer because you can't bring yourself to cut your losses. The rest of the team will resent you for shackling them with an albatross who slows the organization down and causes it to underperform.

Beware of Hubris, Especially Your Own

For the first decade, FINCA led a charmed existence. Every program we had in Latin America and Africa was the best-performing microfinance program in the country (and sometimes the only one). Many of our programs had perfect repayment rates, and those that didn't were still in the high nineties. All our directors were stars. Raising money was almost as easy as printing it ourselves. I remember going on trips and coming home with millions in new donor commitments, just on the strength of a half-hour meeting. Every move we made was the right one. We could do no wrong.

Or so it seemed. When things appear to be going really well, rest assured disaster lurks just around the corner. As a manager, you should keep yourself in a constant state of skepticism. This is really hard when all the evidence suggests everything is going swimmingly.

The swag box "I Tried to Warn You, but You Wouldn't Listen" recounts how the author, buoyed by nearly a decade of everything going right, grew overconfident and failed to heed warnings from several people that FINCA's programs were not as solid as they appeared.

||||||||||||||||||||||||||||||||||||||||||||||||||||||||||||||||||||||||||||||||||||

I Tried to Warn You, but You Wouldn't Listen

In 1993, Carol, a consultant hired by AID to conduct a mandatory mid-term evaluation of our institution-building grant, tries to warn me that FINCA is growing faster than its rudimentary internal control and management information systems can manage. Invest in better systems, she warns, or the FINCA car will shake apart the next time you step on the gas. I smile in amusement. What do consultants know?

In the same year, a German consulting firm, IPC (which will later go on to found Procredit, a premier microfinance network), evaluates FINCA's star programs in Honduras and El Salvador. Their conclusion: FINCA's accounting and information systems are grossly inadequate and, if not improved, could lead to a major fraud.

I dismiss these warnings as typical scare tactics of consultants, out to justify their pay and perhaps win a follow-up contract to fix the problems they identified. They had to find *something* wrong, right? And in the case of the German firm, there is an element of professional rivalry. FINCA is, after all, riding high. Our repayment rate is 99.9 percent, or so claim the reports from the field. What benefit could an investment in better systems bestow, an improvement of another 0.1 percent? Not worth it.

Then comes 1994. One by one, our programs in El Salvador, Mexico, and Guatemala crash and burn. My life becomes a living hell of auditors, lawyers, and smirking consultants telling me "I told you so!"

Dragging myself from the flaming wreckage, I swallow my pride, go back, and reread the reports. Gulp. I conclude that I didn't heed the warnings of the consultants because I wasn't *ready* to listen, nor was I willing to look beneath the surface to see if things were really as well as they appeared to be.

Postpain, I can admit "they were right" and devote myself to fixing the problems so we don't make the same mistakes twice.

▌▌

Learn from Your Mistakes, but Don't Overlearn

While you must learn from your mistakes, it is possible to learn too well. As the old aphorism goes, sometimes the cure can be worse than the disease.

In the wake of the El Salvador million-dollar embezzlement, FINCA and I became obsessed with preventing fraud. I deployed armies of internal auditors to the countryside, with orders that they audit every village bank and verify that all the clients were real. I told them to be present at the moment the loans were disbursed and to make sure someone from the finance department was there to check the clients' IDs to make sure these were the same people signing the loan agreements. At the affiliate board meetings, I grilled the country directors for hours, making sure that when they did detect a fraud they acted quickly and pursued the perpetrators without mercy.

It worked. Another decade passed before we suffered anything close to the million dollars we lost in El Salvador. But it worked too well. Years later, I realized that the price of crushing down fraud risk to zero came at the expense of focusing on the larger strategic questions. While FINCA was playing defense, other microfinance organizations, especially in Latin America, were looking for ways to improve their products and increase their market share. As a consequence, FINCA programs fell behind the competition, threatening their very survival.

Success Kills: Managing Growth Before It Manages You

You came up with a Big Idea, a Killer App. People are beating down your door in such numbers you don't have to spend a dime on promotion or advertising. All you have to do is build a big enough oven and the warm bread will fly off the shelves on its own. Congratulations!

Let me list the FINCA programs that have had growth spurts in the number of clients and size of portfolio, followed by major collapses and contractions: Mexico, Honduras, El Salvador, Guatemala, Nicaragua, Haiti, Tanzania, Malawi, Congo, Kosovo, Armenia, and Afghanistan. That is more than 50 percent of our programs. We had to learn the same lesson twelve times, in other words. What lesson is that?

First, your people and systems that have brought you this far are almost never the same ones that can take your organization to the next level. If you have the resources, build the capacity you need before you need it. If you don't—more often the case with mission-driven organizations—try stress-testing your rapidly growing programs *before* you give the green light for implementation. This means sending in a team to audit the systems and personnel you have in place to confirm whether you have ones you need to manage rapid growth. Things can still go wrong, but at least you have identified potential weaknesses and created awareness among the staff that you will be watching.

Second, understand that incentives play a role. Remember the Golden Tree Award and how effective it was in stimulating growth in our outreach? Today, two GT recipients, Afghanistan and Ecuador, have dropped below fifty thousand clients. Take a fresh look at what you are rewarding in your organization. If it is only growth, with no quality component, you may inadvertently push people beyond their management capabilities.

The Transparency Trap: You Show Me Your Cards, and I Won't Show You Mine

Total transparency in communication, reporting, and promotion is the ideal. But is it realistic?

Some of the biggest liars I have known have been those who spoke most passionately about the need for transparency—in others. Some were high-performing psychotics with so little self-awareness I think they truly believed themselves paragons of transparency. For others, it was nothing more than a poorly disguised way to smoke out their adversaries and get them to reveal their plans while keeping their own agenda secret.

As a more practical strategy, I advocate an approach I call "contingent transparency." Give people the benefit of the doubt initially, but the first time you catch them holding something back from you, scale back your own level of confidence accordingly.

Exceptions to this code are your levels of disclosure to your board, donors, partners, or regulators. With these stakeholders, anything short of full transparency is asking for trouble. They may or may not reciprocate, but you have no choice.

I define full transparency as following the Golden Rule: What would I want to know were I in their shoes? This means you *don't* need to share all the most remote fears and doomsday scenarios, everything that could possibly go wrong and keeps you up at night. It does mean that when you have passed the "Mama mia!" mark, and the light at the end of the tunnel clearly is a locomotive, you need to come clean.

One thing that makes transparency a difficult code to follow in modern society is the huge legal consequences of full disclosure. What to you and your fellow board members might be considered an honest mistake made by you or your organization could be grist for a future lawsuit. The minutes of your board meetings are not the place to engage in self-flagellation. As you review them, imagine them being read aloud at your trial.

Speaking of which . . .

Get Out of Jail Free or, Better Yet, Don't Go at All

As a director of a number of regulated financial institutions, I have always had as one of my goals staying out of jail. This is not as easy at it might seem. In the developing countries where FINCA works, the norm is for the innocent to go to jail and criminals to go free. One Latin American country in particular has a history of imprisoning its bankers as a first reaction to the frequent collapses of its financial system. Some deserved it, but many were simply those left behind while their superiors fled to Panama or Miami with suitcases of cash.

The bigger problem faced by foreign companies operating in developing countries is that any and all dealings with the government involve a fee—under the table. If you pay it, the U.S. Foreign Corrupt Practices Act says you can go to jail. This is no joke. Ask some of the oil company executives who thought bribing government officials was a good way to land a drilling contract.

So how do you get things done without greasing palms? By being very, very patient. And using the mission. Try to persuade them you are doing something good for their country. It sometimes works. If it doesn't, wait them out. When I was a Peace Corps volunteer, I was hitching from Mexico City back to Guatemala, and I had to go through Belize, the forgotten Central American country on the Atlantic coast. I didn't have any cash, and the immigration official told me, "You're not getting in this country unless you have $100 in cash." I said, OK, but I'm not going back through all of southern Mexico to the Guatemalan border either, so I just sat in his office, opened a book (*One Hundred Years of Solitude*) and started reading. After an hour, with a disgusted, "All right, you can go," he let me through.

If you have a hard deadline and don't have the luxury of waiting them out, you do have the option of escalating it, that is, going over the head of the bureaucrat or minister who is deliberately holding things up. Often, you won't be alone, and there are other companies with someone sitting on their paperwork, soliciting cash in return for his signature. Complaining to the diplomatic community—or even the press—can work, but it can also backfire. It's a hard call.

Your relationship to your general counsel is key to conserving your freedom. There is a wonderful thing called attorney-client privilege, which means you can consult with your GC and say things that you don't have to reveal in a courtroom under oath. (This can help solve the "legal transparency dilemma" described earlier.) Your GC can advise you how you can accomplish your goals without running afoul of the law.

Not all attorneys have the skill or experience to give you useful advice, however. "Baby lawyers"—those fresh out of law school—will likely be very good at telling you all the things you can't do but not so good at advising you as to what you *can* do. But even a very experienced general counsel can only map out your options; she can't make the decision for you. The positive side of the law in developing countries is that it can be very flexible. In some cases, a more aggressive interpretation may be possible than would be in the United States or Europe. Which way you roll on these decisions is a function of your appetite for risk. As social entrepreneurs, we tend to be risk takers. As a Guatemalan colleague of mine once lamented, "If we listen to the lawyers all the time we will never do anything."

Good luck staying out of the pokey.

Build It and They Will Come . . . and Take It

As your organization's net worth grows, it becomes an attractive target for a range of thieves and brigands, both external and internal. As CEO, your job is to fend them off. Fail and you could see a lot of hard work, time, and money go down the drain.

Don't make the mistake of thinking that because yours is a humanitarian organization, you will be exempt from the time-honored practice of some foreign governments expropriating companies or trying to take control of assets. Never forget it is their country, and you are a guest. Their laws are just a convenience for accomplishing their objectives. Taxation of nonprofits, while unheard of in the United States, is common practice in many developing countries. If you have built up a fat income stream from grants or internal sources, they will see this as fair game for the exchequer's gimlet eye.

Uneasy Lies the Head That Wears the Crown: The One Sleepless Night Solution

Sancho Panza, faithful *escudero* and indefatigable source of wise counsel to his master, *el Caballero de la Triste Figura*, Don Quixote de la Mancha, once consoled his knight errant with the following: "If the dogs are barking at us, it's because we are making progress." Think of those words when you hit a hard patch and your critics are attacking you for the decisions you've made or the path you've chosen.

At the apogee of one of FINCA's biggest crises, a member of my management team asked me, somewhat in awe, how I was able to cope with the stress. I think my answer surprised him: "I've learned to enjoy it."

If there is a hierarchy to dealing with crises that begins with allowing them to ruin a good night's sleep and ends in giddy anticipation of the next one, then, after fifteen years at the helm of FINCA, I have achieved the latter. An important milestone on this journey is when you can view problems not as something to dread but as challenging puzzles that are fun to resolve. Key to achieving this state of mind is understanding that the problems will never end, and that if you do manage to keep them at bay temporarily, the next one is incubating somewhere on the near horizon.

If I have one regret it is the time I wasted worrying when I was younger. A certain amount of anxiety about the future is healthy and necessary to our survival, but some of us seem to have it imbedded in our genetic code. I imagine my ancestor as the one who slept at the mouth of the cave, worrying about saber-toothed tigers while the rest of the villagers slept.

The first step on this journey I owe to the women of the marketplace in San Martín Jilotepeque, the Guatemalan town where I lived during my two-year tour in the Peace Corps. I had lived in the town just a few weeks when I began to notice a curious thing about these market women. They would arrive at the marketplace early, having walked many kilometers from their *aldeas*, baskets of onions, tomatoes, or beets on their heads, and in the first hour would sell the majority of their produce. Then they would cover up the remainder and set about gossiping with each other and otherwise just passing the time. Finally, unable to contain my curiosity, I approached one of them and posed my vexing question: "Why don't you just keep selling? You could make all the money you need and then be back in your homes before noon." The women laughed. "That wouldn't be any fun. We like coming to town on market day and selling our produce. If we sold all in the morning, what would we do in the afternoon?"

There it was. To these women, there was no division between work and recreation. It was all just life.

There is another reason I think often of those market women of San Martín Jilotepeque. When I am tempted to feel sorry for myself, lamenting the myriad problems I have to deal with at FINCA, I think of those women and realize how incredibly fortunate I have been both in my life and in my work. Their universe is limited to their small town in the highlands of Guatemala. Mine expanded to embrace the entire world. Any problems I must deal with are problems I have sought.

Finally, remember that all work-related problems are good problems. They all have a solution. It may not be easy and it may cause someone hardship in the short run, but eventually everyone moves on. If we live long enough, we accumulate our share of "bad" problems that have no solution—maladies that affect our family and friends—and that remind us of how trivial our other concerns are.

So the next time a crisis hits, give it one sleepless night, no more.

AFTERWORD

The Next Phase of Social Entrepreneurialism: Expanding, Diversifying, and Scaling the Model

If I have an overarching message in this book it is the following: by thinking creatively and behaving like a business, your nonprofit can accomplish far more than if you simply think of yourself as a charity, dependent forever on donations. Hatch's big breakthrough occurred when he stopped thinking about the poor as helpless victims and, instead, as entrepreneurs and "survival artists" who "just needed a chance" to bootstrap themselves out of poverty.

Another way to look at it is that the majority of people in developing countries are trapped in a deadly crossfire of market and government failures and can't get access to the basic products and services they need to survive. The microfinance industry has been spectacularly successful at addressing the market failure of the global financial system, which a scant thirty years ago had excluded more than one hundred million people who now participate fully in it with access to savings and credit. Our work is not finished, of course, but we have built the business and financial model and need only to scale them up. If governments around the world will enable this process—a big *if*—by creating microfinance-friendly regulatory environments, I have no doubt we can overcome the remaining barriers to open up the global financial system to the rest of the world's population.

What is preventing this from happening now? The usual suspects. Control-minded governments don't want a bunch of independent foreign microfinance companies empowering millions of their citizens through provision of financial services and creating a potential breeding ground for subversive ideas like freedom, democracy, and (sometimes) capitalism. Other governments are beholden to monopolies in the financial sector, owned by the elites who don't want to open their economies to foreign competition.

The Alliance for Financial Inclusion, an initiative by the Gates Foundation and the German Development Agency, aims to launch a soft offensive against these ramparts through a number of initiatives targeted at educating central banks on actions they can take to create more access to the formal financial sector in their countries. So far, fifty countries have signed up. There is hope.

Are there other government and market failures that could be addressed the same way the microfinance industry has approached the failure in the financial sector? Too numerous to count. If the best indicator of the level of development of a society is the number of functioning institutions and service systems, whether they be in the public or private sector, then the converse is also true: you can measure the severity of a country's underdevelopment by the number of institutions and services it *doesn't* possess, or that don't work as they are supposed to. Sometimes, as we have noted, this is by design, as in the case of the legal systems of most developing countries. Rule of law and the justice systems of these countries don't work because the elites don't want them to. They need legal impunity to steal from the poor and eliminate their competition.

Interestingly, the great appeal of Al-Qaeda in Somalia and the Taliban in Afghanistan derives from their imposition of Islamic justice and the rule of law in these failed states. While the local populations don't necessarily appreciate having their hands cut off for stealing and their women shrink-wrapped from head to toe in burkas or stoned to death for adultery, they do value the protection they receive from marauding bands of thieves, rapists, and murderers unleashed when the previous government collapsed. Not only do Al-Qaeda and the Taliban address the failure of formal governments to impart justice, they also provide a range of social and economic services, above all, paid employment in their militias. We call them terrorists, but they are also social entrepreneurs. A question for the future then, is, in countries like Afghanistan and Somalia where the existing governments are weak and corrupt, will the social entrepreneurs of the future come from Islamic extremists or more moderate elements? Nothing short of the future of our global security may hinge on the answer to this question.

In the meantime, we should turn our attention to those places where nonextremist social entrepreneurs can still work—before they lapse into failed-state status. A number of large microfinance organizations and networks are doing just that, taking what is described as a holistic approach to the economic and social development of their clients. This philosophy says that, while financial services are critical to a low-income family's survival, they are not by themselves sufficient to guarantee it. Poor families also need health, education, and access to clean water and energy to sustainably improve their standard of living.

At FINCA, we are going to explore the feasibility of filling these gaps in one of two ways, either through strategic alliances with existing providers of these services or, absent that, through the creation of companies dedicated to that mission. In either case, the objective will be to create financially sustainable businesses that, although perhaps initially funded through grants and donations, will eventually cover all their costs through user fees or other income generated by the "internal pillar."

We anticipate that this will be a far simpler task in the economic arena than the social one. The reason for this is that the wallet of our low-income clients is limited, and although economic services can be self-financing from the income generated by our clients' businesses, social services must either be provided free of charge or else burden the clients' already meager income via user fees. For this reason, we see the greatest potential in the business models of companies like Avarind Eye Hospital and CEMEX, discussed in Chapter 11, which have a mixture of poor and nonpoor customers.

In Search of Failure: Applying the Microfinance Formula to Other Market and Government Failures

If the potential of social entrepreneurialism to address the thorny problem of global poverty is only just beginning to be tapped, could this movement be of relevance to market and government failures in the developed world? Put differently, could social entrepreneurialism, writ large, eventually transform the entire global economy?

The first question to ask is, if social entrepreneurialism thrives in the space created by market and government failures, do these exist on the same scale in the rich countries as in the developing world? The answer is clearly no. In fact, the effort to transplant the microfinance model to the United States, which on a small scale continues to this day, is an excellent example of a solution in search of a problem that didn't exist. Until recently, obtaining a loan for any purpose in the United States was easy, even for low-income people with bad credit histories. When microfinance companies like FINCA attempted to replicate its success in the developing world in poor communities in the States, we found very few people interested in borrowing small amounts to start or grow a business. Those we did find often failed after a few loan cycles and didn't repay. Why? There are a number of reasons.

First, the United States is a developed economy where only 10 percent of the population is self-employed, a fact that automatically limits the potential client base. Second, for most low-income people, who tend to be less educated and skilled, being an entrepreneur is not a viable strategy for escaping poverty. In a developed economy, the barriers to starting a business are much higher than in the developing world, where pretty much anyone with fifty dollars in capital can go to the market and buy and sell vegetables and make a buck or two. In the United States and Europe, to succeed as an entrepreneur you need much more than capital. You need a novel idea, a good business plan, marketing skills, financial acumen, and if your business goes to scale, management skills.

While market and government failures don't exist on the same scale in developed countries, recent changes in our economy suggest that they are present, and growing. An excellent example of a market-failure-in-progress is the inability of small businesses in the United States to get bank financing in the wake of the financial crisis. We are talking about profitable, growing concerns, who, because of new restrictions on capital placed on banks by regulators, cannot get loans to scale up their businesses and create desperately needed jobs. And Congress, of course, is too absorbed with making each other's party look bad to break the impasse.

I grew up in a world accustomed to thinking that, when it came to organizing an economy, you had three choices: communism, capitalism, or the "compromise" system called socialism, wherein private business took care of the productive sector while state-run monopolies addressed the social services of health care and education. After the collapse of the Soviet Union, the assumption was that capitalism and the market economy had triumphed. With the Chinese economy looking increasingly capitalistic, and only a handful of small European nations embracing anything close to a "pure" socialist approach in the health and education sectors, it appeared that the rest of the world would increasingly follow the path of private enterprise.

The recent global economic crisis exposed the folly of relying on a largely unregulated, profit-driven private sector to address all our society's needs. The terrifying ride the financial sector gave us in 2008, plus the massive failure of the U.S. health care system to meet the needs of a huge percentage of the population, begs the question whether the time has not come to put forth some alternative economic models.

Cooperatives: Part of the Answer

Spokespeople for the cooperative movement make much these days of the fact that, as a sector, it survived the financial crisis of 2008 in much better shape than many of its private-sector counterparts.[1] The reason is that, with few exceptions, cooperatives did not speculate with the assets of their owners as did private-sector financial institutions. The fact they did not has to do with the ownership structure of the cooperative model, which is spread among the customers rather than in the hands of profit-maximizing private investors. The not-too-subtle subtext is that the global economy could do worse than pattern itself on this alternative economic model.

I am a great admirer of cooperatives, and just as I owe my political education to the union movement, I attribute much of my microfinance "street cred" to what I learned working as a credit officer for the Flor Chimalteca Cooperative in the highlands of Guatemala.

Cooperatives are already a hugely important component of the global economy. More than 800 million people are members of co-ops, and another 100 million are employed by them. In 1994 the United Nations

---

1. "Cooperatives and the crisis: Our customers are also our owners," July 2, 2010. International Labour Organization website, http://www.ilo.org/global/about-the-ilo/press-and-media-centre/insight/WCMS_142558/lang—en/index.htm.

estimated that cooperatives "secured the livelihoods" of more than three billion people, or fully half of the world's population.[2] Even in the United States, arguably one of the most capitalistic economies in the world, one in every four citizens is a member of a cooperative.

As an economic model, cooperatives work equally well in the productive, social, and service sectors. In the productive sector they are deployed with great success in the agricultural, industrial, and fisheries sectors; in the social sector you find housing, health, and education cooperatives. In the service sector they are represented by utilities (energy) and financial institutions (credit unions and cooperative banks).

One of the most attractive features of the cooperative model from the perspective of the average consumer is its focus on member service and ethical behavior toward its customers. While not a big player in the U.S. market, cooperatives in Europe and Japan are major players in the insurance industry. Imagine dealing with an insurance company whose business model was not to gouge its customers on premiums and cheat them on payouts. Imagine not having to call health insurers fifteen times to get them to pay a claim while they play "let's reject 80 percent of the cost of this procedure and see if he complains." Cooperative insurers don't need to gouge and cheat their customers not only because they don't have to generate high returns to investors but also because they have real ethical standards they adhere to based on their founding principles.

Perhaps the most promising aspect of cooperatives, in the context of their potential as an alternative economic model, is that they function effectively in both developed and developing countries.

The Other Piece

Significant as their outreach is, there are reasons why cooperatives are unlikely to ever fully dominate the global economy. In developing economies, once thought of as a potential solution to poverty, cooperatives have exhibited two important limitations. First, if they are a truly democratic organization, run for and by the membership, they quickly move up the economic ladder and away from the very poor. This is especially true of credit unions, where the more well-to-do members are not willing to risk

2. "Statistical Information on the Co-operative Movement," November 18, 2010. International Co-operative Alliance website, http://www.ica.coop/coop/statistics.html.

their savings by lending them to poor people. In the case of democratically run cooperatives in other sectors—housing, consumer, agricultural services—in order to be a member you need a certain minimum income, whether it be from salaried wages or self-employment. This is because the cooperative enterprise itself needs a certain level of sales to operate above breakeven, and this is difficult to achieve if the member base contains large numbers of poor people with little disposable income.

The other limitation is the case of the undemocratically run cooperatives, where the leadership, emulating the bad example set by the political leadership of the country, "co-ops" the cooperative for its own personal gain. This was the sad fate of the Flor Chimalteca and its sister regional cooperatives affiliated to FECOAR, which became little more than the personal business of the general manager and his chief operating officer.

While cooperatives in the developed world tend not to suffer from these same limitations as their counterparts in developing countries, there are other constraints on their growth. First, like other democratic institutions, in order to function properly they require an investment of time and energy on the part of their members. As the "owners" of their cooperative enterprise, the members have to elect their leaders and remain sufficiently informed to vote intelligently on various resolutions affecting their cooperative as a business. But wait: doesn't a shareholder of a public company have similar obligations? True, but the fact that most cooperatives are small means that, in order to prevent bad things from happening to their shares and the services they receive, members need to be more involved. The fact is, most shareholders of publicly traded companies don't even bother to vote, and the board "recommended" resolutions—many of which deal with their compensation—rarely go down in defeat.

Come to think of it, only a little more than half of the U.S. population exercises its right to vote in presidential elections, even with all that is at stake in those contests. So requiring a high degree of participation in running a business is a lot to ask.

A second limiting factor is the flip side of the advantage conferred by its risk-averse, member-capitalized approach: most cooperatives are small and thinly capitalized. Greed does have an advantage in mobilizing financial capital in a global society comprised of at least some well-endowed citizens, and it goes to where it receives the highest return.

Finally—and this is a personal observation—cooperatives seem to work better in smaller population centers versus the megacities where most of the world's people increasingly reside. This is because, in the context of a small town or city, the cooperative serves a social function as well, bringing people together at regular meetings and creating a social network. In large cities, by contrast, people have less time or need for this kind of interaction. They want to transact their business as quickly, cheaply, and efficiently as possible. As such, many prefer to deal with a faceless corporation for their essential goods and services.

Arise, Social Entrepreneurs! This Is Our Moment!

The social enterprise model offers the same advantages as the cooperative model in terms of social mission, risk aversion, and ethical behavior, but minus the constraints of a self-limiting capital structure and without burdening the customers and management with the inefficiencies of a member-owned governance model. Customers and even investors might not be aware that the business was being operated as a social enterprise. Its ethical, fair treatment of its customers could power its growth beyond that of its profit-maximizing competitors. As such, the outreach of the social enterprise sector, limited only by the richness and variety of its business models, could be vast.

Where might these models—and the social entrepreneurs themselves—come from? Developing countries would be one source. A comparative advantage of the poor countries in this sector is that, in order to succeed, a social enterprise in a developing country must achieve scale and price its products affordably, that is, within reach of the small wallets of the poor. Social entrepreneurs from developing countries could teach their counterparts in the developed world how to apply that principle to sectors like health care, where costs have priced services beyond the reach of almost everyone without insurance.

But most social entrepreneurs and the business models they innovate in developing countries will, I suspect, come from the developed countries themselves. The reason is simple: they live there and know intimately the problems, such as market and government failures, that need to be addressed. The sectors crying out for new thinking and solutions are energy, health care, and the environment. We could add financial services to that, but the problems of this robust and highly creative sector will more likely be found through more effective regulation.

There are more than three thousand schools in the United States offering academic course work in entrepreneurship and even social entrepreneurship, but a good number of social entrepreneurs will probably emerge from the ranks of the already employed.[3] In the health-care sector, they may come from the ranks of the disenchanted, overworked, and undercompensated providers, rebelling against a totally broken, bankrupt system that only the insurance companies love. In the energy sector, they will be young engineers anxious to try their ideas and just in need of a venue and capital.

Where will the capital come from? Probably not from existing businesses with traditional, profit-maximizing business models that don't take into account the environmental or social costs of their operations.

A logical source for capital would be the existing players in the non-profit sector. Unfortunately, most nonprofits are so occupied with their own financial survival, it would take a great leap of courage and faith for them to divert a significant portion of their resources to something so untested. Others, more well endowed, are compromised in other ways. In the health sector, for example, many of the charities are merely raising money for *the existing medical establishment*, not financing social entrepreneurs like Avarind who are experimenting with new business models.

That leaves the "funder of last resort": Uncle Sam. If the movement is to truly gain importance in this country, the money will have to come from the government, in the form of subsidies, loans, and perhaps even short-term capital investments, until the social enterprises become sustainable and attractive investments in their own right. Once that occurs, as is happening in microfinance, the capital markets can take over.[4]

But even if the government makes significant capital available to social entrepreneurs, will the solutions necessarily follow? I believe so. I recall when the microfinance movement was young, and I was sparring with skeptical USAID bureaucrats in the days before Congress allocated money under the Self-Sufficiency for the Poor Act, who told me that even if significant funding were made available, the nascent microfinance movement

---

3. "America's Best Colleges for Entrepreneurs," *Fortune Small Business*, September 2007. CNNMoney.com, http://money.cnn.com/magazines/fsb/bestcolleges/2007.

4. Since I wrote this, another potential source of social venture capital has arisen. Bill Gates and Warren Buffet are purportedly prevailing upon other billionaires around the world to contribute half of their wealth to philanthropy. Time to create "The Billionaire's Global Fund for Social Enterprises"?

didn't have the "capacity" to utilize it. I countered that if they made the money available, the microfinance movement would create the capacity to absorb it, and more. Thirty years and several billion dollars later, the record speaks for itself.

Some Principles

The organizing principles for the social enterprise model in the developed world are the same as those operating in the developing countries:

- Addresses a market or government failure
- Takes a business approach, applying best practices in management, systems, and strategy
- Achieves financial sustainability within a reasonable time frame (three to seven years)
- Is risk averse, not gambling with its capital in order to achieve high returns
- Holds a market-plus-psychic-income compensation strategy (paying with money and good feelings) to attract "the best employees money can't buy"
- Operates with a positive or neutral impact on the environment

Toward a New World Order?

Am I advocating a complete overhaul of the global economy and a whole-sale scrapping of the existing private sector? Of course not. Mankind's basically selfish nature is not going to change overnight, if ever. Capitalism is still the best way to harness that force and direct it as best we can to the greater good.

But we can give social entrepreneurialism at least the benefit of a level playing field and a fighting chance to prove it can come up with solutions that work for everyone, not just shareholders and highly paid executives. And as the old dinosaurs die off, why not replace them with social enterprises? At the very least, let's not keep them alive with our tax dollars. Rather than bail out the outdated models, the government could take a stake in what looks like promising social enterprises in the areas of clean energy, innovative health care, and the environment.

The Last Word

One of the working titles of this book was *Confessions of a Social Entrepreneur*, and here I would like to make a confession: despite its subtitle, I am actually writing this section of the book months before I have completed it. I do it in part to alleviate the anxiety of having to deliver to a deadline, for the first time in my so-called writing career.

I thought that this would be an easy book to write, since it isn't really a book but an extended letter to all the young, idealistic people of the world who want to make a difference but don't know how or where to begin. And it's powered by the realization that it is really their world now, no longer mine, to change for the good. I had my shot, and now all I really have to offer is this collected wisdom.

One thing that is very clear to me is that, with all the "lousy leaders" out there, just looking after their own selfish interest or that of their families and clans, if we are going to change this world for the better, it will have to come from the bottom, not the top. I have a fantasy that maybe one day one of our hundreds of thousands of brave, hardworking, noble FINCA women, like Nayima, will make her way into a position of leadership. If she does, she will carry with her the unforgettable legacy of her own struggle and, hopefully, will fight for the right of her impoverished, oppressed sisters to a less complicated, less obstacle-ridden path to a life with dignity and hope. Since the terrible reality is that it takes only one lousy leader to doom an entire nation of millions to lives of starvation, deprivation, and frustration, I believe that the future of a nation and its people could also be changed for the good if just one good woman or man made it to the top. So I'm rooting for you, Village Bankers. And I'm saying to all you aspiring social entrepreneurs: knowing what you know now about all the human potential that is out there, just waiting to be given a chance to develop, don't rest until you find a way to liberate it.

INDEX

ACCION, 170
Accounting system, 174–75
Advertising and PR. *See*
    Communications campaign
Advisory Board, 216–17
Affiliates, 169–71
Afghanistan, 82, 137, 235, 242, 248–49
AFL-CIO, 25
Al Jazeera, 150
Agency for International Development
    (AID), 32, 33, 137, 138, 240
Alda, Alan, 130
Alliance for Financial Inclusion, 248
Alliances, strategic, 205–6
Al-Qaeda and the Taliban, 235, 248
Amelia, Dona, 34
American Bankers Association, 96
American Institute for Free Labor
    Development (AIFLD), 25, 95
AmeriCorps, 6, 8
Amin, Idi, 97
Angry donor management, 127–29
Apple Computer, 211
Armenia, 60, 182, 242
Attorneys, 244
Auditors, internal, 176, 180–81, 182–83
Audits, 176–77
Avarind Eye Hospital, 140, 249
Azerbaijan, 100, 182, 193

Bangladesh, 32, 205
Bar raisers, 57–60
Bean, Mr. *See* Mr. Bean

Berhorst, Dr., 20
Berkeley, 22
Big Ideas, 19–21
Big pond organizations, 14–15
Board meetings and CEOs, 218–19,
    221–22
Board members
    admitting mistakes to, 220
    adversaries as, 222
    compensation for, 225
    critical Carlos, 223
    evaluation of, 212–15
    ideal, 211–12
    management team and, 221
    risks and rewards for, 224–25
    timing, resources, and recruitment of,
        215–16
Board seats, entitlement, 217–18
Bolivia, 31–33, 114, 170
Borlaug, Norman E., 7
Brangelina, 154–55
Brown University, 109
Builders and maintainers, 46–49, 50–51
Burns, Robert, 180
Business model
    defined, 159–60
    five components of, 160–61
    organizational structure and, 162–65

CARE, 14, 144, 201
Carpenter, The, 33–34, 39, 40, 49, 106,
    179, 214, 220
Catholic Relief Services, 14, 201

Celebrity spokespeople, 153–55
CEMEX, 139–40, 249
CEOs. *See also* Leaders; Managing
  board meetings and, 218–19, 221–22
  crisis management by, 230–34
  earnings of, 225–27
  friends of, 238–39
  relationship between chairman and
    CEO, 220
Certified Fund Raising Executive
  International Credentialing Board
  (CFRE), 113, 117
Chankonse, Mailesi, 146–47
Charity Navigator, 226
Chesbrough, Henry, 160
Chief financial officers (CFOs), hiring,
  63–68
Client stories, 146–47, 208–10
Clinton, Bill, 148, 151
Clinton, Hillary, 148
Coaches, executive, 238–39
Code of conduct, 178
Committees, strategic, 165–66
Communications campaign
  celebrity spokespeople, 153–55
  client stories, 146–47, 208–10
  core constituencies and, 148–49
  name recognition, 143–46, 149
  Web-based Kiva, 120, 122, 149–53,
    170
Compartamos, 227
Competitive strategy, 161
Confianza moment, 7–8
Congo, 68, 242
Cooperatives, 251–54
Corrupt Practices Act, U.S. Foreign,
  243
Costa Rica, 7, 41, 48, 202
Crisis management, 230–34
Crossover employees, managing,
  90–91
Culture, corporate, 177–78

D'Abuisson, Roberto, 94
Dangers and occupational hazards, 1–3,
  234–36
De Veer, Derick, 27

Degata, Marty, 136
Delegation, 87–88
Development Alternatives, 139
Destroyers, 51–53
Direct mail, 111–12
Directors and officers (D&O)
  insurance, 225
Dominican Republic, 32, 94, 139–40
Donors
  management of, 127–29
  respect for, 110
  types of, 122–26

Eads, Darwin, 57, 91, 71, 72, 73, 74, 99
Ecuador, 100, 188, 189, 223, 242
El Salvador, 26, 48, 92, 94, 95, 136, 137,
  182, 183, 192, 214, 234, 236, 240,
  241, 242
Eliot, T. S., 27
Employees, types of
  bar raisers, 57–60
  builders and maintainers, 46–49
  Carpenter, The, 33–34, 39, 40, 49,
    106, 179, 214, 220
  CFOs, 63–68
  destroyers, 51–53
  Essential Visionary, 30, 31–33, 38–39,
    96, 211
  fixers, 49–51
  fund-raisers, 112–17
  heirs apparent (HAs), 80–83
  high-performing psychotics (HPPs),
    76–79
  Monkey in the Middle, 35–37, 39
  Mr. Bean, 34–35, 39, 40, 106
  perfectionists, 87–88
  Too Smart by Halves (TSBHs), 85–87
Enemies, 234–38
Entitlement board seats, 217–18
Entrepreneurial path, 16–17
Evaluations, 73–74
External audits, 177

Failure, permissible, 88–90
Failure rate for philanthropic start-ups,
  17
False innovators, 200

Federacion Nacional de Cooperativas de Ahorro y Credito (FENACOAC), 163

FINCA (Foundation for International Community Assistance)
advertising, 143–55
board, 211–25
business model, 160–61
client stories, 146–47, 208–10
founding of, 31–39
funding, 103–17, 119–32, 135–42
growth of, 241–42
innovations at, 202–3
leadership at, 93–102
managing, 71–83, 85–92
name recognition, 144–45
organizational structure of, 163, 164–65
recruiting at, 41–55, 57–70
strategic alliances with, 205–6
strategic plans, 185–89
systems at, 173–83, 201–2

FINCA Canada, 122
Fixers, 49–51
Flannery, Jessica, 149, 150
Flannery, Matt, 149, 150
Food Industry Crusade Against Hunger, 115
Fraud
corporate culture and, 177–78
employees and, 181–83
punishment for, 179
Freedom from Hunger, 169
Friends, managing, 238–39
Fund-raisers, hiring, 112–17
Fund-raising
dinners, 129–32
direct mail, 111–12
fear of, 107–9
government funding, 134–39
internal sources pillar, 139–42
networks and service clubs, 109–10, 120–22
private pillar basics, 105–7
private pillar pitfalls, 119–32

Gandhi, Mahatma, 96, 97
General Electric (GE), 206

Georgetown University, 22, 86
Goals, articulating, 72
Golden Tree Award, 100, 242
Gossip, malicious, 236
Governance, 179. See also Board members
Government funding, 134–39
Grant-writing skills, 134–35
Gregorian, Vartan, 109
Grove, Andy, 54
Growth, managing, 241–42. See also Strategic planning tips, 189–91
Guatemala, 7, 48, 124, 125, 126, 131, 141, 167, 191, 194, 203, 212, 216, 234, 240, 242, 244, 246, 251

Haiti, 66, 100, 129, 152, 180, 242
Hammer, Mike, 25–26, 234, 236
Harris, Sam, 135
Hatch, Bob, 33–34, 35, 39, 49, 62, 95, 220
Hatch, John, 16, 20, 21, 25, 31–33, 34, 35, 36, 37, 38, 39, 47, 48, 92, 103, 114, 115, 120, 136, 137, 181, 201–2, 247
Hatch, Mimi, 201
Heirs apparent (HAs), 80–83
High-performing psychotics (HPPs), 76–79
Hiring. See also Recruiting
builders and fixers, 50–51
CFOs, 63–68
fund-raisers, 112–17
smart people, 53–55
Honduras, 48–49, 53–55, 221–22, 240, 242
Household word campaign, 143–46, 149
Human resources (resourceful humans). See also Employees, types of; Recruiting
builders and maintainers, 46–49
Carpenter, The, 33–34, 39, 40, 49, 106, 179, 214, 220
Essential Visionary, 30, 31–33, 38–39, 96, 211
fixers, 49–51
fund-raisers, 112–17

mission for attracting talent, 42
Monkey in the Middle, 35–37, 39
Mr. Bean, 34–35, 39, 40, 106
websites for attracting talent, 43
Hurricane Katrina, 15
Hurst, Soledad, 129

Ideas, Big, 19–21
Impact investors, 227
Innovation
  examples of, 202–3
  focus and, 204–5
  good versus bad, 203–4
  mitigating costs of, 204
  questions on, 199
  standardization and, 200–202
  strategic alliances and, 205–6
  tips for managing, 207–8
Inter-American Foundation, 115
Internal auditors, 176, 180–81, 182–83
Interviewing candidates, 69–70

Jagger, Mick, 149
Jail, avoiding, 243–44
Jobs, Steve, 211
Jolie, Angelina, 154

King, Larry, 155
King Abdullah of Jordan, 155
Kiva program, 120, 122, 149–53, 170
Kosovo, 59, 182, 183, 242
Kristol, Nicholas, 151
Kyrgyzstan, 129, 180, 202

Lanao, Aquiles, 31
Lawyers, 244
Lay, Kenneth, 144
Leaders
  commitment of, 94–95
  as conductors, 93
  lousy, 97–99
  praise from, 99–101
  traits of, 95–97
Lee, Michelle Kydd, 81
Little, Tom, 235
Little pond organizations, 11–12
London Economics, 22

Malawi, 166, 187, 205, 242
Management by committee, 165–66
Management team
  board members and, 221
  structuring the, 168–69
Managing
  basics of, 71–72
  crossover employees, 90–91
  evaluations, 73–74
  friends, 238–39
  by "getting out of their way," 74–76
  growth, 241–42
  heirs apparent (HAs), 80–83
  high-performing psychotics (HPPs),
    76–79
  mistakes, 88–90, 220, 241
  perfectionists, 87–88
  Too Smart by Halves (TSBHs), 85–87
Manuals, 175–76, 201, 202
Market segment, 161
Matrix organization, 162, 164, 165
McKeon, Mr., 101
McQueen, Steve, 82
Mentors, 23–26
Mercy Corps, 14
Mexico, 100, 121, 122, 139, 145, 147,
    188, 189, 202, 205, 206, 227, 240,
    242
Micro Finance Solutions Incorporated
    (MFSI), 89
Microcolumbia, 22
Microsoft Project software, 187, 190
Mission and new hires, 42, 60–63
Mistakes, handling, 88–90, 220, 241
Money and board members, 213
Monkey in the Middle role, 35–37, 39
Motive of board members, 213
Mr. Bean, 34–35, 39, 40, 106
Mugabe, Robert, 98
Murphy, Ben, 101
Museveni, President, 148

Name recognition, 143–46, 149
Networks, structuring, 169–71
Networks and board members,
    213–14
Nicaragua, 202, 247

Nongovernmental organizations
(NGOs), 6, 8, 9, 21, 163, 169, 188,
206
Nonpartisan organization, being a, 45

Oprah, 143, 144, 151, 155
Organizational structure
structure traps, 167–68
types of, 162–65
Otero, Pancho, 170

Peace Corps, 6, 7, 8, 9, 20, 31, 32, 96,
163, 234, 246
Perfectionists, 87–88
Peru, 116, 141, 145, 170
Pitt, Brad, 154
Policies and procedures, 175–76
Portman, Natalie, 22, 81, 129, 147, 155,
210
Poverty experience, 8–10
Prahalad, C. K., 139
Praise, as motivator, 99–101
Previn, Andre, 93
Principles, organizing, 256
Procredit, 169, 170, 171, 240

Queen Rania of Jordan, 81, 130, 155

Recognition, 99–101
Recruiting
bar raisers, 57–60
builders, maintainers, and fixers,
46–51
chief financial officers (CFOs),
63–68
destroyers, 51–53
interviewing and, 69–70
mission and, 42–45
smart people, 53–55
Revenue generation and margin, 161
Ripken, Cal Jr., 130
Risk management, 179–80
Rivers, Stephen, 81
Rosenbloom, Richard, 160
Rotary Clubs, 106, 109, 115, 120–22
Rulfo, Juan Carlos, 147
Rural Development Services, 32

Salary and benefits for social
entrepreneurs, 225–26
Sarbanes-Oxley Act of 2002, 212
Save the Children, 14, 144, 201
School for Advanced International
Studies (SAIS) at Johns Hopkins,
22
Self-Sufficiency for the Poor Act of 1987,
135, 136, 255
Sinatra, Frank, 30
Small organizations, 11–12
Social Enterprise Program at Columbia
Business School, 22
Social entrepreneurs
earnings of, 225–26
entrepreneurial path, 16–17
future for, 254–57
ideas and, 19–21
mentoring for, 23–26
poverty experience for, 8–10
risks for, 27
training for, 21–23, 255
Social investors, 227
Software, banking, 192
Somalia, 2, 178, 248–49
South Africa, 187, 230
Sponsorship programs, 119–22
Stalin, Joseph, 96–97
Standardization and innovation,
200–202
Stanford, 22
Stonier School of Banking, 96
Strategic alliances, 205–6, 207–8
Strategic plan
FINCA's first, 185–87
FINCA's second and third, 187–89
Strategic planning tips, 189–91
Strategy and technology, 191–95
Stress, coping with, 101–2, 245–46
Struthers, Sally, 144
Subsidiaries versus affiliates, 169–71
Survival, physical, 1–3, 234–36
Systems
accounting, 174–75
audits, 176–77
code of conduct, 178
cost of, 181

fraud and, 181–83
governance and, 179
importance of, 173–74
policies and procedures, 175–76
risk management, 179–80

Tanzania, 139, 178, 230–32, 242
Taxation of nonprofits, 245
Teamwork Piggy, 100
Technology implementation, 191–95
Thunderbird School for International
    Business, 22
Toffler, Alvin, 187
Too Smart by Halves (TSBHs), 85–87
Training for social entrepreneurs, 21–23,
    255
Transparency, 242–43, 244

UCLA, 22
Uganda, 1, 2, 186, 202, 205, 208, 210
UNICEF, 149
United Nations Capital Development
    Fund (UNCDF), 191
United Nations High Commissioner for
    Refugees (UNHCR), 154
United States, microfinance model in, 250

University of Wisconsin, 32
U.S. Foreign Corrupt Practices Act,
    243
U.S. Green Building Council
    (USGBC), 12–13, 21
USAID, 15, 16, 33, 138, 255
USC, 22

Value chain structure, 161
Value proposition, 160
VISA, alliance with, 206
Visionary, Essential, 30, 31–33, 38–39,
    96, 211

Welch, Jack, 88
Wharton, 22
Wisdom of board members, 214
Women for Women, 143
Women's World Banking, 169
World Vision, 14

Yunus, Muhammad, 20, 21, 32, 95, 135,
    200

Zambia, 146–47, 187
Zeitinger, Dr. Claus Peter, 171